REMAKING GOVERNANCE

Peoples, politics and the public sphere

Edited by Janet Newman

First published in Great Britain in September 2005 by

The Policy Press
University of Bristol
Fourth Floor
Beacon House
Queen's Road
Bristol BS8 1QU
UK

Tel +44 (0)117 331 4054
Fax +44 (0)117 331 4093
e-mail tpp-info@bristol.ac.uk
www.policypress.org.uk

British Library Cataloguing in Publication Data
A catalogue record for this book is available from the British Library.

Library of Congress Cataloging-in-Publication Data
A catalog record for this book has been requested.

ISBN 1 86134 640 9 hardback

A paperback version of this book is also available

Cover design by Qube Design Associates, Bristol.
Printed and bound in Great Britain by MPG Books, Bodmin.

Contents

List of tables and figures

Table

Figures

Acknowledgements

Six of the contributions to this book originally took the form of papers to the 'Governing the Social' strand at the conferences of the European Social Policy Association Research Network. Our thanks to the organisers of these events for enabling us to meet and share ideas.

Our thanks also to The Open University's Research Centre on Citizenship, Identities and Governance who helped to support an international colloquium at which the authors presented and discussed draft chapters.

Notes on contributors

Henrik Bang is Associate Professor in Comparative Politics and Director of the Centre for Studies in Public Organisation and Management, University of Copenhagen, Denmark.
E-mail: hb@combs.anu.edu.ac

Emma Carmel teaches social policy at the University of Bath, UK and is editor of the *Journal of European Social Policy*.
E-mail: e.k.carmel@bath.ac.uk

John Clarke is Professor of Social Policy in the Faculty of Social Science, The Open University, UK.
E-mail: john.clarke@open.ac.uk

Bjørn Hvinden is Professor of Sociology at the Department of Sociology and Political Science, Norwegian University of Science and Technology, Trondheim, Norway.
E-mail: bjorn.hvinden@svt.ntnu.no

Håkan Johansson is a researcher and lecturer in social work at the School of Social Work, Lund University, Sweden and the Department of Health Sciences and Social Work, Växjö University, Sweden.
E-mail: hakan.johansson@soch.lu.se

Noémi Lendvai is a doctoral student at the University of Bristol, UK.
E-mail: noemi.lendvai@bristol.ac.uk

Janet Newman is Professor of Social Policy in the Faculty of Social Science, The Open University, UK.
E-mail: j.e.newman@open.ac.uk

Michael Saward is Professor of Politics in the Faculty of Social Policy and Social Science, The Open University, UK.
E-mail: m.j.saward@open.ac.uk

Rebekah Sterling is a doctoral student in the Department of Political Science, University of California, Los Angeles, USA, and was formerly (2002–04) a research fellow with the Scottish Centre for Research on Social Justice, University of Glasgow, UK.
E-mail: rs1@ucla.edu

Introduction

Janet Newman

'Modernisation', 'globalisation' and 'privatisation' are each terms that signal profound shifts in the process of governance. Across Western Europe governments are seeking to dismantle the contract between state and citizen that was inscribed in the social democratic welfare state and to build a more 'modern' contract based on responsibility and choice. Governmental power is both retreating – with state institutions being slimmed down, 'hollowed out', decentred and marketised – and expanding, reaching into more and more of citizens' personal lives: for example, their decisions about work, health and parenting. At the same time, actors – partnership groups, community organisations and citizens themselves – are being 'empowered' by those same policy reforms and new political spaces potentially opened up.

This dynamic – the remaking of peoples and publics as both the object of governance but also as the subjects of new forms of agency – forms a central focus of this book. It brings together a number of authors whose work is opening up critical forms of analysis and debate in social policy, public policy and political science. Originating as a way of capturing shifts in the character of political rule, governance as a concept has been stretched to encompass a range of different transformations, including the increasing emphasis on 'governing the social': drawing citizens and communities into the process of collaborative governance and constituting new forms of governable subject. However, governance theory tends to conceptualise the social through frameworks in which governance forms the primary analytical concept and the social a residual category. The social is viewed as something defined by its 'otherness' to the state and economy, as an entity to be governed, a resource to be mobilised or the site of social reproduction. The result tends to be a 'thin' conception of the social (Newman, 2004). In this book we draw on strands of social and cultural theory that view governance as meaning-making as well as institutional practice; that contest the image of the social actor as a rational resource-maximising individual; and that offer critical perspectives on ways in which 'the people' who are to be governed and the 'public' domain of governmental activity are understood. We highlight ways in which new governance relationships and practices may reshape patterns of identity and belonging. We focus on the remaking of the contested boundary between public and private domains of responsibility and activity, as European welfare states reconfigure benefit entitlements and services. We are interested in how notions such as 'the people', 'citizenship' or 'community' are being reconstituted in an attempt to form new social settlements that are supposedly suited to the requirements of globalisation. We are concerned with how ideas of the 'active citizen', 'worker-citizen' and 'participating citizen' are being shaped and enacted. Finally, we explore how questions of identity may be implicated in new governance forms and relationships; in particular the kinds of social and political imaginaries that may be opened up or closed down.

Themes and structure of the book

Themes

Two main strands of argument and analysis are developed in the chapters that follow:

- the new formations of peoples, publics and politics that are produced in the remaking of governance. We begin with a focus on the contested constitution of 'Europe' as a governable entity and move through other spatialised or identity-based formations, interrogating the ways in which the boundaries of the public sphere are being redrawn and the implications of this for the sites and practices of politics;
- the contradictory and contested process of remaking governance – a process which both produces new governable subjects and potentially opens up new sites of agency.

Here we begin by introducing our use of the three core concepts – peoples, publics and politics – and then go on to address how these and the contradictory dynamics of the process of remaking governance are reflected in the structure of the book. The second half of this Introduction traces the theoretical approaches that we draw upon in tracing the dynamics of remaking governance.

Remaking peoples

Notions of the people are usually associated with membership of a nation-state. This often 'forgets' or obscures the complex historical struggles which took place in the formation of nationhood and the contested concepts of the people condensed into the boundaries of nationhood (Clarke, 2004). In the late 20th and early 21st centuries we can trace the ways in which the simple unities of nation-states, governments and peoples – although always problematic – have been challenged by the growing significance of transnational bodies such as the European Union (EU), the rise of regional or ethnic claims for self-determination and patterns of migration across national borders. Yet the shift of power from national governments is strongly contested. At the time of writing, the proposed EU constitution has been rejected by the citizens of France and the Netherlands, and new cleavages are opening up between 'old' and 'new' Europe. At the same time, the UK government has announced future plans for local government based on the idea of neighbourhood governance, extending the emphasis on 'community' and 'partnership' in its policy agenda. The governance regimes of the EU, nation-states and specific institutions or locales interact in a dynamic way, as struggles take place over the boundaries of the 'people' as both an object and resource of governance.

Remaking publics

The constitution of peoples as unities forms the basis for collective forms of social welfare and a common public domain of action. We use the idea of 'the public' to denote the sphere of activity that is assumed to be a collective responsibility (rather than the personal responsibility of households or individuals, or subject to the logics of the market). These distinctions between 'public', 'private' and 'personal' domains are being redrawn as a result of the modernisation of welfare states, in which governments are expanding their enabling, regulating and coordinating activities while reducing their role as the direct provider of public services. Network governance tends to dissolve or obscure the distinctions between public and private sectors and the emphasis on collaborative governance fudges the boundary between what issues are considered to be the domain of collective public responsibility (and thus subject to the formal processes of politics and policy) and what are the responsibilities of individuals, families and households.

The remaking of governance also has consequences for the ways in which citizens are constituted as actors in the public sphere. We can trace the emergence of new categories of social citizenship: the active citizen, participating citizen, responsible citizen, the citizen-consumer, the worker-citizen and others. In the process we can see how citizenship is undergoing a transformation from a supposedly passive (rights-bearing) to a more active (performing) subject, taking on new responsibilities as the public/private/personal boundaries are reconfigured. Like the public/private distinction itself, such conceptions are, of course, profoundly gendered and racialised and the potential source of new forms of inclusion and exclusion into notions of 'the people'.

Remaking politics

Governance "speaks to important political transformations of our time. As a field that is always in flux, politics threatens to escape the terms we have to comprehend it" (Walters, 2004, p 31). Governance theory offers an account of the dispersal of power beyond and within the state, undermining the privileged place of representative democracy as the means of channelling citizen interests and legitimising governmental actions. The image of a hierarchical relationship between state and citizen – with the state above and beyond the reach of the citizenry – is displaced by the idea of multiple parallel spaces in which power is encountered and negotiated. This dispersal of state power opens up new ways in which citizens can engage in the politics of localities and regions and participate in 'project politics' on specific issues. At the same time, the remaking of the public sphere recasts definitions of what counts as 'political' and what is identified as merely a question of 'good governance'.

The remaking of peoples also has profound implications for the practice of politics. For example, the development of the EU as a policymaking and legislative body opens up the question of the extent to which Europe constitutes a transnational public sphere in which citizens can debate and participate: a shared space of public communication with institutional support for the expression of interests (Scharpf, 1999). Many writers point to a democratic deficit at the core of the legitimacy problems of the EU, a deficit that is attributed not only to the institutional weakness of the European Parliament but also to the limited Europeanisation of public discourse in comparison with nation-states (Peters et al, 2005). Within nation-states, too, the growing importance of network and collaborative forms of governance brings into question the centrality and authority of representative institutions. At the same time, 'community' is emerging as both a site of governmental intervention and participation in the public sphere (see Sterling in Chapter Seven of this volume).

However, the remaking of governance is not just concerned with institutions and policies. Walters uses the concept of 'political imaginary' to direct attention to "the scale and space of social thought" (2002, p 381). In this volume the term political imaginary is used to denote how we imagine the spaces through which we engage with political power and the selves that we bring to that engagement.

Structure of the book

Chapters One, Two and Three are concerned primarily with the dynamics of remaking peoples as an object of governance and the consequences for the policy process, focusing on 'Europe' as a contested social and political unity. John Clarke begins by analysing European governance both as the management of difference and the expression of coherence in the form of an imagined unity. The borders and boundaries of this unity are the site of political contestation around our understanding of the people who are the subjects of governance strategies and policy interventions. In Chapter Two, Emma Carmel explores the attempt to bring a 'European' social into being through the ways in which the EU engages with social policy issues. She traces the ways in which formal policy goals and governance processes interact to delineate the limits of the social, noting a number of ambiguities and tensions around the form that the social should take. In Chapter Three, Noémi Lendvai recounts the experience of 'joining' Europe from the perspective of one of the Accession Countries, Hungary, as it encounters and attempts to interpret the governance strategies of the EU. Across each of these chapters the importance of understanding new forms and relationships of power can be traced – both institutional (for example, the powers of the EU as a legislative or policymaking body) and cultural (the power of new discourses to constitute ideas of 'modern' European states and peoples fitted for a globalised world).

Chapters Four and Five are concerned with the dynamics of remaking publics and the public sphere through new strategies of social and welfare governance (a topic introduced in Chapter Two on European social policy). The modernisation of welfare states redraws the boundary between public (the domain of collective responsibility for welfare) and private (the domain of market relationships and services). This boundary is one which has been the focus of feminist debates and critiques, and in Chapter Four Janet Newman provides a gendered analysis of the changing relationships between state, market, networks and self-governance as domains of governance. She notes in particular how 'networks' open up new questions about gender and gendered work and highlights the significance of issues of identity and agency in welfare governance. In Chapter Five, Håkan Johansson and Bjørn Hvinden highlight the pressures 'from above' and 'from below' that are shaping the transformation of welfare states and outline the dynamic relationship between the different conceptions of citizenship that are produced in these transformations. They contrast the different forms of citizenship that are implicated in the modernisation of welfare states – liberal, libertarian and republican – and capture the tensions between the active and passive dimensions of each. In doing so they trace the ways in which social policy reforms not only constrain social actors, subjecting them to new forms of governance and new technologies of power, but also open up the possibility of new forms and sites of social agency.

This theme is taken up in Chapters Six to Nine, whose primary concern is with the dynamics of remaking politics. The idea of active citizenship discussed in Chapters Four and Five is not only associated with labour market activation, it is also linked to a redrawing of state–citizen relationships through new collaborative governance strategies. In Chapter Six, Janet Newman highlights the significance of public participation as a strategy which invites citizens to collaborate with state and non-state actors in shaping public policy or taking decisions on public services. She traces the ways in which the public domain of participation and deliberation is produced and reproduced, opening up questions of public and private to critical scrutiny. She also traces the contradictory implications of the new technologies of power associated with participation and collaboration. These arguments are developed further in Chapters Seven and Eight, both of which assess the potential of collaborative or participative governance to produce new forms of political imaginary and agency. In Chapter Seven, Rebekah Sterling argues that the emergence of partnership working as a key governmental strategy reflects a complex intersection of governance trends. These have paradoxical implications for democracy: while not intrinsically democratic and offering very circumscribed opportunities for public participation, partnerships have the potential to draw citizens into new domains of power. Chapter Eight highlights the importance of studying informal, as well as state-sponsored, forms of democratic participation. Henrik Bang addresses the problems of individuation and the decoupling of states from citizens, but argues that governance strategies designed to enhance social capital have resulted in a growing division between what he terms 'expert citizens' and 'everyday makers'. In Chapter Nine, Michael Saward explores the new spaces and places in which political representation happens in the fragmented fields of power of network governance, analysing the significance of new kinds of representative claims.

The Conclusion reviews the contribution of the book to theorising the remaking of governance both in terms of the constitution of new governable subjects and new sites and possibilities of social agency. Here, it is argued that governance shifts are profoundly political in that they reshape the public realm of welfare-state provision and redraw citizenship rights and responsibilities. They offer new ways of conceptualising the 'people' around imaginary unities of interest or identity. They create new patterns of inclusion and exclusion. But they also open up the possibility of changing the terrain of political engagement and action. Rather than a view of politics as separate from society, the book suggests a *politics of the social*. It explores how new strategies of governance rest on cultural projects concerned with reconstituting peoples and publics as governable entities, while also holding on to the idea that these cultural projects are subject to contestation, struggle and dissent. In doing so it engages in a process of rethinking key concepts – 'states', 'citizens', 'democracy', 'representation', 'participation', and so on – in a way that we hope enriches them.

The dynamics of remaking governance

The term 'dynamics' has appeared frequently in setting out the themes of the book, serving as something of a shorthand way of talking about one of the book's central preoccupations. We set out not to describe large-scale, generalising processes of change – the emergence of the EU as a transnational tier of governance, the rise of network-based patterns of coordination, the emergence of new governmentalities that constitute the 'empowered' citizen, and so on. This has been done extensively elsewhere. Rather, we focus on teasing out the dynamics of *remaking* governance, theorising the instabilities and contradictions that may be produced in the process of reform. As such, we engage critically with those political science and social policy traditions that assume a universal – and universalising – narrative of change. In what follows, four such narratives and our response to them are highlighted:

- the shift from government to networked, multi-level processes of governance;
- the process of welfare-state transformation in response to globalising pressures;

- the development of new technologies of power through which the subjects of governance are constituted;
- the emergence of collaborative governance.

From government to governance?

What Rhodes (2000) calls the "governance narrative" provides an account of how hierarchical government has given way to a differentiated polity characterised by network-based processes of coordination. This opens up important questions about institutional change and new forms of political power. The emergence of network-based patterns of coordination, whether informal or in more formally inscribed partnership bodies, implies a shift in governmental power towards the use of influencing and enabling strategies rather than direct authority. The idea of a shift from government to governance provides the context for a number of the shifts that we trace. Here I set out a number of critiques of the governance narrative that form the starting points for the analyses which follow (for further discussion, see the reviews in Newman, 2001; Walters, 2004).

The first critique centres on the notion of a decentring of state power. I argue that, in emphasising the 'hollowing-out' of the nation-state and the demise of authority as a means of governing, the governance literature both ignores the continuing role of national governments in exercising coercive forms of power and underestimates the significance of the role of the state in 'metagovernance' – setting the rules of the game within which networks operate and steering the overall process of coordination (Jessop, 2000; Kooiman, 2000). Although the shift to networks and 'enabling' policy approaches may be evident in many areas of social and public policy, there is still plenty of governing (in the form of direct control by states) in evidence. Despite the importance of the EU's attempts to reshape policy, the nation-state still serves as a political entity which takes the primary role in (re)distributing resources and delivering social protection for citizens (see Chapters Two and Three of this volume). The 'hollowing-out' thesis also tends to flatten differences between nations, ignoring differences between strong and weak states, Eastern and Western Europe and different national welfare regimes.

The second critique centres on its depiction of change as unidirectional (from 'government' to 'governance') and as simple, rather than compound. The contributors to this volume have attempted to capture some of the more subtle and complex – and often contradictory – dynamics involved in these processes of change. This is particularly evident in our approach to understanding 'multi-level' governance, a concept that draws attention to the vertical interface between transnational bodies such as the EU, the nation-state and so-called 'sub-national' tiers of governance. Such a reading of change focuses attention on the institutions of governance: the redistribution of power and resources between 'levels', the processes of negotiation among actors and the outcomes in terms of institutional adaptation or path dependency. A rather different reading – and the one with which we are concerned with in this book – emphasises the shifting practices of governance that cut across different scalar levels: the emphasis on partnership and collaboration (Chapters Six and Seven), or the more fundamental 'modernisation' of welfare governance and the recasting of concepts of citizenship that it produces (Chapters Four and Five). This is not to say that such processes are uniform or produce equivalent outcomes. The literature on comparative social policy provides a rich repertoire of conceptual tools for understanding difference as well as similarity, divergence as well as convergence, among nation-states. But such realignments produce shifts in governing practices and power relations and not just a reorganisation of scale; that is, it influences the *how* and *who* of governance as well as the where.

The third critique is that the idea of multilevel governance tends to focus on the institutional rather than cultural dimensions of change: the interaction between EU institutions and national governments, between the nation-state and the dispersed array of institutions acting on its behalf, and so on. In this book, we focus on the cultural constructions of 'levels' and the policy ideas that flow across, between and within them. John Clarke, Emma Carmel and Noémi Lendvai explore, in different ways, the struggle to establish Europe itself. This is not just a question of political negotiations between the EU and nation-states. As John Clarke argues in Chapter One: "Constituting Europe is a process of spatial construction … the 'borders' of Europe are not merely mapping the external boundaries of Europe: they are inscribed – and contested – within." In Chapter Seven, Rebekah Sterling notes three different governance trends that are condensed in governance through partnership – the drive towards integration and collaboration; the reconfiguration of governance around territory; and the renewed emphasis on 'bottom-up' processes that stress participation and community. Each, she argues, has its own internal tensions and, as they converge, may produce points of conflict as well as synergy.

Finally, the governance narrative is derived from a Western European – especially British – account of change. It is by no means the only way of describing the 'remaking' of governing institutions, including the institutions of the nation-state. Noémi Lendvai's chapter illuminates what happens when states already experiencing the transition from communist control engage in another set of transformations as Accession Countries to the EU, an EU that is itself undergoing major change. As a result of enlargement, this 'double dynamic' suggests a much more troubled and unsettled process of change. The experience of Eastern Europe also brings into question the salience of theories developed in 'strong state' countries – especially the UK – for other contexts.

The modernisation of welfare governance

The social policy account of the modernisation or transformation of welfare states intersects with the governance narrative described above, in that both view change as deriving from or determined by the 'new realities' of globalisation and the rise of neo-liberal economic pressures. However, the impact of globalisation on welfare governance has been widely debated and the arguments of Gough (2000), Clarke (2004) and others suggest that contemporary changes in welfare governance are not simply the results of either pressure from above (where the external pressures of globalisation, mediated through supranational bodies such as the EU or World Bank, produce new governance strategies), or pressures from below (as a product of changes in citizen capabilities and demands, the individuation of society, more consumerist orientation, and so on). Rather, as Håkan Johansson and Bjørn Hvinden argue in Chapter Five, these dynamics must be captured as mutually reinforcing processes. Nevertheless the *idea* of globalisation has had a profound impact on the assumptions underpinning welfare reform (Hobson et al, 2002), producing the instrumental approach to welfare discussed in Chapter Three, the processes of commodification and decommodification highlighted in Chapter Four, the activation policies outlined in Chapter Five and a range of emerging European policies on employment, pensions and welfare benefits discussed in Chapters Two and Three.

The discourse of modernisation underpinning the transformation of welfare states draws its legitimacy from a number of narratives about the poverty of 'old' ideas for 'new' times. Both academic writings and policy texts trace the new global realities in which states must operate and set out the need to challenge 'outdated' assumptions about universal access to social protection schemes or rights-based notions of citizenship. But this is not just situated in supposedly 'external' forces such as globalisation. The work of Giddens (1998) and others argues that the fabric of societies has been transformed as the old solidarities of class, community, family and nation have been weakened and as people have become more individuated and consumerist, producing new patterns of social risks, needs and demands. These ideas have been appropriated readily in policy texts and political speeches and inform a number of shifts in the public sphere, for example the idea of the 'worker-citizen' around which gender relations are being reformed (Chapter Four) and the 'active citizen' subject of modernising welfare states (Chapter Five).

This means that it is important to trace the delineation of new policy paradigms and the assumptions that they make about the changing character of social issues and problems as well as economic imperatives. However, these shifting paradigms may contain internal contradictions or lines of tension. The dominant focus in EU policy is on flexible labour markets and competitiveness. But this is overlaid on a subordinate narrative on work–life balance, parental leave and increased state funding of childcare. The tensions between these different paradigms might be conceptualised as a tension between an 'efficiency'-oriented approach to state welfare, in which the role of the state as a provider is minimised, and a 'social investment' approach, in which the state acts as an enabler in order to improve the stock of human capital through training and personal development strategies and thus to equip the future workforce for the demands of a globalised economy. Such policies may be in tension with those designed to improve *social* capital through the citizen involvement and community participation strategies discussed by Janet Newman in Chapter Six, Rebekah Sterling in Chapter Seven and Henrik Bang in Chapter Eight.

Technologies of power

It is one thing for policies to set out new conceptions of citizenship and community, responsibilities and relationships. It is another for these to be realised in social action. One way of accomplishing this is through the steering or 'meta-governance' role of the state as it attempts to coordinate a dispersed array of network and partnership arrangements or deploy its powers to shape new governance practices (Jessop, 2002; Kooiman, 2003). In terms of welfare governance, coercive policy instruments may be deployed – for example, changing the criteria which enable people to claim welfare or work-related benefits and access state-funded services. However, steering or coercive strategies may fail to bring about the cultural shifts that governments desire: that is, the shifts in who people think they are, how they should relate to each other, what they can legitimately expect from the state and what the state can legitimately expect from them in return. The fostering of new identities, relationships, expectations and aspirations is accomplished – with more or less success – through new technologies of power.

Such an approach displaces, or decentres, government and/or the state within the analysis by insisting that governing takes place through multiple agencies, relations and practices (Dean, 1999; Petersen et al, 1999; Rose, 1999; Larner and Walters, 2004; Marston, 2004). Rather than the reduction of government promised by neo-liberal regimes, such changes can be understood as the dispersal of governmental power across new sites of action. Rose (1999) argues that what are termed 'advanced liberal' societies construct new forms of governance (or governmentalities) that draw apparently empowered subjects into new fields of power based on autonomy coupled with responsibility. Here, governance takes place through a range of strategies and technologies – directed towards what Foucault (1991) terms the "conduct of conduct". This kind of approach is one that Emma Carmel draws upon when, in Chapter Two, she defines governance as "historically contingent ensembles of practices and procedures" that are capable of making some forms of activity thinkable and practicable both to its practitioners and those upon whom it is practised. Rather than debating whether the power of the state has been 'hollowed-out', the approach directs attention to the kinds of knowledge and power through which social activity is regulated and through which actors – citizens, workers, organisations – are constituted as self-disciplining subjects.

As such, post-structuralist theory provides a sharp contrast with the normative view of networks as the preferred mode of governance, capable of overcoming the disbenefits of both market and hierarchy; or of welfare governance reform as simply a response to new social risks or citizen expectations. The view of power as productive also presents an important challenge to ideas of the empowered subject in new governance regimes: the ways in which state practices of empowerment – of actors to participate in decision-making, of citizens to be responsible for their own health decisions, or households for the provision of their own welfare needs – might be understood, rather, as new strategies of regulation and control. Many of the chapters in this volume trace the constitution of new forms of governable subject: the degendered active citizen, participating in society through work (Chapters Four and Five); the construction of specific populations through public participation strategies (Chapters Six and Eight); or of communities taking responsibility for solving their own problems (Chapter Seven). Indeed, as is argued in Chapter Four, social policy reforms are often introduced in ways that assume that new modes of citizenship – for example, the individuated, adult worker freed from the ties of family or community and ready to take their place in the global, flexible labour market – already exist.

However, we might also highlight some problems in the governmental approach. First, some forms of post-structural work on governmentality tend to produce an over-simplistic view of change in which 'old' forms of governing are displaced by new forms of power. Rather, new discourses draw on and rework older understandings into new configurations. For example, Johansson and Hvinden note that:

> Whether the forms of active citizenship are 'new' in a strict sense is debatable. They may represent a return to ideals or principles present in earlier stages in the history of the welfare state in question, principles which were later marginalised or eroded in the face of competing ideologies. (Chapter Five)

Second, new governmental strategies do not necessarily present coherent rationalities (Rose, 1999). This lack of coherence means that the assemblages may embody internal contradictions and points of fracture. For example, in this volume we trace several different sets of ideas about 'active' citizenship – workforce activation, community activation, active participatory citizenship, active consumerism – which do not necessarily 'hang together' and may exist in tension with one other. General theories of the constitutive power of discourse fail to capture the complexity and diversity of the ways in which conceptions of the public are negotiated and remade.

In *Remaking governance*, then, we trace how large-scale social, political and cultural changes are being enacted. But we are careful to avoid any suggestion of a simple narrative in which old ideas, practices and institutions have been supplanted. Our approach is one that does not assume the effectivity of new discourses of welfare governance, citizenship or democracy, but that attempts to unpick what happens as different ideas and pathways of change intersect and as new discourses confront and interact with older ideas. This means that our understanding of the remaking of governance is one of compound, contested and unstable social and political formations. We also want to avoid any suggestion that these processes are universal, taking the same form across different nation-states. The 'social' of social governance is shaped by and through the specific histories of particular cultures and places. The 'everyday maker' described by Henrik Bang in Chapter Eight is deeply rooted in the traditions of Danish democratic practice, while the successful embedding of the consumerist discourse in the UK is unsurprising, given its place in the rolling out of neo-liberalism. There is a need, then, to pay attention to the specificity of how new governmental discourses are elaborated within different national formations and the ways in which they draw upon, and are articulated with, existing cultural resources. This does not set out to be a comparative book, but it offers a number of analytical frameworks which might contribute to the work of tracing the dynamics of remaking governance in different locations. We do so by embracing both 'cultural' and 'institutional' ways of understanding governance, since we believe that this forms a productive site of intersection and theoretical development.

References

Clarke, J. (2004) *Changing welfare, changing states: New directions in social policy*, London: Sage Publications.

Dean, M. (1999) *Governmentality: Power and rule in modern society*, London: Sage Publications.

Foucault, M. (1991) 'Governmentality', in G. Burchell, C. Gordon and P. Miller (eds) *The Foucault effect: Studies in governmentality*, Hemel Hempstead: Harvester Wheatsheaf.

Giddens, A. (1998) *The third way: The renewal of social democracy*, Cambridge: Polity Press.

Gough, I. (2000) *Global capital, human needs and social policies*, Basingstoke: Palgrave.

Hobson, B., Lewis, J. and Siim, B. (2002) *Contested concepts in gender and social politics*, Cheltenham: Edward Elgar.

Jessop, B. (2000) 'Governance failure', in G. Stoker (ed) *The new politics of British local governance*, Basingstoke: Macmillan, pp 11–33.

Jessop, B. (2002) *The future of the capitalist state*, Cambridge: Polity Press.

Kooiman, J. (2000) 'Societal governance: levels, models and orders of social–political interactions', in J. Pierre (ed) *Debating governance: Authority, steering and democracy*, Oxford: Oxford University Press, pp 138–66.

Kooiman, J. (2003) *Governing as governance*, London: Sage Publications.

Larner, W. and Walters, W. (eds) (2004) *Global governmentality: Governing international spaces*, London: Routledge.

Marston, G. (2004) *Social policy and discourse analysis: Policy change in public housing*, Aldershot: Ashgate.

Newman, J. (2001) *Modernising governance: New labour, policy and society*, London: Sage Publications.

Newman, J. (2004) 'Through thick or thin? The problem of "the social" in societal governance', paper presented to the Contemporary Governance and the Question of the Social Conference, University of Alberta, 11–13 June.

Peters, B., Sifft, S., Wimmel, A., Brüggmann, M. and Königslöw, K. (2005) 'National and transnational public spheres: the case of the EU', in S. Liebfried and M. Zürn (eds) *Transformations of the state*, Cambridge: Cambridge University Press.

Petersen, A., Barnos, I., Dudley, J. and Harris, P. (1999) *Post-structuralism, citizenship and social policy*, London: Routledge.

Rhodes, R.A.W. (2000) 'Conclusion: transforming British government – the governance narrative', in R.A.W. Rhodes (ed) *Transforming British government, vol 1: Changing institutions*, Basingstoke: Macmillan, pp 254–66.

Rose, N. (1999) *Powers of freedom: Reframing political thought*, Cambridge: Cambridge University Press.

Scharpf, F.W. (1999) *Governing in Europe*, Oxford: Oxford University Press.

Walters, W. (2002) 'Social capital and political sociology: re-imaging politics?', *Sociology*, vol 36, no 2, pp 377–97.

Walters, W. (2004) 'Some critical notes on "governance"', *Studies in Political Economy*, vol 73, spring/summer, pp 27–46.

ONE

Reconstituting Europe: governing a European people?

John Clarke

Introduction

European integration remains one of the most controversial political projects of the current period. It is the focus of much political conflict and considerable academic debate. Integration through the institutions of the European Union (EU) is often represented as the expression of an underlying European essence – a unity of place, people or culture. Such imaginaries have proved to be persistently unstable and contestable, providing an imperfect basis for conceiving of an integrative 'European-ness'. In this chapter, the inherent problems of these imagined sources of unity are examined briefly, before attempts to define European-ness in contrast to its 'Others' are considered. Instead of searching for a unifying European 'character', it is argued that Europe is being constituted in the institutions, apparatuses and practices of European governance itself. In the emergent governance arrangement of the EU, we can see a conception of European diversity being constructed as an object to be governed. This view depends on seeing governance arrangements as political–cultural formations, rather than as constitutional or institutional systems whose meaning is self-evident. In the last part of the chapter, some of the limitations of this conception of European diversity and their implications for notions of a 'social Europe' are considered.

In search of unity

My approach to opening up the apparent, or imagined, unity of Europe to critical investigation draws upon previous work on the invention or construction of Europe as a social, political, economic and cultural space (for example, Christiansen et al, 2001; Fink et al, 2001; Balibar,

2002; Leontidou, 2004). Such authors have enabled an understanding of 'Europe' as an imaginary unity with several distinctive features:

- like all socially produced unities, it is necessarily a *unity in difference* – the product of attempts to organise coherence out of multiplicity. At its simplest, this can be grasped as attempts to define what is European, rather than national, in terms of culture, identity, space and forms of attachment or belonging;
- defining European-ness implies the relational definition of the non-European: Europe's 'Others'. In basic terms, this articulation of what Europe is not is worked through the definition of other people, places and cultures. For example, often European-ness is defined axially – it is not the 'South', and nor is it 'American';
- constituting Europe is a process of spatial construction (Hudson and Williams, 1999; Jonsson et al, 2000; Leontidou, 2004). This process involves the construction and alignment of different types of space: economic, political, cultural, for example. This uneven construction of European space is most visible in the shifting borders of different types of Europe: the EU, the Schengen territories[1]; 'Euroland'; and even 'Europe in waiting' – the would-be members of the EU.

The emergence of an integrated Europe as a political project in the second half of the 20th century provoked a search for unifying images through which its coherence could be imagined and projected. The search for European unity mirrored processes of nation-formation in earlier periods – the attempts to define the unity of people, place and culture that both gave birth to and was expressed in the singularity of the nation (Eley and Suny, 1996). The fusion of cultural and territorial unity and integrity was a foundational mythology for what have been called 'Westphalian nation-states': an essentialising and naturalising image of unified sovereignty that has dominated approaches to nation-formation and the international state system (Biersteker and Weber, 1996). It also underpins most constitutionalist discussions of the EU, posed as they are in relation to its consequences for national sovereignty.

We can see this "assumed isomorphism of space, place and culture" (Gupta and Ferguson, 1992, p 7) being scaled up from the national to the supranational level in discussions of the singularity of Europe. The 'people of Europe' have been identified variously with a unique space, a unique history and a unique culture (see, for example, Llobera, 2001). Each of these 'unique' qualities has proved problematic as a basis for constituting 'European-ness'. The conception of a European space is profoundly unstable, not least because the expansive dynamic of the EU itself has ensured that the borders of Europe remain mobile in a number of different directions. To the north, the ambivalence of the UK towards Europe bedevils the 'continental' definition; to the west, Atlantic territories and ex-colonies 'stretch' the boundaries of Europe in disconcerting ways; to the east, the dissolution of the Soviet bloc has reopened discussions about how the West and East are to be distinguished; while to the south, the Mediterranean is simultaneously a border and a past and potential future constituent of Europe (see Balibar, 2002, pp 230-5; Leontidou, 2004, pp 600-3). The conflicts over Turkey as a potential EU member have hinged, in part, on a disputed conception of the space of Europe.

At times, then, the concept of a European space serves to unsettle rather than solidify the idea of an integrated European-ness. While the borders remain mobile and subject to renegotiation, Europe cannot be a settled space. Its unsettled quality invites more evaluative mappings: of the 'real' Europe; of the European 'heartland' (as opposed to peripheral territories); of the 'old' (rather than 'new') Europeans, and so on. This sort of shifting and contested alignment emerges from the problem of stabilising the European space. Not surprisingly, efforts to define European-ness have tended to prioritise formations of people and/or culture.

However, it has also proved difficult to forge a coherent conception of a European people. The spatial instability noted above is one source of problems: since the space is expandable, so too is the range and variety of peoples who may have to be included in the 'European'. Even if the biological and cultural imaginary of colonial racial hierarchies could be maintained in the present, Europe would still lack a 'racial unity': it is cross-cut by a *mélange* of old and new differences. An 'Anglo-Saxon' European model of unity clearly lacks both empirical and political plausibility, no matter the attempts that are made to reinvent it as a locus of both national and European regression. But the spaces of Europe are already:

- *multiracial* – even in the colonial figuring of racial characters and hierarchies, 'Mediterranean' and 'Slavic' peoples coexist with the 'Anglo-Saxon';
- *multi-ethnic* – through the colonial and post-colonial diasporas and in the blurrings of East and West, for example; and
- *multinational* – as people and places have become increasingly interpenetrated by the migrations to, and within, 'Europe'.

So, like the spatial imaginary, the racial imaginary of a European people cannot provide a foundation for a unifying European-ness, even without addressing the conventional problem of whether national identity outweighs or renders impossible a European identity. As Llobera remarks:

> The results of successive editions of the *Eurobarometer* show that in most EU countries only a very small percentage of people (around 5 per cent) declare having an exclusive European identity, while up to 50 per cent do not have any sense of European identity ... there is little doubt that the sentiment of belonging to an entity called Europe is rather limited. (2001, p 173)

But if there is no unifying conception of a European people as a racialised entity, then what about the appeal to a common culture, or the sharing of a common history of European civilization? Here, there are rather more fulsome efforts emanating from the EU and related agents that attempt to imagine a Europe formed of common cultural orientations, values and experiences. Fernandez-Arnesto's (2002) commentary identifies seven forms of this argument. A 'European civilisation' may be marked by a shared religion, language, political culture, intellectual culture, economic culture, the Enlightenment or a shared historical experience. He argues that neither history nor the present configuration of Europe allows any of these to define an essential and integrative European-ness. Religion has been internally divisive (within and between nations), while there are three major language groups (Romance, Germanic and Slavonic) and over 70 languages spoken within the countries of the EU (Llobera, 2001, p 189).

Nevertheless, at times, claims to a common cultural heritage have played a critical role in identifying a European identity. As Llobera observes, "from this perspective, European culture is what people like Dante, Michaelangelo, Goethe, Mozart, Beethoven, Goya, Dostoevsky and many others produced" (2001, p 184). In this discussion, we might want to disentangle three things:

(1) the existence of European cultural networks from the 17th century which produced and circulated art and artists of various kinds;
(2) the limited penetration of high cultural forms and practices into 'European' (and other) popular cultures; and

(3) the selective production of cultural canons to define and perpetuate high culture as the site of civilised people and practices.

The work of *inventing* a European civilization, based in high cultural production and consumption, might be seen better as a continuing process, rather than the expression of a deeply-embedded, unifying cultural heritage.

Europe and its Others

Often, the attempt to imagine a European unity has been worked through implicit or explicit distinctions between Europe and its Others. We can identify three main axes of European distinction: civilisation/ barbarism, West/East and America/Europe. As we will see, these are not entirely distinct and all articulate a conception of a Europe cohered by history and values against its Others. The dominant trope here is European civilisation contrasted against backwardness or barbarism. This is a conception that was strongly formed in the colonial period, as forms of European rule were exercised over subordinated colonial populations. As Balibar insists, this is the inextricable connection of the European nation-state and colonialism. The very form of the nation-state, its mode of citizenship and its conception of universalism were the products of this combination:

> One could now show that ... there is a material correlation between the development of the nation-form, its progressive triumph as a specifically 'bourgeois' form of political life (thus a form of institution of 'bourgeoisie' or citizenship) over other competing forms (urban republicanism, dynastic empire and so forth), and the dominant position occupied in the world-economy by the nations in the course of formation ... But what is of more interest to us here is the way in which this historical correlation is translated into the very formulation of universalism: first in religious language, as a mission of evangelization, then in secular terms through the discourse of the Enlightenment, as a mission of civilization of the whole of humanity with which, each on its own account and all together, 'European' nations, bearers of a certain idea of Man, the *polis*, Culture and so forth, would have been invested on behalf of the rest of the world. This represents an *extensive* (or assimilationist) universalism whose relation to an imperialist

politics (in the double sense of economic-political imperialism and cultural imperialism, formation of an 'Empire of Truth') cannot seriously be denied. (2002, p 57; emphasis in original)

This civilisation/barbarism axis mobilises many of the unifying threads noted previously. They are woven together in a conception of Europe as older and wiser than other places and peoples. In the post-colonial period, the articulation of Europe-as-civilisation requires a work of remembering this connection between the civilising mission and colonial rule. The universals of European civilisation have to be separated – or salvaged – from their implication in colonialism. Colonialism is historicised, remembered as the errors of the past (where it is remembered at all). Civilisation is then universalised anew, free from any taint of power, exploitation or oppression. This conception of a transcendent culture remains contested in relation to forms of European and national governance within Europe, not least in the disturbed spaces inhabited by diasporic populations.

Although elaborated primarily in and through colonialism, this distinctiveness of Europe as a political–cultural entity has been significant also to conceptions of East and West. The projection of a shared political–cultural character enabled the alignment of Europe as part of the West (against both the East and the rest; Hall, 1992). Most clearly, Europe was sutured into an East/West division between 'communism' and the 'free world' after 1945. This gave primacy to 'values' (the persistent imagery of freedom-as-markets plus liberal democracy) over space, in that 'central and eastern' Europe became non-European, or de-Europeanised (Leontidou, 2004, pp 604-5).

More recently, this image of Europe has been aligned with the 'clash of civilisations' imagery of a world divided between Christianity and Islam (Huntington, 1996). However, it has also been resisted around a different axial alignment of Europe versus America. Although this formulation took shape conjuncturally around the proposed invasion of Iraq, it has deeper roots in conflicts over different places and trajectories in contemporary forms of globalisation. The US commitment to a neo-liberal form of globalisation – an insistence on free trade 'opening up' national economies and reducing (if not subverting) national political institutions – was both institutionally and politically in tension with EU conceptions of a social market, and hostile to social democratic and Christian democratic conceptions of the social, social rights and social welfare. This antagonism has been played out in a number of ways: in conflicts in the World Trade

Organization; in conflicts over policy formation and direction; and in images of an older and wiser (if less powerful) Europe constraining or mediating a new US imperialism.[2]

None of these images of Europe has proved sustainable, not least because of the interpenetration of Europe and its imagined others. The colonies were always partly constitutive of the imperial centres, never just their passive product (Hall, 2002). Their existence shaped the institutions, imaginaries and politics of the imperial cores. European political cultures were formed in and through the colonial encounter, and were reformed as the periphery began to migrate to the centre. In a different way, the conception of East versus West, produced as a Cold War distinction, was always uncertain. Listen to the shifting 'Europes' evoked in Llobera's attempt to see whether Europe can be defined 'against its enemies':

> In the past, one way of looking at what united Europeans was to consider who they were fighting against. Historically Islam was the classical enemy. In the twentieth century, it was the struggle first against fascism and then against communism. (2001, p 178)

As Guibernau remarks, the period of the 'crusades' against Islam cannot be made to fit a simplifying conception in which Europe equals Christian:

> [E]arly Europe as Christendom already contained significant religious minorities (Jews and Muslims) – and it barely included the rural masses, whose peasant status was closely linked with a 'pagan' (and thus non-Christian) outlook that presented a constant challenge to the consolidation of any regional Christian realm. (2001a, p 8)

There is a critical point here about how we understand the 'interior' of Europe, in that it always contains parts of what is apparently 'external'. We can see this even more emphatically if we look at the other 'enemies' identified by Llobera. Fascism was hardly an external enemy – originally, the struggles over fascism were internal to Europe, only subsequently engaging other places and peoples into mass warfare. Equally, communism had a decisively European location and line of development – however much the capitalist democracies of the West attempted to construct an East/West distinction that orientalised communism. Communism and communists persisted inside the West, to the irritation of non-communist western governments. In short, Europe's apparent 'Others' (including the military, economic and cultural formations of 'America') are always deeply ensconced within the Europe that tries to separate itself from them. Europe is never 'pure'.

At the border

Europe has become increasingly concerned with questions of border maintenance, particularly in the face of flows of migrants and asylum-seekers, as well as movements within the EU itself. The project of defining a European social and economic space has led to an increased concern to differentiate 'citizens' from 'aliens'. The formation of European citizenship is shaped by the approaches of member governments, such that the conditions of citizenship remain nationally defined (with the EU identifying European citizens as the citizens of Member States). A whole battery of distinctions and differentiations have been put to work in constructing 'citizens' – what Balibar (2002, p 60) calls an apparatus of "anthropological differences" that justify exclusion from citizenship. In one sense, this intensified concern with borders and the management of membership is widely understood (see, for example, Layton-Henry, 2001). Integral to the process of constructing the space of Europe has been the solidification of borders, popularly construed as the building of 'Fortress Europe'. Partly because of the shifting frame of the EU itself, and partly because of different national policies towards the relationship of migration, residence and citizenship rights, the image of Fortress Europe has overstated and oversimplified the border question – since different borders have been unevenly permeable to differently identified groups of would-be citizens. Borders are also the site of complex transactions, mobilities and intensities where cultures, commodities and peoples are complexly intertwined (Leontidou and Afouxenidis, 1999).

Nevertheless, border control has remained a central question for the formation of Europe, most often posed in a range of racialised forms against migration from the South and the East. The legacy of the colonial imagination is the capacity to racialise differences, producing new formations of subordinated Others (ethnicised, minoritised and made objects of suspicion). In most cases, the racialised difference overrides other positions (including residence), such that racialised Others are identified as properly belonging 'elsewhere' even if they are second- or third-generation inhabitants of European space. In the administrative management of border zones, the identification of 'aliens' or 'suspect' figures involves the thoroughly routinised classification of persons in momentary encounters. As Miles (1999) observes, these processes (and their necessary speed of classification) produce stereotypical criteria for differentiation: who looks as though they belong here?

We are used to thinking about borders and their management as positioned at the intersection of the external and internal worlds: taking place at the edge of the nation or the EU. However, the complexly constituted and turbulent populace of a multi-ethnic Europe means that borders and boundaries are also policed, regulated and enforced in the interior as well as at the edges. In particular, the production of the category 'illegal immigrant' at the intersection of European citizenships and migration flows produces a policing of the interior that deploys the characteristic (and characteristically racialised) categories of normal citizen and abnormal alien. Balibar argues that we have seen a proliferation of (state) apparatuses and practices designed to control the internal space of Europe (in its different national formations) through the question of immigration:

> An endless spiral links the refusal to consider residency rights as a *democratic norm*, the repression of 'illegals', the amalgamation of different phenomena of illegality and criminality (it is particularly serious that 'unlawful residency' is designated and punished as a *crime*), the syndrome of collective insecurity, the stigmatization of foreigners in general (or, rather, those 'foreigners among foreigners' who come from the South including Africans, Arabs and Turks) and the normalization of violence against them. (2002, p 63; emphasis in original)

This internalisation of borders, he suggests, is a European phenomenon, even though it is administered through the bureaucratic and policing apparatuses of nation-states within Europe. Balibar and others have argued that Europe (in contradistinction to nation-states) may be a political terrain on which the question of citizenship might be reworked in less repressive and more emancipatory ways, not least because of the regressive and exclusionary forms of nationalism which hitherto have framed access to citizenship (see also, for example, Soysal, 1994).

What is clear is that these issues of borders and the management of the relations between domestic and external populations challenge the idea of a 'European people' distinguished by a shared 'race' or culture. The world, so to speak, is already within Europe. This is the distinctive characteristic of the post-colonial condition: people no longer know – or are bounded by – their 'proper place'. The better management of the border (at the edge or internally) cannot restore a European 'essence' or preserve it from 'contamination'.

A European governance?

Let us summarise the argument so far. Although it is possible to see a variety of imaginaries that claim a distinctive European-ness, none of these has provided a compelling, coherent or uncontested unity for Europe. History, culture, space and 'race' have failed to deliver – even though they go on being tried. Trying to hold back the 'Others' absorbs a lot of attention, effort and emotion and has corrosive and degrading effects on the political and public spheres of contemporary Europe. Instead, let us suggest that a reading of EU governance institutions and practices offers a different view of European-ness, as a political–cultural project inscribed in the arrangements developed to govern 'Europe'. European governance can be treated as a *constitutive* formation – one that makes Europe, even as it claims to reflect European-ness. William Walters has argued recently that most studies of European integration have failed to explore its 'discursive' character:

> Scholars of the EU have not been particularly interested in the discursive aspect of European integration. Whether European integration is analysed in terms of a dynamic interplay of geopolitical and economic 'interests', as an unfolding process driven forward by increasing socioeconomic and political 'interdependence', or as a shift from a system of 'state-centric' to 'multilevel' governance, one thing is quite constant. It is that questions of the discursive framing of 'Europe' have been relatively marginal to these endeavours. (2004, p 157)

Elsewhere, I have argued for treating states and other governance arrangements as political–cultural formations, the outcome of projects to imagine the world, and to construct the world in that image (Clarke, 2004). In what follows, I will argue that the multiple modes of European governance define their object of governance – a united Europe – and attribute to it a set of characteristics which both need to be governed and shape the mode of governance appropriate to those characteristics. This approach to governance defines the character of European-ness as the 'civilised' reconciliation of inter-nation differences through institutionalised processes of negotiation, compromise and persuasion. This united Europe is contrasted with Europe's 'past' – a shared history not of civilised values, but of recurrent dissension, violence, conflict, invasion and war. The result is a system of governance in which European 'diversity' must be reconciled. Nation-states are clearly one embodiment of this diversity, and have long been the focus of the distinctive concerns of governance: integration, harmonisation and coordination (see, for example, Emma Carmel in Chapter Two of this volume and Dale, 2004 on the Open Method of Coordination). Walters (2004) draws out a number of governmental apparatuses and strategies in the construction of an integrated Europe:

- the technising identification of Europe as a project of modernisation;
- the construction of new apparatuses of planning for the EU which had to coexist with national centres of power;
- the logic of harmonisation (rather than standardisation); and
- the institutionalisation of integration as a bureaucratic conception and practice.

Leontidou also foregrounds the 'bureaucratic/institutional narrative' of Europe-as-EU, arguing that this narrative

> includes anniversaries, days of celebration in Europe, and landmarks in its development (eg, 9 May 1950), as well as heroes and visionaries of European integration, such as Robert Schuman and Jean Monnet, giving their names to metro stations, streets and University Chairs.... By implicitly equating 'Europe' with the European Union after successive territorial formalizations, the new narrative influences the construction of new spatialities in cultural and social life. It attempts to place 'Europe' as a constructed spatiality in parallel with the nation-state, by-passing legislation, regulations and treaties in the EU. (2004, pp 605-6)

Both Leontidou and Walters highlight the persistence of nations as governmental objects and categories within the EU, with nations and their characteristics formalised, modelled and calculated. Thus EU governance codifies the object of its integrative strategies. Walters argues that "through the harmonization of national standards Europe is to be constituted as a relatively smooth space, open to the free movement of professionals, goods, services and much else" (2004, p 166). But he is emphatic that this is not the same as standardisation, which implies the dissolution of national differences. For Leontidou, there is a constant movement between integration and nations:

> The principle of 'subsidiarity' was partly devised as the pole opposite to 'Europeanization' within one and the same institutional discourse, in order to calm rising euroscepticism in the face of centralistic decision-making processes. This contradiction is mirrored in the tendency of a postnational political culture to essentialise the nation-state in the context of the EU dominant bureaucratic narrative. (2004, p 608)

This system of governance for constituting and reconciling European diversity is not exactly liberal democracy in the form that European (or western) values usually celebrate. Although there is an elected assembly, it is by no means the most influential element of the combination, flanked as it is by the European Commission, the European Court and the Council of Ministers. The 'voting citizens' of Europe are doubly represented – not only through the direct election of members of the European Parliament, but also by their national leaders in the Council of Ministers. The European Court and European Commission provide countervailing powers to these representative processes, forming the second element of Gramsci's (1971) description of the state as the 'democratic-bureaucratic complex'. For Gramsci, the bureaucratic element was always a critical element of the capitalist state, insulating policy, direction and power from the uncertainties and vagaries of popular politics. In the EU, too, the weight of the bureaucracy is a reminder of Europe's ambivalent relationship to popular politics, a testimony not just to the elite character of the EU's invention and development, but also to the fears of an incursionary democratic politics of Europe (whether regressive or emancipatory). Doing Europe's business – and doing business in Europe – both have been seen as processes that need protecting against politics.

Nevertheless, the citizens of Europe appear in other rights-bearing modes in this combined system of European governance: as 'legal citizens' and 'social citizens'. The European Court has been a mechanism for claims-making individuals to work at the tensions between national and supranational government, using 'European' conceptions of equality and human rights to resist, challenge or overturn national policies and practices. However, as noted earlier, its 'European-ness' is limited by the convention that European citizens are construed as citizens of Member States – so non-citizens are not rights-bearing individuals. Both the European Court and the European Commission have embodied and developed conceptions of a social Europe. We may note two different things about this social Europe: first, concerning the meaning of the social; second, concerning the relationship between the social and modes of European governance.

Constituting 'social' Europe

As Janet Newman argued in the Introduction, the 'social' is a contested domain, rather than a simple distinction between the social and the economic or political domains of contemporary society (Clarke, 2004, Chapter 3). In one critical sense, the 'social' denotes that which may be changed, remedied, regulated or managed by intentional policy and intervention. Much energy has been expended from a post-Foucauldian point of view on whether the 'social' has been diminished or dissolved in advanced or neo-liberal governmentality (Rose, 1999). But in its different incarnations, Europe has been a site of (highly contested) expansive conceptions of the social. Although originally this took the form of a corporatist view of the 'social', articulating the social partners of business and labour in the regulation of employment and working conditions, other struggles have left their traces on the European 'social'. These have been centrally around gender equality (Geyer, 2000) but have included other struggles around 'race'/ethnicity, the politics of time, sexualities and the environment.

I do not mean here that the EU has been transformed by radical and progressive social movements (although its critics sometimes suggest that it has deviated from the proper political–economic business of governing a European 'economic space'). Nevertheless, the movements have had an impact on European self-conceptions as a site of 'progressive' and not just 'civilised' values. The European Commission and the European Court have proved partially open to such socialising conceptions of what is to be governed – particularly those formulated as challenges to unwarranted, unreasonable and inappropriate 'discriminations' (for example, discriminatory differences in employment conditions, or retirement policies and practices). In its imaginary of a European social space, the EU seeks to overcome distinctions that stand in the way of creating a European people (whether they are based on nation, gender, age and – uneasily – 'race').

Social Europe is profoundly linked to the multiple modes of European governance, because the EU has supplemented the representative channels of parliamentary and ministerial processes with an attempt to foster the engagement of 'civil society' in its workings. For some commentators, the concept of governance itself denotes a shift away from the state-centric processes of government to a more diverse and differentiated set of processes articulating state and society. For example, Guibernau argues that the concept is particularly relevant to the study of the EU because it

> is closely connected to the growing complexity of the governing processes and the number of actors involved. Governance involves the emergence of autonomous self-organizing networks of actors. These self-organizing networks come to centre stage as a result of the shift from government to governance, and include regions, ethnic minorities, feminist groups, green groups, labour movements, elites, pressure groups, family associations, media organizations and many other social actors. (2001a, p 29)

She goes on to argue that this mode of governing is seen as having both functional and symbolic value:

> The main advantage of encouraging the emergence of governance processes is that self-organizing networks are seen as more effective than government-imposed regulation, and that they have the potential to enhance democratic practice through greater contact between state and civil society. It is in this sense that governance can be defined as a mechanism that enables people to participate in governing processes. (2001a, p 30)

This formulation encapsulates the significance of how the social (here understood as people freely associating in civil society) and governing are forged into a sort of unity in the EU. It also begs a few questions about the relationships between people, politics and power. The 'governance narrative' (Rhodes, 1997) typically blurs some issues of causation: does the shift to governance reflect the rise of increasingly potent 'self-organising networks' in civil society; or does it create the conditions in which they can flourish? In the context of the development of the EU, such associations have been actively *sponsored* by the EU as a deliberate supplement to national political representation. Non-governmental organisations (NGOs) have been required as part of the EU's view of consultation and participation, and have taken local, regional, national and transnational forms. But at the same time, social movements and associations have been a source of innovative pressure on the bureaucratic complex, as Barnett argues in the case of EU cultural policy:

> The grafting of an 'ethic of participation' onto elite-driven policy processes has changed the patterns of consultation and representation through which EU cultural policies, including audio-visual policy, have developed.... The shaping of EU initiatives for media and culture around a discourse of citizenship, when connected to institutional changes in opportunities for the participation of a broader range of policy actors, has provided a foothold for different actors to challenge and contest dominant conceptions of citizenship, media and democracy. (2003, p 145)

The EU commitment to reflecting – and creating – a European 'civil society' offers a further example of the institutionalisation of a European-ness in the apparatuses of governing. It reflects the enlargement of the European 'social' beyond its original labour market focus in which the primary social partners were labour and capital. It envisages a European citizenry engaged with a range of social issues that are not always captured in the politics and policies of national governments (for example, environmental, regional, urban and familial issues). It imagines that such issues and interests may be organised and articulated in associational forms, and seeks to aid and foster such 'self-organisation'. While this forms part of the repertoire of voices, interests and possibilities that might constitute Europe, consultation and participation remain notably *indeterminate* governing processes and relationships (see Newman, Chapter Six of this volume). The people of Europe might be encouraged to speak, and they may be listened to respectfully, but the multiplicity of voices creates a precise space in which decisional power can be exercised centrally. In this context, governance denotes a more complex and ambivalent set of relationships between people and power; between state(s) and societies; between forms of representation and modalities of decision-making. The multiplicity of forms, sites and processes in the governance of Europe speaks to the problem of articulating an economic, political and social space that is European – and to the symbolism of what Guibernau (2001b) calls 'governing European diversity'.

Conclusion: governing a European people?

Here I have attempted to argue that, rather than search for a single dominant and integrative European imaginary, we might look instead at the ways in which the multiple modes of governing in Europe are framed by the challenge of producing Europe in a European way. What is European is not to be derived from statements about European culture, character or civilisation, although such claims abound. In the contemporary period, every claim to discern the essence of European-ness – whether addressed to 'race', place, culture or history – is essentially contestable, and is usually contested in practice (see, for example, the arguments over Turkey's potential membership of the EU). Instead, I have tried to argue that it is in the modes of 'governing European diversity' that we can see an attempt to define European-ness – *how* Europe is to be made (a project, not a reflection) is what expresses the character of Europe. This multimodal apparatus of governing is itself understood as a dynamic of movement between unity and multiplicity (a dynamic that is permanent, because 'Europe' itself will never be settled). This final section draws out two sets of issues about this view of 'governing diversity'.

First, it requires some attention to the articulation of the apparatuses, processes and relationships of governing. This assemblage both addresses and expresses the multiplicity of Europe, primarily but not solely conceived in national terms. Europe is to be governed through mechanisms which embody (aspirationally European) integrative values – collaboration rather than conflict, negotiation rather than violence, subjection to legitimate authority (and the rule of law) rather than wanton (national) individualism, and an investment in building a multivocal, diverse and tolerant European civil society. The multiplicity of the European Commission, European Court, Council of Ministers and European Parliament reflects the problem of reconciling the multiple interests that form the economic, political and social spaces of Europe. Both the bureaucratic and juridical apparatuses constrain the risks or fears of popular democracy, while the associational voicing of civil society offsets the potential ossification of representative politics into party or other blocs. The 'genius' of European governance, then, is to create apparatuses that embody a vision of European values which might prevent Europe from repeating its history – whether conflict and war, imperial aggrandisement or the violent 'irrationalities' of popular politics.

Second, this view of governing diversity requires some attention to what is included in the conception of diversity – and what is not. The core focus of European diversity is the multiple nations that constitute (at any one time) the membership of the EU – and they are the primary object of the multiple modes of integrative governance. But in response to different pressures (from national governments and social movements) the EU has developed a widening conception of the 'social' as a field of intervention and association. Here, however, the foundational problem of European citizenship continues to pose a problem about where the boundary of 'legitimate diversity' is to be drawn. The EU has been drawn increasingly into issues of discrimination and inequalities around formations of 'race' and ethnicity that disturb the 'social space' of Europe. Where governments, businesses and other political–economic agents discriminate or behave unreasonably towards identifiable minorities, EU governance conceptions of equity and tolerance may underpin attempts to remedy such conditions.

However, the social space of Europe is itself multiply constituted: as a geographic space (in which people live); as a multinational space (in which people are or are not citizens); and as a racialised space (in which people have 'anthropological' identities in a colonial or post-colonial formation). The European people who inhabit this social space are the subject of 'splitting' – European by virtue of residence or presence; non-European by virtue of citizenship exclusions (at the national level); European by virtue of archaic racialised classification; non-European by virtue of their evident Otherness. In this splitting, we find the double motif of 'exclusion' and 'tolerance' which embodies post-colonial ambivalence (Lewis, 2002). The contested and unstable concern with 'multiculturalism' is one site of these strains (Hesse, 2001), while questions of immigration, asylum and 'illegality' form the other critical locus. Exclusion and tolerance are densely interwoven, not least in the claim that exclusion is a necessary condition for the maintenance of tolerance.

'Tolerance' is a marker of the civility of Europe, and an invocation as to the mode of governing that is appropriate to the conduct of a civil society[3]. It is a concept that often underpins multicultural conceptions of the social space (for example, in education, socialisation and cultural policy). It oscillates unstably between conceptions of mutuality and hierarchy. At one moment, it is an insistence on 'mutual respect' as a rule that should govern encounters between others, but it is also the voice in which the assumed centre speaks to the peripheral or marginal ('We will tolerate You'). This second voicing of tolerance is the metropolitan position in the post-colonial. It is historically amnesiac: forgetful of how difference was constituted in the process of

European rule; dismissive of old or archaic assumptions about the colonial structuring of racialised distinctions; and at ease with a 'civil' diversity. It is tolerant, in effect, of differences that are not disturbing. But the self-confident voicing of tolerance belies a set of uncertainties and anxieties that are occasioned by the doubling of the world within and beyond Europe. 'The rest', the 'South' (and parts of the 'East') are disputed and disputable objects of international intervention. But they are always understood as separated from 'Europe' – the elsewheres whose past intertwining with Europe is the subject of recurrent amnesia. This is the distinction that enables the announcement of Europe as a tolerant centre.

The 'race'/ethnicity couplet thus comes to play a multiple role in the processes of governing European diversity. It is spoken in the (contested) formulations of official multiculturalism, and governs the regulatory administration and policing of 'legitimate membership' of the social space as the apparatuses of governing classify and control 'the people' of Europe. But it is also denied (at national and European levels) as part of the processes which regulate citizenship in the context of migration and asylum. Governments are profoundly resistant to claims that their approaches to 'managing immigration' may be discriminatory or racist, claiming instead that the policies, processes and practices are merely administrative and juridical: dealing with 'illegalities' on the part of migrants themselves, or the 'criminal gangs' who transport and exploit them.

Here we identify the contested limits of European diversity – in the struggles to include and exclude people within the 'European'. It is not that there is a singular and essentialised European identity – on the contrary, multiplicity and diversity are understood to be characteristics of 'European-ness'. Rather, the profound social conflicts centre on the definition of the range and limits of this multiplicity and diversity. While citizenship remains a field of national systems of inclusion and exclusion; while the condition of presence or residence in the European social space is not a rights-bearing status; and while the criteria of classification of citizen or alien are compounded and conflated with a post-colonial imaginary of racialised difference, citizenship may be a continuing site of ungovernability in the constitution of Europe.

Notes
[1] A group of Member States which have abolished border controls between each other.

[2] It is visible in arguments about whether there is a distinctive 'European' model of welfare states (for example, Leibfried, 2000), and about the relationship or distinction between Europeanisation and globalisation (for example, Beyeler, 2003; Graziano, 2003).

[3] I am grateful to Wendy Brown and Gail Lewis who have led me to think about the governmental significance of tolerance. Neither is responsible for what I have made of it.

References

Balibar, E. (2002) *We, the people of Europe? Reflections of transnational citizenship*, Princeton, NJ: Princeton University Press.

Barnett, C. (2003) *Culture and democracy: Media, space and representation*, Edinburgh: University of Edinburgh Press.

Beyeler, M. (2003) 'Globalization, Europeanization and domestic welfare state reforms: new institutionalist concepts', *Global Social Policy*, vol 3, no 2, pp 153-72.

Biersteker, T. and Weber, C. (eds) (1996) *State sovereignty as social construct*, Cambridge: Cambridge University Press.

Christiansen, T., Jorgensen, K. and Wiener, A. (eds) (2001) *Social construction of Europe*, London: Sage Publications.

Clarke, J. (2004) *Changing welfare, changing states: New directions in social policy*, London: Sage Publications.

Dale, R. (2004) 'Forms of governance, governmentality and the EU's Open Method of Coordination', in W. Larner and W. Walters (eds) *Global governmentality: Governing international spaces*, London: Routledge, pp 174-94.

Eley, G. and Suny, R. (eds) (1996) *Becoming National: A Reader*, Oxford: Oxford University Press.

Fernandez-Arnesto, F. (2002) 'A European civilization: is there any such thing?', *European Review*, vol 10, no 1, pp 3-14.

Fink, J., Lewis, G. and Clarke, J. (eds) (2001) *Rethinking European welfare*, London: Sage Publications/The Open University.

Geyer, R. (2000) *Exploring European social policy*, London: Sage Publications.

Gramsci, A. (1971) *Selections from the prison notebooks*, London: Lawrence and Wishart.

Graziano, P. (2003) 'Europeanization or globalization? A framework for empirical research (with some evidence from the Italian case)', *Global Social Policy*, vol 3, no 2, pp 173-94.

Guibernau, M. (2001a) 'Introduction: unity and diversity in Europe', in M. Guibernau (ed) *Governing European diversity*, London: Sage Publications/The Open University, pp 1-34.

Guibernau, M. (ed) (2001b) *Governing European diversity*, London: Sage Publications/The Open University.

Gupta, A. and Ferguson, J. (1992) 'Beyond "culture": space, identity and the politics of difference', *Cultural Anthropology*, vol 7, no 1, pp 6-23.

Hall, C. (2002) *Civilising subjects: Metropole and colony in the English imagination 1830-1867*, Chicago, IL: University of Chicago Press.

Hall, S. (1992) 'The West and the rest: discourse and power', in S. Hall and B. Gieben (eds) *Formations of modernity*, Cambridge: Polity Press, pp 275-320.

Hesse, B. (ed) (2001) *Un/Settled multiculturalisms: Diasporas, entanglements and transruptions*, London: Zed Books.

Hudson, R. and Williams, A.M. (eds) (1999) *Divided Europe: Society and territory*, London: Sage Publications.

Huntington, S. (1996) *The clash of civilizations and the remaking of world order*, New York, NY: Simon and Schuster.

Jonsson, C., Tagil, S. and Tornqvist, G. (2000) *Organizing European space*, London: Routledge.

Layton-Henry, Z. (2001) 'Migrants, refugees and citizenship', in M. Guibernau (ed) *Governing European diversity*, London: Sage Publications/The Open University, pp 65-102.

Leibfried, S. (2000) 'National welfare states, European integration and globalization: a perspective for the next century', *Social Policy and Administration*, vol 34, no 1, pp 44-63.

Leontidou, L. (2004) 'The boundaries of Europe: deconstructing three regional narratives', *Identities: Global Studies in Culture and Power*, vol 11, pp 593-617.

Leontidou, L. and Afouxenidis, A. (1999) 'Boundaries of social exclusion in Europe', in J. Fink, G. Lewis and J. Clarke (eds) *Rethinking European welfare*, London: Sage Publications, pp 231-48.

Lewis, G. (2002) 'Culture as practice, culture as sign: post-colonial anxiety in the midst of multi-culturalism', paper presented to the Crossroads in Cultural Studies Conference, Tampere, Finland, July.

Llobera, J. (2001) 'What unites Europeans?', in M. Guibernau (ed) *Governing European diversity*, London: Sage Publications/The Open University, pp 169-94.

Miles, R. (1999) 'Analysing the political economy of migration: the airport as an "effective" institution of control', in A. Brah, M. Hickman and M. Mac an Ghaill (eds) *Global futures: Migration, environment and globalization*, Basingstoke: Macmillan, pp 161-84.

Rhodes, R. (1997) *Understanding governance: Policy networks, governance, reflexivity and accountability*, Buckingham: Open University Press.

Rose, N. (1999) *Powers of freedom*, Cambridge: Cambridge University Press.

Soysal, Y. (1994) *Limits of citizenship: Migrants and postnational membership in Europe*, Chicago, IL: Chicago University Press.

Walters, W. (2004) 'The political rationality of European integration', in W. Larner and W. Walters (eds) *Global governmentality: Governing international spaces*, London: Routledge, pp 155-73.

TWO

Governance and the constitution of a European social

Emma Carmel

Introduction

The past 10 to 15 years have seen a transformation in the European Union's (EU) engagement with social policy issues – from the Social Protocol in the Maastricht Treaty to the initiation of a new mode of policymaking, the Open Method of Coordination (OMC). This is designed to allow the EU to engage with social policy issues ranging from employment services to immigration, social cohesion and pension systems. Originally used to manage the process of introducing the single currency and creating the Eurozone (de la Porte and Pochet, 2002a), it appeared to offer a solution to the EU's frozen social policy landscape. The OMC seemed to politicians and scholars alike to offer a new way of overcoming the impasse of Member States' intransigent defence of their existing welfare state arrangements and their resistance to joint measures which would involve them in perhaps unpalatable legal and/or financial commitments. This chapter begins by outlining the ways in which OMC functions as a policymaking process. However, the chapter is less concerned with the process itself than with the interaction of the governance processes and the formal policy goals, and how this interaction delineates the limits of the social in social policy governance within the EU.

While each OMC has particular characteristics, the broad principles remain the same across all policy areas. The common social and social policy problems faced by all EU Member States would be dealt with by adopting common policy goals and through learning from each other regarding the best policy solutions to meet these goals, through benchmarking and comparison using common indicators, and in the European Employment Strategy (EES) common targets. This means that broad agreement on policy goals could be gained, without imposing a uniform 'Euro-solution' onto all Member States for every policy area. The Member States would debate, negotiate and agree these goals at regular meetings, but crucially, they could choose to use and implement whichever means were politically, economically or socially appropriate to the circumstances of their (welfare) state in order to meet those goals. The basic policy mechanisms are the production of regular (annual or biannual) National Action Plans (NAPs) by Member States, which report on how policy goals are being met, followed by a multilateral surveillance of these reports by all the Member States, and a joint report on the NAPs produced by the European Commission. This joint report also refers to the agreed indicators and targets, both jointly and for each Member State individually.

As a generic mode of governance, the OMC is now applied to the areas of employment, social inclusion, pensions, health care and immigration, as well as economic policy and the 'information society'. The principles of the OMCs in social policy were established in the EES, while employment gained legal status as a policy concern of the EU in the 1997 Amsterdam Treaty. The terminology of 'open methods' for other policy areas was endorsed and formalised at the 2000 spring meeting of the European Council in Lisbon. It was at this meeting that the Council agreed a new strategic objective for the EU, "to become the most competitive and dynamic knowledge-based economy in the world capable of sustaining economic growth with more and better jobs and greater social cohesion" (European Council, 2000, p 5), and in consequence of this objective, the social inclusion OMC (OMC/incl.) was introduced.

As a consequence, in recent years there has been flourishing academic interest in the OMCs, focusing on their potential and efficacy as governance instruments, the processes themselves and on their impact in terms of directing policy goals or institutions within Member States (Goetschy, 1999, 2003; de la Porte et al, 2001). Despite the growing amount of research, in many ways these studies are in their infancy: we have few detailed published studies of national impact (de la Porte and Pochet, 2002b and Pochet and Zeitlin, 2005: forthcoming being notable exceptions); there is a great deal that we do not yet know about even the EES, the most-studied social policy OMC; and, for example, the processes of multilateral surveillance and peer review remain largely a black box (de la Porte and Pochet, 2004), despite their importance in the OMCs.

In what follows, the focus will be on the OMCs in the areas of employment and social inclusion, in part because these are the most well established but also because they are associated with developments that appear most clearly to bring a European 'social' into the collective imaginary of Member State and EU policy actors. This chapter asks: is there an identifiable European 'social', however contested and unstable, which can be identified as an object of EU governance, and what does this social look like? What are its component elements and limits?

Governance and the constitution of the social: means and ends

It is the contention of this chapter that all forms of governance constitute that which is to be governed in ways that reveal and, in many cases reproduce, particular forms, divisions and categorisations of the social world. Governance forms can be analysed as a specific ensemble of practices and procedures, "capable of making some form of that activity (of governing) thinkable and practicable both to its practitioners and to those upon whom it was practised" (Gordon, 1991, p 3). Crucially, this historically contingent ensemble of governance procedures necessarily produces the subject categories of those procedures, such as national citizens/EU citizens/immigrants, easterners/westerners, or categories of welfare subjects, such as employed/unemployed/inactive/retired. At the same time, this ensemble establishes limits to what constitutes 'appropriate', 'common-sensical' or 'possible' forms of action by the institutions and actors which comprise this ensemble.

Insofar as governance is concerned with the rationalities and logics of governing in a particular geographical space or specific territory, it is also a central argument of this chapter that the borders of sociopolitical institutions, whether of national states or of 'Europe', are not 'givens'. As Bankowski and Christodoulidis (1998) argue, the EU is identified, understood and formed through processes of contestation. It is through the limits of these contestations that we can identify the political, social and territorial limits of the EU and a European social.

Processes of contestation are partly symbolic struggles about defining what *might be* contested. That is, they are about defining what is public and political, as opposed to what is domestic or privatised, in the sense of being removed to the economic sphere (Fraser, 1989, p 168), or what is a matter for administration, or technocratic 'evidence-based' procedures[1]. The activity of defining problems as domestic, economic, or technical (that is, non-political) is itself a political activity engaged in by political actors.

The production of knowledge and the terms in which such

knowledge is couched is crucial to identifying the limits of political contestation. Political struggle is a struggle for the "recognition which gives the authority to impose the legitimate knowledge of the sense of the social world, its present meaning and the direction in which it is going and should go" (Bourdieu, 2000, p 185). This observation is especially pertinent in regard to the social OMCs: with neither legal enforcement mechanisms nor the formal legitimacy and sanctions of a national state, the political struggle to define both what is political and what is a legitimate object of public governance is enacted through all aspects of the governance processes of the OMCs. In an analysis of the EES, Jacobsson (2004) argues that it institutes discursive regulatory mechanisms as a key mode of governance. Jacobsson suggests that by entering the discursive world of the EES, the Member States and the European Commission directorates involved in it constitute the social world in particular ways. The OMCs make some objects and forms of European governing 'thinkable and practicable', and this process excludes other objects and forms from the remit of public or political action.

Therefore, governance as used here draws attention to the mutually constitutive relationship of political and policy goals, and the means (strategies, procedures, rules and so on) adopted in meeting these goals in a particular territory. Together, the ends of policymaking ('what policy'), and the means chosen to meet these ends ('how policy is done'), define the characteristics and limits of territorial and social space to be acted on, and the subject categories to be regulated within this space (Carmel and Papadopoulos, 2003, pp 32-3).

Yet, as both Janet Newman and John Clarke have indicated (Introduction and Chapter Six in this volume; Clarke, 2004), governance forms are unstable and contested; social subjects are agents and one cannot merely 'read off' the constitution of social subjects and their relations from policy goals, institutions and processes.

Although this chapter is not concerned with those who are the objects of European social governance, as we will see, the European social (as it is constituted through the social OMCs) is contested and contradictory even within these governance institutions and processes. Furthermore, when the OMCs are located historically and in relation to other activities, policies and governance processes within the EU, the 'social' constituted through governance in the EU is revealed not only as 'thin' (in the sense that Janet Newman discusses in the Introduction), but also as ambivalent, largely depoliticised and perhaps already superseded or subsumed by the mechanisms and powers instituted and practised through other governance processes.

The following sections examine the implications of the 'social' OMCs as a form of governance in establishing a European social. First, this is done by reviewing the practices instituted in the social inclusion and employment policy OMCs (policy means); second, through an analysis of the policy goals, and how these constitute categories of social subject. Finally, these analyses are drawn together in order to examine the current outline of a European social, as constituted through these governance processes.

Constituting a European social I: policy means

The territorial extent of particular governance processes can be delineated through particular means: comprising border guards, passports and citizenship laws as well as expressions of ethnic, cultural or civic belonging and exclusion – all of which we see evidence of in the EU, except, perhaps the latter.

For the purposes of this chapter, what is intriguing about understanding how the European 'social' is constituted, is that the boundary of the 'European social' is not simply co-terminous with the formal borders of the EU, but was extended to the new Member States during the process of accession. Following the crucial European Council meeting in 2000, requirements were placed on the then Accession Countries to produce joint assessment reports on employment policies[2] (a point developed by Noémi Lendvai in Chapter Three). Therefore, the EES and OMC/incl. are as geographically extensive, if not more so, than other fields. From the perspective of the governance of the social, then, this 'social Europe' is more extensive than the 'Eurozone', as only 12 out of the 25 Member States currently have the same currency, and more extensive than Schengenland[3] of which the UK and the Republic of Ireland are not members. The new Member States may have fulfilled the criteria of 'hardening' their borders to their non-EU neighbours, but will not have access to 'open borders' to the EU for several years to come (Geddes, 2001, pp 179-80; Kvist, 2004). Indeed, the EES and the OMC/incl. are even more extensive than the legal or territorial borders of the EU itself, as they are applied to countries that are not (yet) part of the EU.

The other striking feature of the 'European social' as it emerges through the OMCs is the 'problem' and 'importance' of diversity. What matters in this case is not 'social diversity' but rather diversity of governance practices and welfare regimes among Member States. Indeed, this is echoed in the reports to various presidencies (Ferrera et al, 2000; Amitsis et al, 2003). Historically, national welfare states have tended to subsume territorial difference and, therefore, when used as a benchmark for assessing the likelihood of European social policy convergence or harmonisation, have pointed to a fundamental hindrance to the development of social policies by the EU collectively. Yet this hindrance does not appear to apply to the 'European social' as a field to be governed as it is constituted by the OMCs.

Indeed, the contrary is the case – a 'social European' space is created, to be the object of regulatory governing by the EU, at the same time as national territorial diversity is integral to the definition of this space. Central to the constitution of any territory to be governed is the data or knowledge that is produced about it (Stone, 1997; Rose, 1999). The knowledge that is produced from OMCs predominantly comprises NAPs and indicators which focus on nationally based, rather than regional or sectoral, comparison (Social Protection Committee, 2001; Atkinson et al, 2002, 2004; Stewart, 2003), thus producing the key constituent elements of the European social: national 'socials'. The constitution of the European social in the OMCs is conceptualised in terms of the congruence of national social fields with a vision of a jointly European social (see, for example, European Council, 2002a, p 5). The diversity within national states and societies is to be contained through the production of knowledge on a primarily national basis (subsuming intranational difference), while diversity between national states is contained through the (sometimes tenuous) congruence of the NAPs and indicators with the guidelines and recommendations agreed by the European Council and European Commission.

The centrality of the national state divisions in this 'European' social is intensified through specific procedures enacted in the OMCs. It is primarily national civil servants and ministers who are involved in drawing up NAPs, undertaking peer review, developing and agreeing targets and indicators. Thus, notwithstanding the potential for increased policy coherence, and policy–goal focus *within* national executives through, for example, interdepartmental coordination (see, for example, Coron and Palier, 2002, pp 128-33; Junestav, 2002, p 171), the social Europe of OMCs appears to be one which predominantly comprises the national executives of Member States. Emerging evidence suggests that national-level social partner and non-governmental organisation (NGO) participation and involvement in the development of NAPs at national level is at best uneven geographically and also varies across time (Jacobsson and Schmid, 2002, p 74; Büchs and Friedrich, 2005). In addition, the compressed timeframe of annual reporting in the OMCs has made it difficult for social partners and other actors to participate in the development of NAPs (see, for example, Büchs and

Friedrich, 2005), and the logic of the timeframe has tended to prioritise the management of intra-executive coordination; Jacobsson (2004, p 365) refers to this as "temporal disciplining".

The 'opacity' of the EU committees concerned with the EES and the OMC/incl. accentuates this constitution of the social as an object to be governed by national executives. The Employment and Social Protection Committees, along with the Economic Policy Committee, which are important in the negotiation of guidelines and indicators, comprise two representatives from each of the Member States, plus members from the European Commission. Despite a rhetorical emphasis on openness and participation in the OMCs, at EU level, this crucial negotiating activity remains closed (de la Porte and Pochet, 2002a, pp 46-7). The European Parliament, which divides along party political rather than national lines, and which therefore might act as a counter to the focus on the 'national' divisions in the EU's 'social', has only a limited consultative role. The executive dominance is compounded within Member States as national parliamentary reporting on the OMCs is weak, and there is little or no discussion of the OMCs in national media (Meyer, 2004).

Thus, in terms of the European 'social', although the procedures and activities engendered by the OMCs are designed to make a particular European realm 'available for governing' and thus an object of public, political concern, the procedures and activities comprising the OMCs remain largely private, closed and technocratic. It seems that the OMCs open a strategic space for policymaking for Member States, both individually and collectively. In the OMCs there is the possibility of strategic policy developments and a new European regulatory capacity of the social, providing Member State executives with some degree of autonomy from domestic 'national' pressures (see Wolff, 1999, pp 243-4).

However, this picture is not unremitting. The European Commission reported shortly after the Lisbon summit on the need to include *local* labour market management and policies in the context of the EES (European Commission, 2000). Following the mid-term review of the EES, the Commission noted once again the importance of the 'territorial dimension', and the possibility of developing regional and local partnerships as a way of improving implementation of the EES (European Commission, 2003a, p 8). Yet this approach does not engage local or regional authorities as full participants in the EES; rather, it suggests a passive role for such authorities in its implementation. As the EU's Committee of the Regions has emphasised, increasing the profile of regional and local dimensions of both the EES and the

OMC/incl. requires a formalised and embedded mandate and tools for regional and local authorities to be effective (Committee of the Regions, 2001). Furthermore, the recommendations to Member States in the Commission's 2004 report, *Strengthening implementation of the EES*, make no mention of the regional or local dimension in implementation, and certainly not in developing or reviewing guidelines or indicators (European Commission, 2004, p 10).

Nonetheless, some regions and localities, in Sweden, Spain and Italy, for example, have begun to develop regional and local action plans, and in combination with the pressures from the Committee of the Regions, this may yet open some greater space for local and regional inflections in the European social constituted through these social OMCs. In support of this we might look at the historical emphasis on providing EU funding to regions, which is likely to cohere ever more closely with the EES and OMC/incl. priorities. If such funding could be used to interpret the OMCs' priorities in locally or regionally innovative and challenging ways, which might create alternative perspectives on these two OMCs, different and less exclusionary forms of diversity might emerge in the European social beyond national state divisions.

In addition, there is an important difference between the EES and the OMC/incl. in the participation of non-governmental actors as partners in policymaking and development of the OMCs. In the social inclusion OMC, reports from national experts have been commissioned and are publicly available, therefore permitting some different voices and perspectives on national developments to be heard, even if they have no formal status. Most importantly, in the OMC/incl., one of the four objectives is to mobilise all relevant bodies in dealing with social inclusion (European Council, 2002a), an emphasis which effectively requires Member States to address this in some substance as part of their National Action Plans for Social Inclusion (NAPs/incl.; see European Council, 2003a, pp 109ff). While this 'participation' appears uneven across the Member States, and has been the object of some criticism more generally (Amitsis et al, 2003, pp 105-7), European networks of NGOs in the social field have provided comments on proposed guidelines, conducted shadow peer-review processes and, as part of the OMC/incl., meet annually at a European round table.

The degree and character of participation that is permitted, even under the social inclusion OMC, has been criticised by EU networks as inadequate, being consultative and rather passive (see, for example, Camarasa, 2004). It is also the case that even the involvement of such organisations represents a limited 'public' dimension to the OMCs.

The importance for 'participation' of informal access to the European Commission and members of the relevant committees by the representatives (European networks) of quasi-representatives (national NGOs) of people living in Europe, suggests that the constitution of the European social remains a largely privately managed one.

To conclude this section, the European social as an object to be governed through the EES and OMC/incl. procedures and practices (policy means) primarily comprises national states. The diversity among national states is to be privately managed among the Member States and with the European Commission. There may be some space for contestation, and indeed there is some evidence for this contestation which, however, remains limited, and is most evident in the OMC/incl. The EES has been integrated most recently into the policy dynamic and trajectory of the Broad Economic Policy Guidelines, which govern economic policy developments in the EU, and recent reports commissioned by the European Commission indicate that this integration will be intensified, further constraining the development of alternative voices and developments within the EES (European Commission, 2002a; Kok, 2004).

Constitution of a European social II: policy ends

Given the importance of data and knowledge in constituting the social to be governed, it is perhaps no surprise to find senior social policy scholars writing reports for the European Council, and acting in advisory roles (Ferrera et al, 2000; Atkinson et al, 2002; Esping-Andersen et al, 2002; Amitsis et al, 2003); neither is it surprising to find some congruence with statements appearing in European Commission and Council documents and proposals. However, as regards the EES, the versions of this knowledge which are evident in the employment guidelines, National Action Plans for employment (NAP/empl.), joint employment reports and presidency conclusions, are quite specific and imbricated in an overarching discourse. This discourse constitutes 'the social' in ways which belie the richness, variety and complexity of the scholarly analyses and, in particular, tends to deny the agency of social subjects at the same time as purporting to enhance or 'encourage' specific forms of agency and particular 'acceptable' behaviours. Of course, one would expect, in the EES, that its procedures and practices would constitute and categorise social subjects according to their employment and labour market position. Yet there are some important features of the particular categorisations in the EES that offer some insight into the ways in which the 'social' to be governed, managed and produced through the EES excludes, marginalises, ignores and renders invisible significant elements of social experience and action.

In particular, the European social is constituted in the EES as an object for governing that comprises individuals who should be made entrepreneurial (European Council, 2001, 2003c); and 'active', where 'activity' comprises engagement in employment. The EES guidelines developed after the 2002 review have three "overarching and interrelated objectives": full employment, quality and productivity at work, and social cohesion and inclusion (European Commission 2003a, p 17). To accompany these three objectives, there are three 'headline' targets – all of which are related to the first objective of increasing employment rates – and despite the improbability of many Member States meeting these, they are reiterated frequently as vitally important (Barbier et al, 2004).

The OMC/incl. objectives also include much emphasis on employment, and although there are no additional targets attached to these objectives, three out of the 10 'primary indicators', and three out of the eight 'secondary indicators', relate solely to employment and education or training. One of the striking differences between the OMC/incl. and the EES is the 'opportunity' and 'facilitation'-orientation of the social inclusion objectives. These involve, for example, "putting in place pathways towards employment", "developing policies to promote the reconciliation of work and family life" and "organising social protection systems to overcome obstacles to employment" (European Council, 2003a, pp 10-11). Furthermore, the European social here includes considerably more pan-European social diversity, with social subjects including not only men and women, employees and the unemployed, but also people with disabilities, children, older people and, more recently, immigrants. What remains unacknowledged is that these may be the same people, so that the debates on social exclusion in the 1980s and 1990s, which specifically addressed cumulative and cross-cutting, structurally produced disadvantage (see, for example, Silver, 1994; Room, 1995), are simplified and the subject categories listed more as groups of people who are all equally vulnerable, marginalised or disadvantaged, and all in the same way. Taken as a whole, the OMC/incl. indicates ambiguity: the social which is to be governed is constituted in part through people's needs beyond their relationship to employment – for example, their need for housing, health care, leisure and participation in social and public life. Yet there is little or no mention of these subject categories as active agents – those simply delineated people in need of inclusion are conceptualised in static categories, as passive recipients of policy. Also, in terms of policy proposals, in the NAPs there is some attention given to policies which address these needs, yet the indicators which form the focus of the OMC/incl. demonstrate a concern with employment which tends to enhance the economic agendas evident in the EU; there has been no agreement on the production of indicators for housing, and those for health are very limited.

In the 2003 EES guidelines, there is an increased emphasis on 'activation', while 'adaptability' is now directed at the adaptability of employees, rather than of employers, as previously (European Commission, 2003a, Guideline 3, pp 18-19). In both the earlier and current guidelines, there is little evidence of the variety of values and goals that apply to 'activation policies' (see, for example, van Berkel and Hornemann Møller, 2002) in different countries, neither of the disputed relationships between 'passive' benefits and incentives to work, for which several indicators have been developed. In the guidelines, and in reports on the then Accession Countries' employment policies, as well as the joint employment reports, there is a durable emphasis on reducing financial disincentives to take up paid employment (see, for example, European Commission, 2003a, 2003b).

In this context, people are seen as 'assets', human resources, capital to be educated and trained – not just for particular kinds of jobs, but also to behave in particular, 'entrepreneurial' and 'active' ways. Future developments of the social are to be managed so as not to 'compound' existing social problems, while tackling 'existing social problems' for social reasons is not part of the agenda (European Council 2002a; also European Commission, 2002b, p 8). Not all subject categories are those of individuals – there are distinctions made between men and women as relevant categories of the social, where the pursuit of gender equality is conceptualised as a matter for promoting equal opportunities to become an active, entrepreneurial individual, with equal pay for this active behaviour.

The tendency to individualise or reprivatise individual responsibility is extended when we explore the meanings attached to 'skills'. The premise of arguments about the importance of 'skills' and 'employability', evident in the EES, is that individuals are held responsible for their designation as either unemployable or underemployable. This produces subject categories which should be intent on skills acquisition and who would be likely to blame themselves, rather than the structures, if they fail to achieve. (Bacchi, 1999, p 85). Paradoxically, while apparently emphasising the agency of the social subjects to be governed, such policy goals and statements simultaneously constitute social subjects as economic goods to be managed and trained according to the demands of a personified market. The 'European social' is to be governed *in order to* maintain economic competitiveness.

Employers are largely absent from this constitution of the social. As one of its objectives, under the heading of 'mobilising all actors', the OMC/incl. aims to "foster the social responsibility of business" (European Council, 2002a, p 13). However, this is given derisory attention in the joint reports on inclusion (see, for example, European Council, 2003a, p 123), neither specified in terms of what this might involve for social inclusion, nor emphasised in the future development of indicators. These market actors are rendered largely invisible from the public realm demarcated for governing in the social OMCs; it is employees and potential employees or the self-employed, who constitute the social, in the OMC/empl. The significance of such tendencies within political discourse lies in the reification and naturalisation of market relations; critically for the case in hand, such discourses draw on particular views of the market as an arena outside public control. The Economic and Social Committee (2002) provides us with an example of how this is achieved in an opinion on immigration policy, quoted at length in a commentary on the 2002 employment guidelines:

> The national employment action plans must include criteria which are helpful in managing migratory flows. With the necessary flexibility, national employment plans must give consideration to immigration forecasts in order to ensure that the labour market functions properly. The employment guidelines ... should embrace the new immigration policy. The guidelines will promote higher quality employment for both Member State nationals and immigrants. (2002, p 4)

This example reveals how the Economic and Social Commitee constitutes the extent of 'the social' to be governed. This social is contained territorially within the borders of the EU, but is at the same time 'beyond' Europe, insofar as it includes those people who are not EU citizens or even current residents. At the same time, there is an ambivalence regarding whether this really involves people at all, given the references to 'migratory flows' and 'immigration', and only finally the dichotomous subject categories of 'nationals' and 'immigrants'. Lastly, the emphasis of this quotation, as in many of the publications produced through the OMCs, reconfirms the emphasis on employment. People migrating from territory outside the EU into EU Member States are produced as social subjects because they are – pragmatically and technocratically – a concern for 'the proper functioning of the labour market', as if 'the' labour market simply exists as a natural feature of the European social landscape. Such statements also sit ambivalently with the identification of 'immigrants' as a group in need of social inclusion in the OMC/incl.

Thus in this European social we find evidence of a productivist, economised vision of social policy. This is not merely about the subordination of social policy to economic goals (for example, Wincott, 2003) but is also about the use of social policies to manage the economy, in particular to manage labour; and to promote economic growth with an underlying imperative of saving 'social Europe' from Americanisation (for example, the low-skilled working poor), which is implicit in the OMC/incl. objectives (European Council, 2002a, pp 10-11) or financial collapse (see, for example, European Council, 2000, para 29). This approach is particularly evident in the EES with the emphasis on opportunities, investment and reskilling, and a considerable emphasis on the pragmatic, technical benefits of increasing employment per se (reinforced at recent spring European Councils, 2003b, p 22; 2004).

In toto, the discursive regulatory mechanisms (Jacobsson, 2004) of the EES and the OMC/incl. establish conditions of possibility for Member States to act in some ways and not others. Indeed, some of these other ways – such as increasing social security benefits, increasing taxes, allowing or encouraging people of 'working age' to leave the labour market in order to care for family members or others – are unthinkable in terms congruent with the EES, and the OMC/incl. does little or nothing to contradict such terms. Yet combined, the discursive regulatory mechanisms effectively require Member States to reconfigure their presentation and analysis of the 'social' and its governance within the national state territory, to the point where the categories of subjects are constituted in similar ways in a social which has European, and not merely national, scope. The constitution of social diversity in the OMC/incl. may represent the characteristics and members of constituent national societies in ways that challenge the Member States (for example, changing approach to policies for people with disabilities). This, of course, assumes that national executives in particular, along with other policy actors, are willing to respond to the redefinition, which is scarcely certain (Büchs and Friedrich, 2005).

The productivist, activating vision so sharply evident in the EES is contested – recent emphases on quality of work in the EES, and indeed the very existence of social inclusion OMC, testify to this. The particular adoption of inequality indicators for social inclusion (for example, gini coefficient and income distribution measures) also opens up the possibility of a less 'economised', labour market focus of European social policy. However, the Broad Economic Policy Guidelines remain the main vehicle for the implementation of the Lisbon agenda of economic growth, and, as mentioned above, the EES is becoming more clearly subsumed by the direction and apparent imperatives of these economic guidelines. As the EES becomes more closely aligned with the Broad Economic Policy Guidelines, which are organised from the finance and economics directorates of the European Commission, the more the facilitative, and (slightly) more complex, open vision of the European social instituted in the OMC/incl. through the Social Affairs Directorate appears on the margins of the European social. It is perhaps no accident that the OMC/incl. appears so marginal and vulnerable in European governance – so are many of the people with whom the OMC/incl. is concerned.

Conclusion: the constitution of a European social

The 'social' of the chapter title is not envisaged as complete, stable or unconstested. This incompleteness is marked in this section by reference to '*a* social'; as has been indicated already, there are many different socials that could be constituted through the social OMCs and through other governance processes in the EU. There are also a variety of institutions with different powers, agendas and interests involved in both the OMCs used as examples here – shifts in these powers and interests could easily result in the constitution of different 'socials' to be the object of EU governance procedures and practices. Indeed, even the sometimes oversimplified debates about the 'Anglo-Saxon model' in the wake of the Dutch, and especially French, 'no' vote in their constitutional referenda, testify to the profoundly strained and contradictory visions of the social that co-exist in the EU. Bearing in mind this proviso, here I outline some notable, contested and contradictory features of the European social as it is currently constituted. In doing so, I return to the two analytical features (means and ends) to assess the characteristics and limits of a European social.

In terms of policy procedures and practices, the territory of the European social is very wide, extending to Accession Countries, while the process is dominated by national executives. The rather limited – or certainly uneven – involvement of regions in NAP formulation also seems evident; the extent of policy inclusion can involve NGOs but not poor people.

In terms of policy ends, contradictory tendencies can be observed; the emphasis on certain policy goals precludes the adoption of some policy instruments. In particular, the emphasis on 'activation agenda', entrepreneurialism and equal opportunities belies the OMCs' emphasis on the ability of Member States to choose policy instruments that are compatible with their welfare regimes and political systems in order to meet common policy goals. Relevant subject categories are limited to employment status, age, gender and now, immigrant.

This chapter has argued that the OMCs are part of a process, and indeed the main means, to constitute a 'European social' realm to be acted upon, managed and governed. That is, the initiation, continuation, revision and contestation around the OMCs are bringing into being a distinctively European social field. The concern in this chapter has been with the ways in which policy space and territorial space has been made available for governing by the EU and the collectivity of its Member States via the OMCs. In the OMCs we can see new definitions and political contestations regarding what is 'social', what is to be governed as 'social', and how this social is to be governed. The 'European social', as it currently appears in the OMCs, rests on an assumption of diversity characterised by distinctions between Member States, which nonetheless is contained and identifiably 'European'. It also rests on an assumption of the need to regulate and steer social subjects defined overwhelmingly, although not entirely, in relation to their employment status. This 'European social' appears new in the context of the development of the EU, but the weakness of the social inclusion OMC, and the subsuming of the employment OMC under the Broad Economic Policy Guidelines, may indicate already the fragility and ungovernability of even the 'thin' European social outlined here.

Notes
[1] My thanks to John Clarke for pointing out the importance of the latter.

[2] Of course, these requirements are not as onerous as the budgetary requirements of the Stability and Growth Pact associated with joining the Euro, but these latter requirements do not apply to all current Member States.

³ A group of Member States which has abolished border controls between each.

References

Amitsis, G., Berghman, J., Hemerijck, A., Sakellaropoulos, T., Stergiou, A. and Stevens, Y. (2003) '*Connecting diversity within the European social model*', background report, Conference of the Hellenic Presidency, Ioaninna, May.

Atkinson, T., Cantillon, B., Marlier, E. and Nolan, B. (2002) *Social indicators: The EU and social inclusion*, Oxford: Oxford University Press.

Atkinson, A., Marlier, E. and Nolan, B. (2004) 'Indicators and targets for social inclusion in the EU', *Journal of Common Market Studies*, vol 41, no 1, pp 47-76.

Bacchi, C.L. (1999) *Women, policy and politics*, London: Sage Publications.

Bankowski, Z. and Christodoulidis, E. (1998) 'The European Union as an essentially contested project', *European Law Journal*, vol 4, pp 341-54.

Barbier, C., de la Porte, C., Baeten, R., Ghailani, D. and Pochet, P. (2004) 'European digest', *Journal of European Social Policy*, vol 14, no 2, pp 183-95.

Bourdieu, P. (2000) *Pascalian meditations*, Cambridge: Polity Press.

Büchs, M. and Friedrich, D. (2005) 'Surface integration: the national action plans for employment and social inclusion in Germany', in P. Pochet and J. Zeitlin (eds) *The Open Method of Coordination in action: The European employment and social inclusion strategies*, Brussels: Peter Lang, pp 249-85.

Camarasa, M. (2004) 'Participation of European networks in the social inclusion Open Method of Coordination', unpublished Masters dissertation, University of Bath, UK.

Carmel, E. and Papadopoulos, T. (2003) 'The new governance of social security in Britain', in J. Millar (ed) *Understanding social security*, Bristol: The Policy Press, pp 31-52.

Clarke, J. (2004) *Changing welfare, changing states: New directions in social policy*, London: Sage Publications.

Committee of the Regions (2001) *Opinion on the proposal for a Council decision on guidelines for Member States' employment policies for the year 2002*, CdR 271/2001 final, Brussels: Commission of the European Communities.

Coron, G. and Palier, B. (2002) 'Changes in the means of financing social expenditure in France since 1945', in C. de la Porte and P. Pochet (eds) *Building social Europe through the Open Method of Co-ordination*, Brussels: Peter Lang, pp 97-136.

de la Porte, C. and Pochet, P. (2002a) 'Supple co-ordination at EU level and key actors' involvement', in C. de la Porte and P. Pochet (eds) *Building social Europe through the Open Method of Co-ordination*, Brussels: Peter Lang, pp 27-68.

de la Porte, C. and Pochet, P. (eds) (2002b) *Building social Europe through the Open Method of Co-ordination*, Brussels: Peter Lang.

de la Porte, C. and Pochet, P. (2004) 'The European Employment Strategy: existing research and remaining questions', *Journal of European Social Policy*, vol 14, no 1, pp 71-8.

de la Porte, C., Pochet, P. and Room, G. (2001) 'Social benchmarking, social policy, policy-making and new governance in the EU', *Journal of European Social Policy*, vol 11, no 4, pp 291-307.

Economic and Social Committee (2002) *Opinion on the proposal for a Council Decision on guidelines for Member States' employment policies for the year 2002*, COM(2001) 511 final – 2001/0208 (CNS), Brussels: Commission of the European Communities.

Esping-Andersen, G., Gallie, D., Hemerijck, A. and Myles, J. (2002) *Why we need a new welfare state*, Oxford: Oxford University Press.

European Commission (2000) *Acting locally for employment. A local dimension for the European Employment Strategy*, COM(2000) 196 final, Brussels: Commission of the European Communities.

European Commission (2002a) *Communication on streamlining the annual economic and employment policy co-ordination cycles*, COM(2002) 487 final, Brussels: Commission of the European Communities.

European Commission (2002b) *Joint employment report*, Brussels: Commission of the European Communities.

European Commission (2003a) *The future of the European Employment Strategy (EES): 'A strategy for full employment and better jobs for all'*, COM(2003) 6 final, Brussels: Commission of the European Communities.

European Commission (2003b) *Progress in the implementation of the joint assessment papers on employment policies in candidate countries*, COM(2003) 37 final, Brussels: Commission of the European Communities.

European Commission (2004) *Strengthening implementation of the EES*, COM(2004) 239 final, Brussels: Commission of the European Communities.

European Council (2000) *Presidency conclusions*, European Council in Lisbon, 23-24 March.

European Council (2001) 'Council decision on guidelines for Member States' employment policies for the year 2001', *Official Journal of the European Communities*, vol 22, pp 18-26.

European Council (2002a) *Fight against poverty and social exclusion: Common objectives for the second round of national action plans*, 14164/1/02 rev 1 SOC 508, Brussels: Commission of the European Communities.

European Council (2002b) *Presidency conclusions*, European Council in Barcelona, 15-16 March.

European Council (2003a) *Joint report by the Commission and the Council on social inclusion*, 7101/04, Brussels: Commission of the European Communities.

European Council (2003b) *Presidency conclusions*, European Council in Brussels, 20-21 March.

European Council (2003c) 'Council decision on guidelines for the employment policies of the Member States', *Official Journal of the European Communities*, vol 197, pp 13-21.

European Council (2004) *Presidency conclusions*, European Council in Brussels, 25-26 March.

Ferrera, M., Hemerijck, A. and Rhodes, M. (2000) *The future of the European welfare state: Managing diversity for a prosperous and cohesive Europe2*, report for the Portuguese Presidency of the European Union, Lisbon.

Fraser, N. (1989) *Unruly practices: Power, discourse and gender in contemporary social theory*, Cambridge: Polity Press.

Geddes, A. (2001) *The politics of migration and immigration in Europe*, London: Sage Publications.

Goetschy, J. (1999) 'The European Employment Strategy: genesis and development', *European Journal of Industrial Relations*, vol 5, no 2, pp 401-18.

Goetschy, J. (2003) 'The European Employment Strategy, multi-level governance, and policy coordination: past, present and future', in J. Zeitlin and D. Trubek (eds) *Governing work and welfare in a new economy: European and American experiments*, Oxford: Oxford University Press, pp 59-87.

Gordon, C. (1991) 'Governmental rationality. An introduction', in G. Burchell, C. Gordon and P. Miller (eds) *The Foucault effect. Studies in governmentality*, London: Harvester Wheatsheaf, pp 1-51.

Jacobsson, K. (2004) 'Soft regulation and the subtle transformation of states: the case of EU employment policy', *Journal of European Social Policy*, vol 14, no 4, pp 355-70.

Jacobsson, K. and Schmid, H. (2002) 'Real integration or just formal adaptation? On the implementation of the national action plans for employment', in C. de la Porte and P. Pochet (eds) *Building social Europe through the Open Method of Co-ordination*, Brussels: Peter Lang, pp 69-96.

Junestav, M. (2002) 'Labour cost reduction, taxes and employment: the Swedish case', in C. de la Porte and P. Pochet (eds) *Building social Europe through the Open Method of Co-ordination*, Brussels: Peter Lang, pp 137-76.

Kok, W. (2004) *Facing the challenge – the Lisbon Strategy for growth and employment*, Brussels: European Commission.

Kvist, J. (2004) 'Does EU enlargement start a race to the bottom? Strategic interaction among EU Member States in social policy', *Journal of European Social Policy*, vol 14, no 3, pp 301-18.

Meyer, C.O. (2004) 'Policy coordination without public discourse? A study of quality press coverage of economic policy coordination between 1997 and 2003', paper presented at the GOVECOR Final Review Meeting, Brussels, 16-17 February.

Pochet, P. and Zeitlin, J. (eds) (2005) *The Open Method of Coordination in action: The European Employment and Social Inclusion Strategies*, Brussels: Peter Lang.

Room, G. (1995) *Beyond the threshold: The measurement and analysis of social exclusion*, Bristol: The Policy Press.

Rose, N. (1999) *Powers of freedom*, Cambridge: Cambridge University Press.

Silver, H. (1994) 'Social exclusion and social solidarity: three paradigms', *International Labour Review*, vol 133, nos 5-6, pp 531-78.

Social Protection Committee (2001) *Report on indicators in the field of poverty and social inclusion*, October, Brussels: Commission of the European Communities.

Stewart, K. (2003) 'Monitoring social inclusion in Europe's regions', *Journal of European Social Policy*, vol 13, no 4, pp 335-56.

Stone, D. (1997) *The policy paradox. The art of political decision-making*, New York, NY: W.W. Norton and Co.

van Berkel, R. and Hornemann Møller, I. (2002) 'The concept of activation', in R. van Berkel and I. Hornemann Møller (eds) *Active social policies in the EU*, Bristol: The Policy Press, pp 45-72.

Wincott, D. (2003) 'Beyond social regulation? New instruments and/ or a new agenda for social policy at Lisbon?', *Public Administration*, vol 81, no 3, pp 533-53.

Wolff, K.D. (1999) 'Defending state autonomy. Intergovernmental governance in the EU', in B. Kohler-Koch and R. Eising (eds) *The transformation of governance in the European Union*, London: Routledge, pp 231-48.

THREE

Remaking European governance: transition, accession and integration

Noémi Lendvai

Introduction

Since 1989, Central Eastern Europe has faced continuous change. The transition from centrally planned to market economies was followed by European accession and subsequent integration into the wider process of European governance. These three processes (transition, accession and integration) are distinct, yet their interrelatedness forms a historically unique meeting point. This chapter explores the dynamics of integrating European and post-communist social policy, using a critical constructivist perspective to explore the dialogue between different social policy traditions that is taking place. As will be argued, the fragility of post-communist social policy manifests itself through dislocation, dissociation and the concept of control.

The chapter is divided into three parts. The first part provides a comparative insight into the development and architectural features of both post-communist and European Union (EU) supranational social policy. It argues that there are numerous similarities between the process of transition and EU integration. The second part provides a critical perspective of EU accession and the nature of this institutionalised dialogue. The final part elaborates on the integrative effects of the three transformative processes and highlights their fragility.

The dynamics of European and post-communist social policy: comparing European integration and post-communist transition

The institutional architecture of European integration – the creation and formulation of European supranational social policy – and the process of transformation in Central Eastern Europe have numerous

Table 3.1: Comparing European and post-communist social policy

Features and dynamics of transition in Central Eastern Europe	Parallels	Features and dynamics of European integration
Post-communist social policy		**European social policy**
'Instrumentalisation' – social policy is not legitimate as an independent field, viewed and justified in political and economic reasoning	Marketisation	Priority is economic integration – social policy dominates negative integration measures
Weak institutional capacities to reinforce law, to implement and monitor policies	Weak institutional capacities	Fragmented institutional system
		'Easier to block than to initiate policies'
State vs market		Nation-states vs EU
State dismantling	State competences questioned	Pre-empted policy space
'Premature welfare state'	Conflict agenda	Genuine ambiguity at the heart of EU documents regarding whether social policy enhances or hinders economic growth
	Competitiveness and social policy	

similarities. Both can be interpreted as the emergence of distinct structures of governance, associated with political, legal and social institutions (Olsen, 2002). Both involve a transformation process that includes developing and strengthening organisational capacities for collective action; developing common ideas, new norms and collective understanding of citizenship (Checkel, 2001). Both are concerned with the creation of social policy and setting up a 'social' agenda in rapidly changing circumstances. In both, the processes of institutional change are substantially different from those characterising the formation of European welfare states. Both EU and post-communist 'quasi-welfare states' lack the cultural aspects of the welfare-state building process which took place at the nation-state level. Thus they need to be understood in terms of a distinct set of dynamics. In Table 3.1, four points of correspondence are traced between the dynamics of (post-communist) transition and (EU) integration.

Marketisation: market-making versus market-correcting social policy?

European integration has been primarily a process of economic integration, the building of a common market. In Eastern Europe the transition from communism has resulted in a shift from command economies to market economies. Market-making, then, seems fundamental in framing the ways in which both European and post-communist social policy have been formulated and developed. Since European social policy is formulated in the context of supranational market-making, where the post-communist welfare states are facing national market-building there are going to be important differences. However, many similarities can be traced in terms of the impact of marketisation on social policy.

In the case of European social policy, the priority of economic integration features 'negative integration', in which social policy serves to remove barriers from the free movements of capital, labour, goods and services. It is fundamentally a market-making, not a market-correcting, social policy with a

> fundamental asymmetry between policies promoting market efficiencies and those promoting social protection and equality … [E]conomic policies have been progressively Europeanized, while social-protection policies remained at the national level. (Scharpf, 2002, pp 665-6)

As a consequence:

> National governments are the bearers of democratic legitimacy, but the transfer of authority that has accompanied the implementation of the Common Market has reduced their power to shape the prospect and safeguard the interest of their national populations. (Offe, 2000, p 11)

The primacy of market-making over the market-correcting at European level social policy and the impairment of the nation level market-correcting social policy

> appear to represent a descent down the ladder that T.H. Marshall proposed as a model for the process of European political modernization. The three rungs of this ladder are

liberal, democratic and social rights, achieved cumulatively. The question is whether in Europe today the social welfare and democratic levels are being passed in reverse, reducing Euro-citizens to the status of mere participants in a neo-liberal marketplace. (Offe, 2000, p 10)

Social policy in Central Eastern Europe has been formed by very similar dynamics. Central Eastern Europe has been described as an experimental field for the global market (Ferge, 2000) with post-communist countries particularly exposed to neo-liberal policies. Deacon (2000) argues, however, that it not economic, but *political* globalisation that had a heavy impact on social policy development in Central Eastern Europe, with global actors such as the World Bank promoting a particular, ideologically driven view of how social policy should position itself in relation to the market. Throughout the 1990s, post-communist social policy was dominated by market-making features and seriously lacked market-correcting visions. Liberalisation was not followed by targeted support for those most hit by the drastic increase in the prices of fundamental goods, the withdrawal of highly subsidised mortgages, the marketisation of the pension system and parts of health care and the cut-back on social security payments and benefits. All served to remove burdens from the market by cutting back public expenditure and inviting private investments into social services and infrastructures. The same struggle appears between liberal and social rights. The 'down the ladder' themes are taking place in post-communist countries as well as in the EU. Despite having been constitutionalised, social rights have been questioned and withdrawn, subjected to economic capacities and their interpretations by economists.

Competitiveness and social policy: the discursive battle

Since social policy is closely linked both to state-making (as a necessary authority to correct market failures and promote public good) and market-making (as a means of removing the barriers to market competitiveness), the constructed trade-off between competitiveness and positive, interventionist social policy occupies both the dynamics of European integration and post-communist transition. Although the issues appear similar, they are occurring in very different circumstances. In Central Eastern Europe the discourse of 'social policy versus competitiveness' is a very new agenda, one which has been opened up by the politics of post-communist transition. In the case of Hungary, the focus of debate centred around Kornai's (1993) concept of the 'premature welfare state', also known as the 'overdeveloped' welfare state (Balazs, 2001). The welfare state is conceptualised as 'over-muscled', where the level of welfare spending is not supported by economic performance, thereby pre-empting fiscal policy space and hindering investment and economic restructuring. Throughout, transition economic and political discourse centred on the trade-off argument: social policy was viewed as a highly unproductive sector, with generous entitlements discouraging market behaviour and attitudes as well as reinforcing paternalistic expectations. The strong discursive pressure that presented the welfare state as overgrown, dysfunctional and harmful played an important role in shaping state–dismantling rather than state–building strategies. The idea of social policy as cushioning the social consequences of transformational recession has been sidelined. The discourse of social policy as a positive factor in economic growth and competitiveness through the improvement of human resources and reducing inequalities has not featured, despite the fact that the welfare regimes in the Central Eastern European countries have played an important role in cushioning the blows of marketisation and privatisation, not to mention the worst economic recession of the 20th century (Kovács, 2002, p 199). The notion of the premature welfare state not only described the post-communist welfare state but also implied the necessary directions for reform.

In deliberations about EU social policy in the same period, very similar arguments to the premature welfare state can be traced. In 1993 the European Commission claimed that: "The current levels of public expenditure, particularly in the social field, have become unsustainable and have used up resources which could have been channelled into productive investment" (European Commission, 1993, p 41). Commenting on the 1994 White Paper on European Social Policy, Kleinman claimed that:

> [T]here is a generally unsatisfactory attempt to present the competitiveness agenda of increased market forces, labour flexibility and reduced entitlements as if there was no conflict between this and a defence and enhancement of the 'European Social Model'. (Kleinman, 2002, p 100)

He noted a 'genuine ambiguity' in the EU documents between the social agenda of high social standards and quality of life on the one hand, and economic competitiveness and a deregulatory economic agenda on the other. And as Emma Carmel argues in Chapter Two of this volume, such ambivalence can be traced in the current strategies associated with the Open Method of Coordination (OMC). The hegemony of the notion of competitiveness is remarkable, considering the notorious elasticity of the concept (Rosamond, 2002) and its emptiness (Krugman, 1994), not to mention the measurement and definition problems that it poses. Yet in the context of transition, EU accession and integration 'competitiveness' is being used as a strategic rhetorical device designed to "lend legitimacy to the project of Europeanising economic governance in a neoliberal direction" (Rosamond, 2002, pp 171-2).

Institutional capacities: institutional deserts and fragmented institutional structures

Central Eastern European transitional states are relatively 'weak' states in terms of their institutional capacity to formulate, implement and enforce policies. They are financially weak in that they have limited capacity to collect taxes and tackle the black or grey economy. They have weak regulatory powers mainly because of the massive legislation work undertaken by parliaments and the burden that this places on policymaking machinery. As a result, there are insufficient capacities to follow up, evaluate and monitor the implementation of even major legislation. Bruszt (2002) describes the post-communist institutional landscape as a 'desert'.

European social policy is also formulated in a fragmented institutional system. In the field of social policymaking the 'lowest common denominator' strategy is dominant. Despite Member States' possession of a key role in decision-making processes, they are constrained by factors such as the accumulation of low profile legal decisions by the European Court of Justice and the accumulative effect of treaty commitments. The emerging multi-tiered governance is characterised by high competition, pre-emption, fragmented policy control and multiplied points of jurisdiction. The overall academic consensus of the 1990s is that the EU is a system in which it is easier to block than to initiate policies (Kleinman, 2002).

State-building: state competences in question

The competences of the state are always embedded in complex institutional and ideological matrices. Two major arguments are presented which undermine European-level state competences. First, the policy space is already occupied by national governments. There is no EU competence in redistribution, a core social policy competence, since it is argued that, among other factors, the EU is neither culturally nor socially homogeneous enough to organise large-scale redistribution. A European welfare state is not on the horizon, because the European Community does not have the "competence to create its own competence", a major characteristic of modern 'stateness' (Leibfried, 2000, p 46).

Second, if at European level the supranational state competences have been pre-empted, the state competences in the post-communist setting have been 'over-empted' and exhausted. Redistributive and many service provider competences have been withdrawn. In real terms most social benefits and services in Hungary lost 20 to 40% of their value between 1989 and 1998 (Ferge, 2001). A great deal of existing social policy-related state competence has been marketised (the pension system and parts of the health care system, such as general practitioners) and new competences (on issues relating to disability, homelessness, single parenthood) have only been slowly taken up. The state was seen as necessarily intrusive, inefficient and wasteful, and consequently regulatory and new institution-building competences have been limited. In general, then, state competences have been subordinated to the market.

EU accession: where transition meets EU integration

European accession is the process that links European integration with transition and engages the two systems in a dialogue. This is a dialogue of two different social, political and cultural traditions. It is a very multidimensional and comprehensive process which has an impact on a number of segments of post-communist social policy governance. From a constructivist–institutionalist perspective, three key aspects of the European accession process are worth considering: EU accession as a meaning-making process; EU accession as an institutional transformation; and EU accession as the emergence of new social policy governance. These three aspects of accession are strongly interlinked but characterised by different dynamics (see Figure 3.1).

European accession: meaning-making and translation

'Meaning-making' is a term adopted by constructivist public policy scholars who are dissatisfied with strongly technocratised understandings of policy. They have argued that we cannot overlook the fact that public policy is always "layered by implicit meanings"

Figure 3.1: A conceptual map for EU accession

KEY PROCESSES OF EU ACCESSION	MEANING-MAKING		INSTITUTIONAL CHANGES	NEW GOVERNANCE
DYNAMIC CHANGES	New vocabulary	New policy concepts	New policy instruments	New modes of policymaking
	New discourses		New policy agenda	New institutions
	'Indigenising' the new terms, concepts, discourses in a meaningful way		Institutionalisation Conditionality	'Modernisation' of post-communist governance Policytaking vs policymaking
KEY THEORETICAL TERMS	Cognitive Europeanisation Socialisation undercarriage Soft social policy Translation and dislocation		'Dissociation' Adaptation pressure Institutional transformation	Multilevel governance Executive bias

(Innes, 2002, p 22); that it creates, transmits and interprets policy meanings (Yanow, 1996); that it constructs social 'facts' (Fischer, 2003); that it offers a way of 'seeing-as' (Rein and Schon, 1993); and that it can be understood as both meaning-making and claim-making processes (Yanow, 1996). Stone views policymaking as "a constant discursive struggle over the definitions of problems, the boundaries of categories used to describe them, the criteria for their classification and assessment and the meanings of ideals that guide particular actions" (2002, p 60). Meaning-making not only constructs boundaries and discursive struggles, but is also an interpretive process which "focuses on the meanings of policies, on the values, feelings and/or beliefs which they express and on the processes by which those meanings are communicated to and 'read' by various audiences" (Yanow, 1996, pp 8-9).

European accession is a meaning-making process for the new Member States; it operates with a set of meanings that were accumulated by decades of European integration of which these countries have not been part. Post-communist Europe, therefore, has to 'read the EU' and has to 'make sense' of and to 'indigenise', all of its new terms, concepts, ideas and structures. In this sense the EU could be seen as a 'semiotic order'. The conceptualisation and understanding of core concepts has been a rather uneasy process for the newcomers, not only because new Member States, Accession Countries and indeed aspirant countries have not been part of the integration process, but also because the 'neutralised language umbrella' of EU discourse is sufficiently 'foggy' and 'blurred' to enable avoidance of EU interference with Member States' social policy competences (Krémer, 2004).

The new vocabulary, concepts and ideas – such as social inclusion, cohesion, 'mainstreaming', joint governance, partnership and social dialogue – are all terms that are culturally and historically embedded in decades of Western European welfare-state development. Some of these terms, such as gender inequalities, social partnership and joint governance, or even social exclusion and poverty, have been silenced as policy issues in the Accession Countries for political reasons, even long after 1989. These 'silences' manifest themselves in languages – many countries for example do not have their own indigenous term for social inclusion. In Hungary, the National Action Plan for Social Inclusion (NAP/incl.) 2004/06 translated itself as the 'National Action Plan for Togetherness', partly because inclusion does not have a consensual translation and partly as a 'resistance', based on the claim that the term 'inclusion' indicates a hierarchical relation between those who include and the included. Moreover, this 'attemptive' translation can be read also as expressing a need to bring back the notion of solidarity and equality into the EU vocabulary, from which these terms have been replaced by the notion of exclusion, inclusion and equal opportunity. In a similar vein, the term 'social exclusion' has generated debates over whether it implies an active exclusion by somebody (such as the state), or whether people just happen to be excluded. In Hungary, there has been a political reluctance to use the active form of the verb 'to exclude', as some have argued that 'nobody excludes anybody in Hungary'.

Meaning-making requires language-making and indeed translation. Therefore, EU accession, European integration or 'Europeanisation' can be seen as a translation process, in which the new Member States begin to develop common understandings and thereby acquire some ownership over EU social policy. However, as scholars of the sociology of translation point out, translation is not only a technical or a linguistic matter – it is a deeply inscribed political and societal process. The sociology of translation is looking at particular ways in which objects, knowledge and facts are produced through displacement or suppression of dissenting voices, or of those "facts unfit to fit" (Gebhardt, 1982, p 405). Translation in this context is seen as a *displacement* process and as a dislocation, whereby the mechanisms of EU accession, such as the institutions, technologies, goals and priorities find themselves in a new context that is alien to them. Besides, "the goal of the translation is to bring together complex entities into a single object or idea that can be mobilised and circulated like a branded commodity or a taken-for-granted fact" (Clarke, 2002, p 115). As a result, the EU is branding itself in post-communist Europe by asserting its own language and discourses.

Translations are complex political, cultural and societal mirrors. They are reflexive of institutional structures and policy practices that operate with their own meanings and understandings. 'Naming' new concepts follows 'framing', a process in which countries make sense of a concept and develop institutional responses and strategies to address the issues.

> The name assigned to a problematic terrain focuses our attention on certain elements and leads us to neglect others. The organizing of the things named brings them together into a composite whole. The complementary process of naming and framing socially constructs the situation, defines what is problematic about it and suggests what courses of action are appropriate to it. It provides a conceptual coherence, a direction for action, a basis for persuasion and a framework for the collection and analysis of data, order, action, rhetoric and analysis. (Rein and Schön, 1993, p 270)

'Soft' social policy is the theoretical concept that is probably the nearest one capable of addressing this above-mentioned meaning-making process. The term 'soft social policy' is associated with cognitive shifts and socialisation processes and refers to the indirect impacts of Europeanisation. For example, Guillen et al (2003) use the term 'cognitive Europeanisation' to refer to the impact of the EU on Portuguese and Spanish social policies. This denotes not so much the direct impacts on the welfare state, but rather the indirect changes around the way in which social issues are handled, discussed, thought of and made. Teague (2000) uses the term 'socialisation undercarriage' to characterise the element of EU social policy which evolves through various policy tools and which builds on commonly developed vocabulary, agendas, policy instruments and institutions. The socialisation undercarriage function of the EU is significantly greater in relation to the new Member States where social policy governance and social policy meanings are so different, so unfit to fit.

European accession: institutionalisation and Europeanisation

Language and meaning-making is directly linked to the institutional landscape and architectures. Meaning-making is not exclusively a process of mental mapping or sense-making, it is also a basis for action guided by understanding and reading. New meanings become institutionalised and are acted upon. At the same time, as March and Olsen (1989) argue, institutions are 'normative vessels': carriers of beliefs, knowledge, understanding and values, as well as 'factories of meanings'; they create, maintain and, if necessary, change meanings. Therefore, it is important to be able to map the two processes (the ideational and material) in tandem.

No doubt, European accession has produced a massive institutionalisation in the field of social policy. The Joint Memoranda on Social Inclusion, or the NAP/incl. of the new Central Eastern European Member States, are indicative of the scale of institutionalisation which took place within a short period. Meeting the need to develop a series of national development plans and various action plans, the Central Eastern European ministries responsible for social affairs established strategic development units for the first time, institutionalising the development of social policy. In addition, inter-ministerial, coordinative committees, boards, councils and working groups have been established; statistical capacity-building and coordination have begun and a number of commissioners and ombudsmen have been appointed in the field of social inclusion in many countries. In Hungary a minister without portfolio responsible for equal opportunities has been appointed to become the 'social conscience' of the government in response to the EU's gender and equal opportunity agenda. Civil dialogue has been strengthened and institutionalised practice has been put in place to enable civil actors to have access to state decision-making processes across Central Eastern Europe.

However, critical perspectives raise rather different issues concerning the constitutive power of institutions. For example, Bruszt and Stark argue that the institutions of *acquis communitaire* provide more than sets of legal standards. They "redefine who and what counts, restructure the distribution of economic opportunities among different economic actors, remake the rules of the game and rearrange the roles these actors play in the domestic and the global economy" (2003, p 78). Cameron views European accession as a process whereby

> new members will be *re-created as states*, committed to processes of policy-making and policy outcomes that in many instances bear little or no relation to their domestic policy-making processes and prior policy decisions but reflect, instead, the politics, policy-making processes and

policy choices of the EU and its earlier member states. (2003, p 25; emphasis added)

This institutionalist approach problematises the way in which a uniformly applied *acquis* and regulative regime is 'imported' into the new Member States and makes it difficult to legitimise internal institutional structures.

Other institutionalist scholars, such as Lindstrom and Piroska (2004), assert that looking at Europeanisation only as institutional adaptation fails to acknowledge the ways in which it is also a process of public contestation, discursive construction and site of political struggle. They challenge mainstream approaches which understand the process of institutionalisation as 'top-down' and universalistic, arguing that Europeanisation is, rather, a dynamic, contradictory and ultimately contestable process. It is important to recognise that institutionalisation is not a straightforward processes with fixed institutional 'scripts' to which to adapt. As the study by Hughes et al (2003) reminds us, institutions themselves are not always unified, but instead multiply-voiced and coded. They argue that in the context of regional policy, the European Commission has not acted as a unified actor; rather, it has been trapped by the conflicting and competing visions between 'democratising' (deliberative and decentralised) and 'technocratic' (efficiency-driven, resulting in centralisation) approaches. The fragility of institutionalisation could be lessened by attachment to indigenous meanings and by adaptation based on extensive deliberation which "does not preclude voting or bargaining, but places the emphasis on obtaining a shared sense of meaning and a common will, both of which are the product of communicative process" (Eriksen and Fossum, 2000, p 18).

European accession: new governance and its critiques

Meaning-making, institutionalisation and the resulting changes in social policy governance are strongly interlinked, interdependent processes. Horizontal institutionalisation and vertical decentralisation change the concepts and practices of post-communist governance (Grabbe, 2001). The difficulty of adapting to this new deliberative, multi-voiced governance structure is not easy:

[T]he biggest problems and concerns in managing European business in Slovenia involve Slovenia's 'European' cadre capacity, above all: (a) the EU personnel deficit; (b) the absence of any previous practical experience of EU cadre; (c) the lack of foreign language knowledge; (d) the lack of a modern organisational, administrative culture; and (e) the only recently acquired knowledge of the EU's 'policy-taking' and the lack of an EU 'policy-making' culture. (Fink-Hafner and Lajh, 2003, p 19)

New players entering the social policy field produce new dynamics, a web of new institutions, interests and ideas. However, the new structures of governance do not emerge in an apolitical context. One of the problems that European accession has generated is that the primary, if not exclusive, nexus of the accession processes has been the national government–EU nexus. During accession the EU had little or no capacity to initiate and maintain EU-wide civil, regional or any other significant communicative domains. As a result, access to the information and knowledge that is crucial for participation and 'inclusion' in the accession process has been very limited for non-governmental organisations (NGOs) and other societal stakeholders. This reinforces previous transitional paths and may contribute to centralisation processes that marginalise civil society and non-governmental voices. My own research on the Hungarian inclusion of OMC processes also indicates that the initial phase of OMC is not only non-participatory, but indeed exclusionary for societal actors.

Grabbe (2001) argues further that the accession process is characterised by tensions: it promotes decentralisation but requires efficiency and control at the same time; the EU emphasises democratic legitimacy but pushes towards fast and full implementation, which increases the weight of central state bodies. She concludes that there is a danger that the EU will import its democratic deficit to post-communist countries through accession. As a result, for many scholars of Central Eastern European governance, European accession represents an exclusivist vision that marginalises non-state actors (Lippert et al, 2001). A multilevel governance approach, then, must be sensitive to power asymmetries in its construction. Furthermore, governance architectures such as OMC need to be 'sensitised' to these power asymmetries in order to be more inclusive, more deliberative and more meaningful for stakeholders.

The fragility of post-accession, post-enlargement social policy

This section will elaborate on the fragility of the processes of transition and accession by pointing to the political, material and discursive factors shaping contemporary post-national as well as national social policy. Jessop (2004) argues for a 'cultural turn' in political economy that combines critical semiotic analysis with critical political economy. He proposes a dialectic relationship between discursivity and materiality, since imaginaries are "discursively constituted and materially reproduced on many sites and scales, in different spatio-temporal contexts and over various spatio-temporal horizons" (2004, p 162). Discourses could be seen as (cognitive) institutions, but also "as institutions in their own right insofar as they can guide political action by denoting appropriate or plausible behaviour in light of an agreed environment" (Rosamond, 2000, p 120; 2002). Therefore, discourses are part of materiality. But at the same time, materiality is also part of discourse: materiality provides cognitive scripts, categories and models for reading and interpreting the world.

Shared factors contributing to the weakness of the 'positive sector'

The materiality of politics is an important factor in explaining both EU and post-communist social policy development. Leibfried (2000), analysing EU social policy, introduces the concept of a 'positive sector', a coalition with an active interest in promoting positive integration and construction of a (pan)-European welfare state. Similarly, Kleinman uses the concept of social-democratic 'power resources':

> In the power resources model of national welfare state development, emphasis is placed on the role of social-democratic forces – Left parties and strong Unions – in overcoming opposition to the establishment of welfare policies. But the political power of organised labour has declined at the national level and has not established itself transnationally or at the European level. Indeed, the reinvigoration of European integration was associated precisely with the emergence in many member states of an anti-social-democratic consensus in economic policy. In contrast with the history of the welfare state nationally, the key institutional and political factors are absent at the European level. (2002, p 129)

The positive sector has been weakened further by the integration process itself. As Streek and Schmitter (1991) emphasise, the system of representation that has emerged during the European integration process has provided privileged access to business interests and incentives for the organisation of 'policy-takers'; making it even more difficult for workers, pensioners, consumers, patients, students and the impoverished to articulate their demands at the supranational level. Offe (2000) also emphasises the fact that the current 'negative' approach to integration works actively against the development of a positive vision.

The 'instrumentalisation' thesis

The initial phase of the market-building process, both in terms of its discursive nature and its institutional materiality, has left little or no room for an interventionist, market-correcting social policy. Residual and market-making social policy have prevailed. As Leibfried and Pierson (1995, p 51) argue: "The EU social dimension is usually discussed as a corrective or a counter to market building, but it has proceeded instead as part of the market-building process." This reduces the scope for the kinds of social policy associated with government intervention which is designed to prevent, mitigate or alleviate the social consequences of economic developments. Such interventions would be intended to modify market outcomes, correct market failures, carrying out regional, interclass or intergenerational redistribution (Leibfried and Pierson, 1995). They would promote goals such as state-building, provision of public goods that the market will not supply, remedying of externalities, and social cohesion across groups (Kleinman, 2002). Further, they would be active agents of social integration, capable of mediating conflicts and preserving stability in divided societies (Banting, 1995). However, market-making social policy does not match any of these definitions. If we assume that social policy serves societal goals or purposes, then EU social policy can be interpreted as a form of social policy that has been diverted from its original purpose and subordinated not to societal, but to economic goals.

The 'instrumentalisation' thesis refers to the phenomenon whereby social policy is not linked to societal aims and social goals such as promotion of social cohesion, solidarity or equality, but instead is instrumental to economic policies and becomes subordinated to it. As Kleinman notes, as far as EU social policy is concerned, there is "an ambiguity about whether social policy is an important policy area in its own right or should be considered mainly as an adjunct or facilitator for economic integration" (2002, p 102). Instrumentalisation refers not only to the subordination of social policy to economic policy, but to the process whereby societal goals and principles are instrumentalised. It has a direct impact on state–market–society relations, pushing the system from a quasi-equal into a more hierarchical market command-driven system. This is not to claim that instrumentalisation is exclusively a market-making-driven phenomenon, as obviously, political and institutional factors play a part. When discussing the transformation of welfare regimes from Keynesian national welfare states into what he calls a Schumpeterian workfare post-national regime, Jessop (2002) argues explicitly that the new construction is:

> [A] workfare regime insofar as it subordinates social policy to the demands of economic policy.... [It] is more concerned to provide welfare services that benefit business and thereby demotes individual needs to second place [and as a result is] associated with downward pressure on public spending. (2002, p 251)

The instrumentalisation thesis is no less relevant to the situation in Central Eastern Europe. Ferge notes that:

> The respect for basic 'western' values like social integration, solidarity or distributive justice is absent from home public policy. Not even lip service is paid to them. This makes it difficult to put them on the agenda of public discourse. (2001, p 125)

Such values have been de-legitimised, related institutions (left-wing parties, trade unions, civil society) have vanished or become seriously weakened, or were non-existent in the early years of transition. Policy formulation has not been driven by negotiated and deliberated social or societal principles, but instead has taken place in a pragmatic, often rushed, ad hoc and non-communicative manner. Offe argues that:

> [T]his instrumental approach of institution building often comes close to being Stalinist in method. That is not to suggest that institution designers in post-Communist societies could actually afford to wait. They rarely can, given the pressing economic needs and the lack of legitimate political authority in their countries. It is only to suggest

that 'copied' and transplanted institutions that lack the moral and cultural infrastructure on which the 'original' can rely are likely to yield very different and often counter-intentional results, in which case ever more hectic and short-breathed further designs must be expected as a consequence. (1994, p 17)

It is the lack of public discourse on fundamental societal principles that leads to the instrumentalisation of social policy. In Hungary, in the first waves of reform, the conservative government (1990-94) used social policy as an instrument of political legitimation and system stability. That meant a status quo-oriented approach, with delayed reforms and a series of non-decisions. The second, socialist–liberal coalition government (1994-98) subordinated social policy to economic policy and launched a strong neo-liberal ideological attack – as a forceful moral agenda – on the welfare state and its 'paternalism'. The Hungarian 'shock therapy' of 1995 involved radical cutbacks which were very similar to the Polish Balcerowicz Plan. This was "one of the great paradoxes of Polish transition that a movement (Solidarity) so clearly guided by the principles of worker self-government, self-management and the 'self-liberation of civil society' should have implemented the radical neoliberal reform package" (Shields, 2003, p 225). The 'shock therapy' was labelled variously as 'modernisatory correction' (Balazs, 2001) by those who saw both the transition and EU accession as a modernisation project. However, 'shock therapy' has been interpreted also as a new revolution:

> Poland wants to be part of the Western European mainstream, but is taking a route via Washington. There is no space for consideration of the advantages for Poland of an alternative process of change and transition remains dominated by the neo-Leninism of the TCC-oriented [transnational capitalist class] 'Shock Therapy'. The new Leninism offers a holistic world view with no sphere of life exempt from its regulation and [is] characterised by simple, fast solutions. 'Shock Therapy' is in effect the new 'revolution' with the attendant moral power. (Shields, 2003, p 238)

The third Hungarian conservative government (1998-2002) was the first to distribute more gains than losses. However, here social policy was oriented to building up a middle class (through tax credits and mortgages with subsidies for high-income earners), which then could become the stable basis for a united conservative party, thus linking the political and economic drivers of the instrumentalisation of social policy.

The deepening and widening of the EU can be viewed in terms of a neo-liberal restructuring of European social relations of production: "in contrast to the project of embedded neo-liberalism shaping the deepening of the EU, the mode of incorporating Eastern Europe up to now has resulted in the export of a much more 'market-radical' variant of neo-liberalism" (Bohle, 2003, quoted by Bieler, 2003, p 11). Social policy faces serious difficulties when trying to reassert itself, because its natural home, 'the state', is itself "the very medium for the articulation of transnational hegemonic concepts of control" (Shields, 2003, p 228).

Conclusion

'Europe in waiting', the very expressive term used by John Clarke in Chapter One of this volume, encompasses a large number of countries: the post-communist new Member States, Accession Countries and indeed aspirant countries. This 'Europe in waiting' is constitutive of the EU, as much as it shapes its institutions, imaginaries and politics. However, it is facing serious realignments of borders and boundaries on its way towards becoming part of the EU. A critical approach is needed to deconstruct the ways in which the dialogue between EU and post-communist social policy is conducted, the ways in which voicing (and indeed silencing), empowerment and disempowerment, formal institutional dynamics as well as informal, implicit processes and new issue cleavages emerge. Indeed, as Diez (1999, p 599) argues, "various attempts to capture the Union's nature are not mere descriptions of an unknown polity, but take part in the construction of the polity itself". New words, new language fragments, are needed to capture EU accession and integration from a post-communist (and indigenous) point of view and more reflexivity is needed to deconstruct the often technocratic or neutral language used to describe European processes of governance.

References

Balazs, P. (2001) *Europai egyesules es modernizacio (European integration and modernisation)*, Budapest: Osiris.

Banting, K. (1995) 'The welfare state as statecraft: territorial politics and Canadian social policy', in S. Leibfried and P. Pierson (eds) *European social policy: Between fragmentation and integration*, Washington, DC: Brookings Institution, pp 269-301.

Bieler, A. (2003) 'European integration and eastward enlargement: the widening and deepening of neo-liberal restructuring in Europe', *Queen's Papers on Europeanisation*, no 8, available at www.queensu.ca/sps/working-papers/

Bruszt, L. (2002) 'Market making as state making: constitutions and economic development in post-communist Eastern Europe', available at: www.columbia.edu/cu/iserp/itcs/nsf/papers/statemaking.pdf

Bruszt, L. and Stark, D. (2003) 'Who counts? Supranational norms and societal needs', *East European Politics and Societies*, vol 17, no 1, pp 74-82.

Cameron, D. (2003) 'The challenges of accession', *East European Politics and Societies*, vol 17, no 1, pp 24-41.

Checkel, J.T. (2001) 'The Europeanization of citizenship?', in M. Cowles, J. Caporaso and T. Risse (eds) *Transforming Europe: Europeanization and domestic change*, Ithaca, NY: Cornell University Press, pp 125-63.

Clarke, J. (2002) 'A new kind of symmetry: actor–network theories and the new literacy studies', *Studies in the Education of Adults*, vol 34, no 2, pp 107-22.

Deacon, B. (2000) 'Eastern European welfare states: the impact of the politics of globalization', *Journal of European Social Policy*, vol 10, no 2, pp 146-61.

Diez, T. (1999) 'Speaking "Europe": the politics of integration discourse', *Journal of European Public Policy*, vol 6, no 4, pp 598-613.

Eriksen, E. and Fossum, J. (2000) 'Post-national integration', in E. Eriksen and J. Fossum (eds), *Democracy in the European Union: Integration through deliberation?*, London: Routledge, pp 1-29.

European Commission (1993) *Growth, competitiveness, employment: The challenges and ways forward into the 21st century*, White Paper, Luxembourg: European Commission.

Ferge, Z. (2000) *Elszabaduló egyenlQtlenségek (Runaway inequalities)*, Budapest: Hilscher RezsQ Szociálpolitikai Egyesület.

Ferge, Z. (2001) 'European integration and the reform of social security in the accession countries', *Journal of European Social Quality*, vol 3, nos 1-2, pp 9-25.

Fink-Hafner, D. and Lajh, D. (2003) 'Managing Europe from home: the Europeanisation of the Slovenian Core Executive', paper presented to the ECPR Conference, Marburb, September.

Fischer, F. (2003) *Reframing public policy*, Oxford: Oxford University Press.

Gebhardt, E. (1982) 'Introduction to Part III: a critique of methodology', in A. Arato and E. Gebhardt (eds) *The essential Frankfurt School reader*, New York, NY: Continuum, pp 255-73.

Grabbe, H. (2001) 'How does Europeanization affect CEE governance? Conditionality, diffusion and diversity', *Journal of European Public Policy*, vol 8, no 6, pp 1013-31.

Guillen, A., Alvarez, S. and Silva, P. (2003) 'European Union membership and social policy: the Spanish and Portuguese experiences', paper prepared for the inaugural ESPAnet conference, Changing European Societies – The Role of Social Policy, Copenhagen, 13-15 November (available at: www.sfi.dk/espanet).

Hughes, J., Sasse, G. and Gordon, C. (2003) 'EU enlargement and power asymmetries: conditionality and the Commission's role in regionalisation in Central and Eastern Europe', Working Paper no 49/03 ESRC, 'One Europe or Several?', available at: www.one-europe.ac.uk

Innes, J. (2002) *Knowledge and public policy* (2nd edn), New Brunswick, NJ: Transaction Books.

Jessop, B. (2002) *The future of the capitalist state*, Cambridge: Polity Press.

Jessop, B. (2004) 'Critical semiotic analysis and cultural political economy', *Critical Discourse Studies*, vol 1, no 2, pp 159-74.

Kleinman, M. (2002) *A European welfare state?*, London: Palgrave.

Kooiman, J. (2003) *Governing as governance*, London: Sage Publications.

Kornai, J. (1993) 'Transzformacios visszaeses' ('Transformative recession'), *Kozgazdasagi Szemle*, vol 25, no 3, pp 7-8.

Kovács, J. (2002) 'Approaching the EU and reaching the US? Rival narratives on transforming welfare regimes in East-Central Europe', *West European Politics*, Special Issue 2, no 1, pp 175-205.

Krémer, B. (2004) *Uniós politikák és Nemzeti Akciótervek a szegénység és a társadalmi kirekesztettség elleni küzdelemre* (*EU politics and the national action plans in the fights against poverty and social exclusion*), Budapest: STRATEK, Füzetek.

Krugman, P. (1994) 'Competitiveness: a danger obsession', *Foreign Affairs*, vol 37, no 2, pp 28-44.

Leibfried, S. (2000) 'National welfare states, European integration and globalization: a perspective for the next century', *Social Policy and Administration*, vol 34, no 1, pp 44-63.

Leibfried, S. and Pierson, P. (1995) *European social policy: Between fragmentation and integration*, Washington, DC: Brookings Institution.

Lindstrom, N. and Piroska, D. (2004) 'The politics of Europeanisation in Europe's southeastern periphery, Slovenian banks and breweries on s(c)ale', *Queen's Paper on Europeanisation*, no 4, available at: www.queensu.ca/sps/working-papers/

Lippert, B., Umbach, G. and Wessels, W. (2001) 'Europeanisation of CEE executives: EU membership negotiation as a shaping power', *Journal of European Public Policy*, vol 8, no 6, pp 980-1012.

March, J. and Olsen, P. (1989) *Rediscovering institutions*, London: Sage Publications.

Offe, C. (1994) 'Designing institutions for East European transitions', *Political Science Series*, no 19, Vienna: Institute for Advanced Studies.

Offe, C. (2000) 'The democratic welfare state. A European regime under the strain of European integration', *Political Science Series*, no 68, Vienna: Institute for Advanced Studies.

Olsen, J. (2002) 'The many faces of Europeanization', *Journal of Common Market Studies*, vol 40, no 5, pp 921-52.

Rein, M. and Schon, D. (1993) 'Reframing policy discourse', in F. Fischer and R. Forrester (eds) *The argumentative turn in policy analysis and planning*, Durham, NC: Duke University Press, pp 162-85.

Rosamond, B. (2000) *Theories of European integration*, Basingstoke: Palgrave.

Rosamond, B. (2002) 'Imagining the European economy: "competitiveness" and the social construction of "Europe" as an economic space', *New Political Economy*, vol 7, no 2, pp 157-77.

Scharpf, F. (2002) 'The European social model: coping with the challenges of diversity', *Journal of Common Market Studies*, vol 40, no 4, pp 645-70.

Shields, S. (2003) '"The charge of the right brigade": transnational social forces and the neoliberal configuration of Poland's transition', *New Political Economy*, vol 8, no 2, pp 225-44.

Stone, D. (2002) *Policy paradox: The art of political decision-making*, New York, NY: Norton.

Streek, D. and Schmitter, P. (1991) 'From national corporatism to transnational pluralism: organised interests in the single European market', *Politics and Society*, vol 19, June, pp 133-64.

Teague, P. (2000) 'EU social policy: institutional design matters', *Queen's Papers on Europeanisation*, no 1, available at www.queensu.ca/sps/working-papers/

Yanow, D. (1996) *How does a policy mean? Interpreting policy and organizational actions*, Washington, DC: Georgetown University Press.

FOUR

Regendering governance[1]

Janet Newman

Introduction

One of the strengths of governance theory is that it draws attention to flows of power that traverse the boundaries of state/society, public/ private and economy/civil society. It recognises that processes of governing take place in and through families, workplaces, communities, schools and other sites beyond the domain of institutional politics. As such, it seemingly connects with strands of feminist analysis that have long problematised the distinctions between public and private and that have drawn attention to forms and flows of power beyond the state. However, the study of governance has remained relatively immune to a gendered analysis. This chapter highlights some of the ways in which transformations of governance are explicitly and implicitly gendered. In doing so it draws on concepts from both political science and social policy, but especially from critical feminist perspectives from across the social sciences.

My starting point is the typology of market, hierarchy and networks that has informed the study of governance. Following Newman (2001), I want to add a fourth domain – that of self-governance – because of both its political significance and its increasing importance as a governmental strategy. The process of 'remaking' governance in the context of the new policy agendas discussed in Chapters Two and Three involves a shifting relationship between these domains. State power is not dissolved – hierarchical forms of governance remain significant – but the idea of the state as a unitary actor is problematised, with more emphasis being placed on market mechanisms, network patterns of coordination (governing through partnerships and collaborative strategies), and the constitution of citizens as self-governing, responsibilised subjects. The chapter traces the ways in which each of these domains is gendered and how each contributes to the contradictory gender order of neo-liberal governance.

However, in setting out the framework – hierarchy, markets, networks, self-governance – let me stress several important points. First, as ideal types the domains denote a logic of organising rather than a sphere of activity. Governmental policies and strategies are likely to cut across them in complex ways, and organisations and individuals may be subject to contradictory logics (Newman, 2001). Second, the domains, although often spoken about as if they are singular entities, each condense different politics, policies and orientations. Even the market – the domain that appears to be the most impersonal, governed by questions of supply and demand, competition and price – must be understood as a social mechanism that disrupts particular forms of relationship and offers new forms of identity.

Third, and most importantly in the context of this chapter, both the typologies themselves and the domains that are constructed within them are gendered. They 'fix' particular identities, relationships and forms of power in temporary – albeit often relatively long-lasting – gender orders: for example, the gender order that underpinned the male breadwinner model of many post-war welfare states, or the gender order emerging in the new service economy of globalised markets. In each, gender is articulated with 'race' and class in complex ways. The post-war welfare settlements of some European states are viewed often as class settlements between capital and labour, but are inscribed not only with gendered formations of family and work but also racialised constructions of nationhood (G. Lewis, 1998). The emerging service economy is one that opens up new labour markets to women, but the ways in which this forms the basis of new patterns of inequality is deeply classed and racialised (Kingfisher, 2002).

Finally, in foregrounding political and economic forms of practice, the typologies serve to obscure social and cultural dimensions of . governance (Newman, 2004). As such, as numerous feminist scholars have argued, they also tend to overlook the importance of the domestic, familial or personal domains (Williams, 1995; Daly, 2000; Daly and Rake, 2003). This has produced a vigorous set of debates between welfare regime scholars – notably Esping-Andersen – and feminist critics insisting on the importance of 'family' as a domain alongside state and market in order to emphasise the gendered distinctions between 'public' (state) and 'private' (familial) in welfare work (J. Lewis, 1992).

As well as the gendered form in which typologies divide social and economic phenomena into domains, each of the domains is itself already gendered. The following sections trace some of the dimensions of change taking place in the shifting configurations of governance.

Of course, these will be experienced in different ways, and to different extents, in specific nation–states and in different sites of governance within them. For example, there are marked differences between the gender orders of so-called 'conservative' and 'liberal' welfare states, and between those of Central and Eastern European Accession Countries and the European Union (EU) as a policymaking body (see Chapter Three of this volume). The aim here is not to try to tease out such differences, but to highlight the gendered implications of the governance shifts that are produced as states attempt to modernise themselves in order to respond to the presumed pressures of globalisation or the policy imperatives of the EU. As such, the chapter provides an analytical framework through which the specific dynamics of particular welfare states might be mapped.

Restating the state: the gender dynamics of welfare governance

It is of course impossible to generalise about the state. While some commentators in political science point to the hollowing-out of state institutions and the decentring of state power, others highlight the continued salience of the state (Pierre and Peters, 2000). Across the literature there has been a vigorous industry of categorising states into different regimes and debating the extent of their convergence (see J. Lewis, 1992; Sainsbury, 1999; Mahon, 2001 for critical feminist work on welfare regimes). Here, the focus is on the new forms of relationship between state and citizen that are predicated on social changes that have dismantled the hierarchical social order of the past and have introduced a more individuated society. The concept of individuation, developed by Beck (1986) and Beck-Gernsheim (2002), describes an erosion of traditional ties that opens out the possibility of new, more differentiated and reflexive forms of identity. This offers enhanced possibilities of autonomy and choice, in part due to the benefits and support introduced by welfare states. However, Beck-Gernsheim also drew attention to the ways in which women's individuation was hampered by those same welfare states, opening up a series of debates about how far the move towards women's further integration into the labour market (what is often termed the 'commodification' of women's labour) might offer enhanced gender equality and overcome the problems of poverty experienced by many groups of women, especially older women and lone mothers – groups traditionally dependent on state benefits or disadvantaged in a benefits and pension system that is predicated on the primacy of the male breadwinner.

The notion of individuation has been highly influential in debates about welfare reform and restructuring. The emergence of the 'adult worker' model[2] at the core of social policy in the EU and many welfare states reflects the changing pattern of family forms which has undermined the validity of the male breadwinner model of social policy. However, the adult worker model also derives from New Right assumptions about work as the basis of social integration and inclusion, especially in relation to groups such as lone mothers, while globalisation has directed the attention of governments to the need to promote policies that focus on the development of human capacities and skills. This means that concerns about gender equality have been articulated – often in uncomfortable ways – with concerns about how to modernise welfare states in the context of globalisation and the competition between nation-states to attract investment and resources[3]. As J. Lewis (2001) notes, states operate as if individuation in the form of an adult worker model has already been achieved or is about to be achieved, shaping policies around assumptions that disadvantage many women whose lives do not reflect such a template, usually those who are already most disadvantaged.

The ideas of Esping-Andersen have been critical in setting the terms of the debate and influencing policy discourse in the EU, being deeply implicated, for example, in the employment strategies integral to the EU's Open Method of Coordination (OMC) (see Chapter Two of this volume). The blueprint set out by Esping-Andersen et al (2002) for a new welfare state architecture is based on the idea of social investment in order to respond to the challenges of competitiveness, provide for the funding of social protection schemes and combat forms of social exclusion, especially that of lone mothers. This legitimates the withdrawal of state benefits associated with the male breadwinner model and the introduction of a range of policies to incentivise and support women's greater participation in the labour market. It also reflects the shift to a more instrumental and productivist orientation in social policy (which was commented on in Chapter Three of this volume).

But the main focus here is on the ways in which the adult worker-citizen opens up new forms of contract between state and citizen. Gerhard et al (2002, p 122) suggest that: "Once policymakers assume an individualized adult-worker citizen model, it becomes possible to construct a contract based set of policy frameworks involving state and citizen and state enforcement of citizen/citizen arrangements." New contractual relationships emphasise the responsibility as well as the rights of citizenship: the responsibility to work, the responsibility to take up opportunities in exchange for support and, in some countries, the responsibility to insure oneself in preparation for retirement or ill-health. But Gerhard et al conclude that "while feminists have always insisted on the recognition of women's capacity to enter into contract, the process of contractualisation based on a citizen-worker model and assuming full individuation will pose major problems for women" (2002, pp 134-5). This is due to the assumption that women can act independently now as worker-citizens and thus can be incorporated into the masculine model of work and welfare (J. Lewis, 2002). The 'degendering' dynamic of this discourse presents major problems for women in that it assumes that gender inequalities have been largely eradicated, apart from a few residual groups that are encompassed in those other gender- and class-neutral discourses of 'social exclusion' or 'family poverty'. As a result, the new gender-neutral contract between state and citizen has contradictory effects. On the one hand, it recognises women as full citizens, taking their place in the public groups of paid work, politics and community in their own right. On the other, however, the model assumes that equality – especially in the private domain of family – has been realised already and leaves the question of the role of men in care and domestic labour unproblematised (Kilkey, 2004).

The nature of the ways in which these contradictions are played out will vary in form as well as extent, depending on the political as well as social formations of specific welfare states: for example, between so-called 'conservative' and 'liberal' welfare regimes. The dominant dynamics of welfare reform are underpinned not only by assumptions about the changing character of the social and, in particular, of family forms (the individuation thesis), but also by the impact of New Right policies in some European states, leading to the introduction of more conditional benefit structures tied to employment (the shift from welfare to workfare thesis). They are also underpinned by the forces of globalisation, which have led governments to focus on the need for a more flexible, skilled and productive workforce (the social investment state thesis). These different formations are overlaid on each other in complex and often contradictory ways.

The significance of the *politics* of modernisation, its form, pace and combination of ideological imperatives, means that the state must be understood not only in terms of its new, 'steering' form, shaping the actions of the plurality of agencies involved in dispersed governance, but also in its traditional role as legislator, regulator and policymaker. Here, as well as unsettling and remaking the gendered dynamics of work and welfare, the state is deeply implicated in the construction and regulation of gender and sexuality, the reproduction of hetero-normative family forms, the regulation of the body through control of reproductive technologies, the categorisation of legitimate and unlawful sexualities, and so on. In addition, the reordering of gender relations of work and welfare will be deeply influenced by the ways in which the state looks to the market to solve supposedly 'residual' problems of gender inequality, not only by providing new, equalising opportunities to work but also in supplying the domestic and care services that enable women to take up their new roles as worker-citizens.

Going to market: the gender dynamics of commodification

The shift towards greater reliance on markets – a seemingly impersonal domain of exchange – collapses a number of different dynamics:

- the privatisation of public goods;
- the introduction of market-type principles into public services;
- the processes of contracting for goods or services;
- the introduction of concepts of choice and consumerism into welfare services; and
- the shifting processes of commodification and decommodification.

This last refers to different kinds of phenomena. One is concerned with the ways in which work is commodified. As individuals enter labour markets, they become entitled to a range of work-related benefits that grant them future entitlements – periods of decommodification such as paid maternity leave, retirement pension – independent of market participation. Processes of commodification and decommodification also refer to the ways in which services previously provided by the state (including care) are being recommodified into the marketplace or decommodified into households or communities.

Each of these dynamics is profoundly gendered and produces new conceptions of women and men as citizens, workers, carers and social actors. In social-democratic welfare states such as Sweden, there has long been state support for a dual-earner model of the family, while in 'conservative' regimes such as Germany, commodification may mark a welcome demise of the dependence of women as mothers on a male breadwinner and may be viewed by feminists as a route to autonomy, independence and financial equality. However, where the adult worker model is associated with liberal welfare states – notably the UK – it has become the focus of a number of feminist critiques (J. Lewis,

2001; Rake, 2001; Williams, 2004), pointing to the ways in which such policies "ignore the care preferences of women and obscure gender inequalities in the home and the gendered part time/full time distribution of work" (Williams and Roseneil, 2004, p 185).

Focusing on women's participation in the labour market also tends to ignore questions of how the market itself is changing and what the implications of this might be. The term 'market' suggests a natural, essentialist phenomena based on the dynamics of demand and supply, modified at the margins by state policies of regulation and intervention. That is, the commodification of work is associated with the (presumed) economic rationality of the market; a sphere in which questions of value that are associated with the 'private' sphere of bringing up children or caring for others in and beyond the family has little place. However, it forms a set of practices and relationships deeply inscribed with social and cultural norms. As Knijn and Ostner argue, the concepts of commodification and decommodification are ambiguous and refer to equally ambiguous empirical phenomena: "Wage dependents can be empowered but also weakened by commodifying and de-commodifying processes. Trade Unions ... employers and the state, too, have regularly used these policies to create the notorious insider–outsider cleavages" (2002, p 162). For example, some trade unions have been notoriously slow in taking on women's concerns about the dominant patterns of working time or in supporting equal value claims. Such social processes derive from historical assumptions about what counts as paid work, the organisation of working time and the structure and norms of the workplace. The hierarchy of value placed on different forms of paid work and the norms of working time and work–life balance all tend to be man-made and are all subject to alternative possibilities.

Policies on the modernisation of welfare governance which involve significant shifts of functions and services from the public sector to the private sector or personal domains have a very significant impact on the dynamics of labour markets, opening up new forms of commodification in the form of marginal and vulnerable workers in low-paid work. For example, in recent years there has been an enormous expansion in the service sector – characterised by part-time, insecure employment and low rates of pay – and a sharp reduction in the kinds of public sector jobs traditionally staffed by women. In some countries social care work is moving out of the public sector and into highly exploitative and low-paid work in agencies with whom the state now contracts to deliver services. As Mahon (2001) notes, states have been active in supporting the growth of employment in the service sector, thus opening up greater consumption of personal and care services. However, this growth of personal and social care services tends to produce greater – gendered and classed – inequalities, since the workforce is likely to be lower paid and more vulnerable to short-term shifts in the economy. Indeed Esping-Andersen saw it as inevitable that the growth of employment in the personal and social services could only take place at the expense of increased inequality because of the productivity gap between goods-producing and service sectors. This is likely to have a negative impact on the value that is placed on women's labour, since such jobs typically represent "a marketised version of conventional domestic tasks" (Esping-Andersen, 1999, p 104).

The processes of marketising domestic and care work produce new chains of interdependencies that flow across national borders, especially between Europe and its former colonies or between northern and southern nations. The capacity of many women in Western and Northern Europe to pursue a career is often dependent on migrant and other women's labour in the marginal economy of commodified care services. These are unlikely to have access to the benefits afforded to those in the mainstream labour force, including access to periods of decommodification in relation to sickness, holidays, the birth and care of their own children and, indeed, retirement. The result is "new cleavages, not only between women and men, but also between women workers in the rapidly emerging globalised post-industrial (service) societies" (Knijn and Ostner, 2002, p 163).

The language of commodification and decommodification, then, misses the complexity of the relationship between different forms of women's labour – between paid and unpaid care work, between the production and consumption of domestic labour, between different forms of emotional labour in households, families and workplaces. The commodification of women's labour and the commodification of care services are not neat processes that complement each other in some functionalist account of welfare state transformation; they are the sites of unevenness and disjuncture as welfare states juggle tax, welfare, economic, immigration, education, pension and a host of other policies. This is a deeply political process. Pascall and Lewis (2004, p 387) conclude that "gender equality in the labour market alone is unattainable, because of systematic connections to inequalities in families, politics and civil society".

Networks and emotional labour: remaking the gender order of care

As the introduction to this chapter noted, while the social policy literature tends to collapse the idea of the state into a singular entity (the welfare state), governance theory offers a more problematised conception of forms and flows of state power. A key focus has been the processes of marketisation and the fragmentation of previously monolithic institutions into a plurality of agencies that cut across public, private and civil society domains in complex ways. The literature also highlights the flows of power to supranational bodies such as the EU and to subsidiary tiers of governance in regions and localities; and the emergence of collaborative forms of governance that draw voluntary organisations, community groups and the public itself into new relationships with government. This dispersal of power opens up the need for new forms of coordination and much of the governance literature focuses on the flows of power associated with network governance. As I have argued elsewhere (Newman, 2002, 2003), networks obscure issues of equality and inequality: formal power and the clarity of position, status and rights that this bestows becomes less significant than flows of influence in interpersonal and inter-organisational relationships. However, my focus here is on what kinds of work are carried out within networks and by whom, highlighting the work of *coordination* that is overlaid on the work of *care*.

This is becoming increasingly important because of the restructuring of state services around the twin principles of managerialism and marketisation (Clarke and Newman, 1997). Managerialism places organisations in competition with each other, either for users, contracts or prestige in terms of their position in government league tables. This places a premium on cost containment (one of the main criteria against which they are judged by government) and on gatekeeping activities (the capacity to select those service users – patients, pupils and so on – on advantageous criteria). Such processes mean that service users with complex or long-term needs may be shunted off to 'the community' and family. Other forms of shunting are also evident: for example, in order to secure greater efficiency, many health treatments are now provided in a single day rather than requiring in-patient hospital care, shifting convalescent or recovery needs from hospital to home.

Overlaid on this are the effects of marketisation. This produces a fragmented array of services which then need to be coordinated, and this work of coordination takes place in networks that cut across frontline workers in public sector organisations, the staff and members of voluntary organisations, informal carers and service users themselves. Care services – for children, the frail and elderly, children with additional needs, people with disabilities, mental health service users and others – are no longer simply provided by the state: assessment and gatekeeping roles may be retained but actual service delivery now takes place through an array of organisations and groups so complex that the boundaries between public and private sector provision are almost impossible to delineate. This fragmentation means that care work has to be composed, managed and coordinated by those in need of care, or their carers. While childcare is the example which has preoccupied feminist commentators most significantly, policies on care for the elderly are moving centre stage as welfare states grapple with the changing demographic profile of populations and seek to reduce expenditure by experimenting with new models of social care. Care services for older people in the UK, for example, are based on a 'package' of services from multiple providers across public, private and voluntary sectors. Health needs are met by yet another set of services, with general practitioners, out-of-hours medical services, occupational health professionals, district nurses, physiotherapists and others all needing to be organised and coordinated. There may be voluntary, community or church organisations providing support, social and care services. Then there are the personal services providing security, cleaning, transport and shopping as well as visiting professionals providing everything from hairdressing to financial advice: all part of the burgeoning service economy targeting the needs of the growing elderly or housebound population.

In the main, the work of coordination is done by women working in the gendered networks that cut across frontline public sector jobs and paid and unpaid care work. As the state retreats into the new governance role of steering, shaping and providing (conditional and often short-term) funding, while the market picks and chooses where it might be profitable to fill the gaps left by the state's retreat, so new coordination needs arise. This takes place in families, households, communities and friendship networks that organise care and welfare and negotiate with state professionals to manage the interface between the gaps in state provision and the consumption of commodified services. Women in paid work, then, may have shed some of their direct care responsibilities. Yet the work of organising patchy, imperfect and unreliable networks of care, and filling the gaps when they fail, remains gendered work because of the persistence of gender inequalities in the distribution of domestic and care work in the home. The work of coordination forms yet another element of the 'emotional labour' that characterises care work (Newman and Mooney, 2004).

It is here that the interaction between the commodification of women's labour and the fragmentation of state services is felt most sharply. Just at the point where women are being addressed increasingly as the degendered, adult workers of the modern state, so those same processes of modernisation, with the managerialisation and marketisation that they produce, are exacerbating the need for informal care in the home and community. Kingfisher (2002) notes the contradictions produced by welfare state modernisation: the 'privatisation' of more and more functions to the home and family at the same time as welfare-to-work imperatives squeeze the capacity of women to engage in informal care work. Drawing on Elson (1994, 1995), she argues that such tensions are resolved in the 'infinite elasticity' of women's labour.

Self-governance, identity and agency: remaking the politics of gender

As earlier sections of this chapter have illustrated, strategies of welfare reform offer new – and degendered – subject positions for women as individuated citizens and adult workers. This is only one of a series of new forms of subject that have incorporated ideas from women's struggles and other social movements (albeit partially and conditionally) into state policies and practice. Women's social movements were crucial in the formation of the much-criticised male breadwinner model inscribed in many European welfare states (Orloff, 2005: forthcoming). While campaigns to support mothers are waning, other claims – notably those around childcare – are being amplified and many European states are now seeking to guarantee places for all children of a certain age. Other social movements have been recognised and incorporated into state practice. For example, the category 'carer' – produced by the de-institutionalisation of care for people with disabilities, the frail elderly and mental health service users – became the focus of collective action which brought issues of care from private to public spheres. As a result, carers are now a target for state support and – that frequent corollary of support – regulation and supervision. More recent social movements have advocated greater attention to domestic violence issues, better treatment for the victims of rape and other forms of violence, care and treatment for those with HIV/AIDS and others.

Many of these movements have their origins in self-governed forms of provision, with care, self-help, advocacy and campaigning being closely interwoven. In their formation, such movements were often based on values and practices which sought to avoid the paternalistic and patriarchal norms associated with state practice. However, a number of tensions arise where women's or other movements have been influential in shaping state policy. Some tensions derive from conflicting conceptions of appropriate practice: for example, those between the norms of disability activists and forms of state practice based on medical models; or those between feminist-based support to women experiencing domestic violence or rape and the practice of police, courts and other state services. Others arise as a result of the unintended costs of incorporation into state policy and practice. Social movements themselves can be appropriated by states – the feminist discourse on individuation as a means of enhancing greater autonomy for women and securing enhanced gender equality has been appropriated and reworked in social policy, where it has taken the form of a modernising rationale.

New modes of provision, for which women's groups and others may have campaigned for years, become intertwined with regulatory practices that "not only constrain individual behaviour but also mobilise and enforce a limited set of subjectivities that accommodate the political projects of bureaucrats and social elites" (Padamsee and Adams, 2002, p 194), and in so doing shift the gender dynamics associated with the movement concerned to one more containable within the state. Padamsee and Adams argue for the importance of tracing the 'privileged subject' of welfare regimes – the male head of household, the housewife, the working mother. Such subjects are formed through discourse and institutionalised in welfare practice. In recent years we have seen some shifts in which subjects are so privileged. For example, there has been a shift in discourse from 'teenage mothers' to 'lone parents', implying not only an apparently gender-neutral recategorisation but also some shift in the emphasis of state policies. But the process of degendering welfare subjects (adult workers, parents) is accompanied by a highly selective attention to gender in the targeting of state intervention on particular groups: not only the 'usual suspects' of lone mothers and absent fathers, but also girls who are deemed to be at risk of early pregnancy, criminal activity or future ill-health due to smoking, alcohol, drug abuse or obesity. Particularly notable has been the focus on fathers in welfare practice, where debates around caring fatherhood and parental leave have produced policy innovation in some countries (Hobson, 2001; J. Lewis, 2001, 2002). By encouraging or coercing them to contribute financially to a child's care and enabling them to take a fuller role through parental leave policies, the targeting of fathers has been accompanied by greater concern with the quality of parenting – what Daly (2003) terms a 'professionalisation' of parenting buttressed by training courses in parenting skills and new forms of professional and state support. This can be linked to the increased focus on the child-as-welfare subject in the 'social investment state' (Lister, 2003).

Alongside the conceptions of women as worker-citizen and responsible parent, women are also implicitly addressed in a range of policies concerned with the creation of cohesive communities. The 'responsibilising' thrust of new forms of social policy in nations such as the UK produces expectations that citizens (often women) will take greater responsibility for social issues and participate in neighbourhood initiatives, children's schooling and various forms of local partnership. This set of policies stresses the importance of stable, responsible families as the basis of strong communities. At the same time, the collaborative governance trend (discussed in Chapter Six of this volume) is based on a model of active citizenship which requires the free availability of time and other resources that are unequally distributed.

Thus, we can trace a number of new identities that are being discursively formed in the remaking of citizens as self-governing subjects in the process of state modernisation. These are shaped in the intersection of economic and moral discourses, with moral responsibilities (to participate in social welfare provision as carers, parents, families, communities) eliding with economic freedoms (to engage in paid work and to free oneself from domestic or care responsibilities through consumption of new services) in a discordant and often contradictory way. However, as John Clarke has argued, new subjects may be called but they may refuse to respond. They may recognise themselves when power calls but may also "ignore it, refuse to listen, or tune in to alternative hailings that speak of different selves, imagined collectivities and futures" (2004, p 158).

In order to assess the relationship between policy discourse and the complexity of social and political imaginaries, we have to turn to more ethnographic, qualitative forms of research. Such approaches make it possible to explore the values that women – and society – afford to different kinds of work, and to highlight the relationship between questions of care and paid work in the personal lives of individual women, families or social groups. For example, Himmelweit and Sigala (2004) explore the ways in which mothers with pre-school children take decisions about paid employment and conclude that "neither identities nor behaviours are fixed, but adapt to each other in a process of positive feedback, both at an individual level and at a social level" (2004, p 471). That is, neither identities (as adult workers) nor choices (to take up paid employment) flow directly from new governmental strategies; rather, identities are enacted which reflect the behaviour of others and which subsequently become inscribed into new institutional norms. A different programme of research[4] focuses not on the choices that women make but on shifts in values and practices and their implications for the future of social policy. One study within this programme explored the values of a series of UK voluntary organisations involved in issues of parenting, partnering and child welfare. The results show a clear distinction between the values and orientations of the voluntary organisations and those of government, although the organisations concerned were seen to be adapting to New Labour's policy programme and adopting elements of gender-neutral and child-centred discourses.

Such approaches open up more complex ways of approaching questions of governance. For example, seemingly common discourses that may appear in the vocabularies of policymaking in different nation-states – or indeed of the EU – may mask tensions and inconsistencies. The ideas of 'social investment' or 'capacity building' may take on very different inflections not only across nation-states but also in their interpretation by different policymaking groups within national and European policy networks, including those social or voluntary organisations seeking – often successfully – to influence policy. Such approaches remind us that we cannot read the transformation of welfare states as simply a response to neo-liberal pressures that produce a tendency towards convergence, neither can we view national policies as uniform and coherent. They highlight the ways in which the tensions and unevenness in the process of remaking the gender order of governance are lived out in the daily experiences of those called to new, often contradictory, subject positions, and how such positions may inform patterns of social agency.

Conclusion

This chapter has attempted to open up questions about how governance might be 'regendered' as an analytical concept. It has focused on how different trends and tendencies – the fragmentation of state power, the increasing importance of markets, shifting patterns of work, family and community and the changing social formations that produce new forms of identity and agency – may constitute and be constituted by formations of gender, 'race' and class. Its primary analytic lens has been gender, especially the ways in which governance shifts apparently degender concepts of citizenship, work and care while potentially opening up new patterns of gendered inequality. Inevitably, this chapter has operated at a high level of generality and the ways in which the shifts that it depicts are played out can only be understood in the context of specific social and cultural formations. Many of the changes are ambiguous – it is possible to read, across national boundaries, for similarities in policy texts and discourses or even in empirical evidence of shifts in women's participation in the labour force, but this leaves questions unanswered about the forms of work, and the processes of inclusion and exclusion as well as the equalities and inequalities, that these produce.

However, the chapter has highlighted important tensions in the interaction between different forms of governance: state, market, networks and self-governance. Government may design policies on the assumption that gender inequalities have been largely solved and that women can now take their place as fully individuated worker-citizens. This in turn implies a shift from dependence on the state to greater autonomy, with the associated responsibilities of self-governance. More care functions are moving out of the state and additional expectations are being made of 'community', at the same time that the adult worker model reduces the capacity of women to 'fill the care gap' or to have time for new forms of active citizenship. There is an assumption, too, that the market can now provide many of the care needs which were formerly the responsibility of the state. As has been argued here, this is not only the source of new patterns of inequality, but also the source of new forms of coordinative work that rely on women's labour in managing a dispersed array of care services. Thus the commodification of women's labour and its relationship to other policy domains, including (but not restricted to) care, is highly ambiguous in its effects. The focus on 'family' in the social policy literature may obscure the complexity of other forms of relationship through which care and welfare are provided; it may miss something of the significance of women's work beyond the family, sustaining the relationships of neighbourhood and community and forming the bedrock of social capital on which network forms of governance often depend.

However, despite these ambiguities, some dominant trends can be highlighted:

> By commodifying personal care without proper decommodification policies and by abdicating responsibility for the quality and quantity of care services to the invisible

hand of the market, the welfare state no longer adopts the role of defender of the public interests against the capitalist economy. (Knijn and Ostner 2002, p 161)

This has a profound effect on those who care for those left behind by the retreating state, whether in paid or unpaid work. The contradictions of neo-liberalism – between, for example, the imperative for women with children, older people, people with disabilities and other groups to (re)enter the labour force and the 'dumping' of social welfare functions onto individuals, households and communities – have to be managed in the private sphere, not only in families but also in the personal lives of individuals as they manage the tensions between citizenship, care and work. As such, the delineation of the boundaries of what is a matter for public concern and what is a private or personal matter – a boundary that feminists have long problematised and contested – is deeply political. The ambiguities, oscillations and contradictions played out across that boundary cannot be contained by those easy formulations of public and private inscribed in the typologies of governance or welfare states with which this chapter began.

Notes

[1] This chapter was written while I was a visiting professor at the University of Bremen. My thanks go to the staff of the ZES Institute for the facilities and support that they offered.

[2] The emphasis on women's integration into the labour market has been described in a number of ways: as the emergence of a 'citizen-worker' model (Rake, 2001), an 'adult worker model' (J. Lewis, 2001) or a 'universal breadwinner model' (Fraser, 1994).

[3] The ways in which these tensions have been reconciled (or not) in specific nation-states have been rather different (see the discussions in the special issue of the journal *Social Politics*, January 2004).

[4] The Study of Care, Values and the Future of Welfare at the University of Leeds in the UK (the CAVA project).

References

Beck, U. (1986) *Risk society: Towards a new modernity*, London: Sage Publications.

Beck-Gernsheim, E. (2002) *Reinventing the family: In search of new lifestyles*, Cambridge: Polity Press.

Clarke, J. (2004) *Changing welfare, changing states: New directions in social policy*, London: Sage Publications.

Clarke, J. and Newman, J. (1997) *The managerial state: Power, politics and ideology in the remaking of social welfare*, London: Sage Publications.

Daly, M. (2000) *The gender division of welfare*, Cambridge: Cambridge University Press.

Daly, M. (2003) 'Changing conceptions of welfare and gender relations in European welfare states', in J. Lewis and R. Surrender (eds), *Welfare state change: Toward a third way?* Oxford: Oxford University Press, pp 135-54.

Daly, M. and Rake, K. (2003) *Gender and the welfare state*, Cambridge: Polity Press.

Elson, D. (1994) 'Micro, meso, macro: gender and economic policy analysis in the context of policy reform', in I. Bakkar (ed) *The strategic silence: Gender and economic policy*, London: Zed.

Elson, D. (1995) 'Male bias in macro-economic policy: the case of structural adjustment', in D. Elson (ed) *Male bias in the development process*, Manchester: Manchester University Press.

Esping-Andersen, G. (1999) *The social foundations of post-industrial economics*, Oxford: Oxford University Press.

Esping-Andersen, G., Gallie, D., Hemerijck, A. and Myles, J. (2002) *Why we need a new welfare state*, Oxford: Oxford University Press.

Fraser, N. (1994) 'After the family wage: gender equity and the welfare state', *Political Theory*, vol 22, no 4, pp 591-618.

Gerhard, U., Knijn, T. and Lewis, J. (2002) 'Contractualization', in B. Hobson, J. Lewis and B. Siim (eds) *Contested concepts in gender and social politics*, Cheltenham: Edward Elgar, pp 105-40.

Himmelweit, S. and Sigala, M. (2004) 'Choice and the relationship between identities and behaviour for mothers with pre-school children: some implications for policy from a UK study', *Journal of Social Policy*, vol 33, no 3, pp 455-78.

Hobson, B. (ed) (2001) *Making men into fathers: Men, masculinities and the social politics of fatherhood*, Cambridge: Cambridge University Press.

Kilkey, M. (2004) 'The "citizen-worker" model and assumptions about men, work and care', paper presented to the European Social Policy Association Network Conference, Oxford, July.

Kingfisher, C. (ed) (2002) *Western welfare in decline: Globalisation and women's poverty*, Philadelphia, PA: University of Pennsylvania Press.

Knijn, T. and Ostner, I. (2002) 'Commodification and de-commodification', in B. Hobson, J. Lewis and B. Siim (eds) *Contested concepts in gender and social politics*, Cheltenham: Edward Elgar, pp 141-69.

Lewis, G. (1998) 'Welfare and the social construction of "race"', in E. Saraga (ed) *Embodying the social: Constructions of difference*, London: Routledge, pp 91-137.

Lewis, J. (1992) 'Gender and the development of welfare regimes', *Journal of European Social Policy*, vol 2, no 3, pp 159-73.

Lewis, J. (2001) 'The decline of the male breadwinner model: implications for work and care', *Social Politics*, summer, pp 152-69.

Lewis, J. (2002) 'Gender and welfare states', *European Societies*, vol 4, pp 331-57.

Lister, R. (2003) 'Investing in the citizen-workers of the future: transformations in citizenship and the state under New Labour', *Social Policy and Administration*, vol 37, no 5, pp 427-43.

Mahon, R. (2001) 'Theorizing welfare regimes: towards a dialogue?', *Social Politics*, spring, pp 24-35.

Newman, J. (2001) *Modernising governance: New labour, policy and society*, London: Sage Publications.

Newman, J. (2002) 'Changing governance, changing equality? New Labour and the modernisation of public services', *Public Money and Management*, vol 22, no 1, pp 7-14.

Newman, J. (2003) 'New Labour, governance and the politics of diversity', in J. Barry, M. Dent and M. O'Neill (eds) *Gender and the public sector: Professions and managerial change*, London: Routledge, pp 15-26.

Newman, J. (2004) 'Through thick or thin? The problem of the social in societal governance', paper presented to the Governing the Social Conference, Alberta, Canada, July.

Newman, J. and Mooney, G. (2004) 'Managing personal lives: doing welfare work', in G. Mooney (ed) *Work: Personal lives and social policy*, Bristol: The Policy Press, pp 39-72.

Orloff, A. (2006, forthcoming) 'Farewell to maternalism? State policies and mothers' employment', in J. Levy (ed) *The state after statism*, Cambridge, MA: Harvard University Press.

Padamsee, T. and Adams, J. (2002) 'Signs and regimes revisited', *Social Politics*, summer, pp 187-202.

Pascall, G. and Lewis, J. (2004) 'Emerging gender regimes and policies for gender equality in a wider Europe', *Journal of Social Policy*, vol 33, no 3, pp 373-94.

Pierre, J. and Peters, G. (2000) *Governance, politics and the state*, Basingstoke: Macmillan.

Rake, K. (2001) 'Gender and New Labour's social policies', *Journal of Social Policy*, vol 30, no 2, pp 209-32.

Sainsbury, D. (ed) (1999) *Gender and welfare state regimes*, Oxford: Oxford University Press.

Williams, F. (1995) 'Race/ethnicity, gender and class in welfare states: a framework for analysis', *Social Politics*, vol 2, no 2, pp 127-59.

Williams, F. (2004) *Rethinking families*, London: Gulbenkian Foundation.

Williams, F. and Roseneil, S. (2004) 'Public values of parenting and partnering: voluntary organisations and welfare politics in New Labour's Britain', *Social Politics*, vol 11, no 2, pp 181-216.

FIVE

Welfare governance and the remaking of citizenship

Håkan Johansson and Bjørn Hvinden

Introduction

Dynamic change in the relationships between states and citizens is a feature of countries undergoing programmes of welfare reform and restructuring. Such changes involve new ways of 'governing the social' in which citizens are expected (or themselves expect) to play more active roles in handling risks and promoting their own welfare. In this chapter we trace the implications of active citizenship for welfare governance. Following Kjær (2004, pp 12–15), we define governance as "the setting, application and enforcement of the rules of the game" in a way that enhances legitimacy in the public realm. We use the term 'dynamics' advisedly: we argue that contemporary changes in welfare governance and citizenship are not the result of a simple one-way process where, for example, external pressures on nation-states bring about new forms of governance and citizenship, or where changes in citizens' capabilities and demands force states to change. Rather, these dynamics must be captured as mutually reinforcing processes, transforming modes of governance as well as the scope for citizen choice, participation and self-directed activity.

The turn to active citizenship leads to a more complex and diversified relationship between states and citizens, opening up new strategies on the part of both. Some strategies can result in an intensification of the practices through which some groups are marginalised or excluded (for example, along lines of gender, ethnicity, disability or previous labour market experience), while other strategies may produce more inclusive forms of welfare governance. The implications of active citizenship will vary between different national welfare states, reflecting established patterns of state–citizen relations. Hence we need to analyse the emerging relationship between welfare governance and active citizenship in ways that are sensitive to the ambiguities and paradoxical effects of reform in specific national – and transnational – contexts. The chapter is based on research in the Nordic countries, but provides frameworks through which the dynamics of change in other nations can be understood.

The turn to active citizenship

Contemporary welfare states face pressure from many sources. A widely shared understanding is that the 'stateness' of welfare states is challenged 'from above', whether this process is framed as globalisation, Europeanisation or denationalisation (Beck, 2000; Rieger and Leibfried, 2003; Wincott, 2003). Such pressures are assumed to constrain the sovereignty of national governments, enforcing stricter budgetary discipline and new regulative measures. This produces a circumscribed range of legitimate policy options and instruments at state level.

The expanding field of transnational governance is one source of such pressures. For European welfare states, the European Union (EU), and to lesser extent, the Organisation for Economic Co-operation and Development (OECD), are of special importance. A core of the Europeanisation project has been to remove all barriers to the free movement of goods, services, capital and labour, as expressed in the 1997 Stability and Growth Pact and the Lisbon process since the summit of 2000. It includes ambitions to build structures of joint decision-making as well as forms of governance that seek to secure appropriate forms of market regulation and to handle the imperfections and undesirable consequences of free market competition. The European Court of Justice plays an ambiguous role in this respect, both limiting national governments' scope for introducing new expensive provisions and forcing them to provide benefits and services to economic migrants and their families (Leibfried and Pierson, 2000; Pollack, 2003). Similarly, as we saw in Chapter Two, the European Commission has also been given a more significant and proactive role within the field of social policy. The 1999 Amsterdam Treaty gave the EU competence to combat discrimination on a number of different grounds and to initiate joint action programmes in this field (European Union, 1997). The overall ambition of these programmes has been to achieve greater convergence between the welfare and social policy programmes of Member States, mainly through the Open Method of Coordination (OMC) (de la Porte and Pochet, 2002). The OMC means that Member States will agree on some overall objectives but are free to choose the means necessary to reach them. The programmes based on the OMC aim to promote higher levels of employment, social inclusion and sustainable pensions. Recent initiatives from both the EU and the OECD have also emphasised (with slightly different wording) the need to shift from 'passive' to 'active' policies, meaning that the primary goal of social protection schemes should be to promote labour market participation among people of working age. Only for those who cannot work at all should the main objective be to provide adequate and secure income support.

Several changes promoted by European integration are perceived to constrain the freedom of national governments to design their systems of welfare provisions as they would wish. In many European welfare states the aim has been to reduce costs and increase the effectiveness of existing public services. Even in Nordic countries, with a long tradition of public authorities being the main provider of services, one can see a shift towards a greater reliance on markets and private providers. This trend may become even stronger if some of the current proposals for an international agreement on the liberalisation of trade with services become reality (General Agreement on Trade in Services – GATS). These trends imply a weakening of earlier ambitions to provide collective protection against the risk of losing income and to correct the inequality-generating tendency of the market through universal and redistributive schemes of benefits and services. However, we should be careful not to overstate the degree to which the decision-making capacity of welfare states has been actually diminished through European integration:

- 'social issues' and 'social policy' are still marginal areas within the joint policymaking of the EU, as the establishment of the internal market is still the main concern. The overall focus of the EU 'social dimension' has been to ensure that national schemes and their administration do not impede the free movement of labour and services within this market;
- Member States have largely retained control over national welfare policies including redistributive schemes such as social security, employment, health and social services, drawing on the principle of subsidiarity to resist EU pressure for welfare reform;
- the emerging regime of international human rights, as well as the more particular development of institutions and legislation at European level, have introduced new substantial rights for citizens and stronger protection against discrimination. Whereas these rights appear to originate 'from above' through supranational processes, national governments are left largely to deliver, supervise and enforce these rights and secure new forms of protection. The implementation

is monitored and assessed by transnational bodies and regulated through the court system;
- even if one could demonstrate a weakening of the redistributive effects of national welfare schemes or increased inequalities after taxes and transfers, it is debatable whether such changes can be attributed to the expansion of the European social dimension.

In addition, welfare states are faced with 'pressures from below'. According to the widely accepted diagnoses of late-modern societies we see a trend towards individualisation and de-traditionalisation (Beck and Beck-Gernsheim, 2002). These are complex concepts which involve something other than individuals being viewed as more egoistic, self-centred or simply occupied with their own well-being. One key argument is that traditional and more spontaneous forms of community, collectivity and solidarity between people have lost much of their practical significance (see Chapter Eight of this volume). Higher than average levels of educational qualifications and knowledge have made citizens less deferential towards public authorities. Generally, people have become more self-confident and conscious of their rights in their dealings with agency staff and health professionals. They expect to be able to influence decisions on their own welfare, whether this is expressed through the rhetoric of co-determination, user involvement, informed consent or freedom of choice. As a result, citizens are challenging bureaucratic or paternalistic modes of administration, the rigidity and inflexibility of some social protection schemes and the arbitrary exercise of discretionary powers in others.

At the same time, minority groups and others in marginal positions have increased their demands for recognition, redress and more responsive public policies. Often, people in these situations – for example, those with disabilities, lesbians and gays, minority ethnic people – have been made invisible and silent as a result of indifference, neglect or discrimination. However, these and other sections of the population have been fairly successful recently in mobilising political support and being heard in the public sphere. Their increased visibility and more active participation in the public arena may modify the degree of marginality that they experience, even if their inclusion in mainstream society remains partial.

Individualisation does not preclude popular support for, and acceptance of, the kind of solidaristic or redistributive public provisions that have played a key role in several modern welfare states. Arguably, political and organisational rationales and objectives will have to be renewed and reaffirmed in order to sustain legitimacy and popular support. This will be a particular challenge in schemes that presuppose a long-term perspective and a fairly stable joint understanding among the affected parties, such as pension schemes based on a fictional 'intergenerational contract'. The individualisation thesis indicates that one cannot take for granted the legitimacy of social protection systems established in the past. As a consequence, governments are faced with the challenge of stimulating and facilitating broad public involvement and participation in discussions about the premises, objectives, ambitions and time horizons of redistributive welfare schemes.

Uncertainties about how national governments should interpret and adjust to these diverse challenges render existing social protection systems more precarious. In some countries there have been calls for substantial reform and restructuring. This has led to a selective retreat from the commitments and responsibilities previously taken on by the state, changing the division of labour between public and private welfare. Efforts to introduce such reforms – singly or in combination – produce complex changes in the relations between state and citizens: neither the welfare state nor citizens remain the same. But even less dramatic changes in the relation between the state and citizens may imply new definitions of roles and responsibilities. We argue that these complex challenges have fostered a variety of attempts to develop or revitalise active forms of citizenship. In the next section we map three forms of citizen activation before proceeding to explore their implications for the dynamics of welfare governance.

Three dynamics of citizenship activation

Periods of change in the role of nation-states tend to unsettle established notions of citizenship. Different versions of active citizenship may be combined in order to establish new settlements between states and citizens. Most forms of active citizenship concepts can be captured with the help of three ideal-type understandings: socio-liberal, libertarian and republican citizenship (Miller, 2000). Each expresses a specific view of the roles of states and citizens and each offers a distinct active–passive dynamic. Recent changes have stimulated interest in the active aspects within each conceptualisation. Whether the forms of active citizenship now taking shape in several European welfare states are 'new' in a strict sense is debatable. They may represent a return to the ideals or principles that were present in earlier stages in the history of the welfare state in question, principles which were later marginalised or eroded in the face of competing ideologies. Thus, over time, there may have been a movement back and forth between active and passive aspects of citizenship, rather than clear progress from one to the other.

The dynamics of socio-liberal citizenship

As formulated originally by T.H. Marshall (1965[1950]), the principle of the socio-liberal conception of citizenship is that citizens should enjoy a minimum level of rights (economic security, care, protection against various risks, and so on) and in return fulfil legal duties and normative obligations vis-à-vis the community. Everyone who is a citizen of the community in question enjoys equal rights and obligations. The exact content of these rights and obligations may vary, but liberal citizenship suggests a fair balance between rights and obligations. The latter may include contributing to the welfare of society, performing paid work, taking responsibility for and undertaking care for children and other dependants and participating in other socially valuable activity. As everybody is to be granted a minimum of economic and social welfare, an element of redistribution of resources between citizens is required. The rights and obligations in question may be formalised in legal rules as well as recognised as social norms. A reciprocal relationship between citizens and 'the community' is assumed to create conditions for social integration.

Established conceptions of socio-liberal citizenship are currently under pressure. As we have discussed earlier, stronger external and internal pressures are perceived to prevent national welfare states from keeping up the ambitions of tax-financed redistribution. Consequently, individuals and families need to take greater responsibility for their own protection against risks. Moreover, it is claimed that a proliferation of unconditional social rights, underpinned by welfare provision, leads to widespread passivity, economic and social exclusion and a weakening of the work ethic. Although mutual rights and obligations were a central theme in the socio-liberal conception of citizenship, it is argued that in practice the obligations side has become dormant, and that social policy researchers have contributed to this one-sided understanding of social citizenship. For example, Esping-Andersen has made a direct link between Marshall's concept of social citizenship and 'decommodification', where the latter entails "that citizens can freely and without potential loss of job, income or general welfare, opt out of work when they themselves consider it necessary" (1990, p 21).

Many have called for a new conception of citizenship involving a better balance between rights and duties. Whatever flag these arguments sail under, for example, 'Third Way' or 'communitarian', the essence is the slogan 'No rights without responsibilities' (Giddens, 1998, p 65). These views have gained wide resonance within contemporary welfare reform. Many welfare states have initiated reforms that place stronger or renewed emphasis on citizens' duties and responsibilities. The redefined obligations mean that everyone should seek to be financially self-sufficient, through gainful employment and/or family maintenance and take greater financial responsibility for their children. Recent changes in social security legislation or the switch from passive to active measures in social protection schemes reflect such concerns. Moreover today, the fulfilment of obligations tends to be defined as a condition for receiving particular income benefits. People may be denied benefits, have them reduced or taken away if they do not comply with requirements such as participation in training or jobseeker courses. These obligations are imposed on the individual, with the intention of inducing her or him to become a responsible agent. This responsibilisation is expressed most clearly in the efforts to involve claimants in the formulation of an individual and tailor-made action plan, specifying the steps to be taken in order to find work and become self-sufficient. This plan is meant to serve as a quasi-contract between the individual and the activation agency, as representative of 'society'.

The original target group of active labour market policies (in those countries such as the Nordic ones where they traditionally played an important role) tended to be limited to the unemployed sections of the core male working class. Now the aim of activation appears to include almost all people of working age who claim income cash benefits (or potentially may do so). Thus it is not limited to people who may claim unemployment insurance but also includes people who are claiming social assistance, disability or lone-parent benefits. This means that we see a generalisation of the work ethic to all segments of the adult population. Yet the enforcement of obligations and use of sanctions tend to be punitive for some segments of the population, such as the poor, long-term unemployed and/or homeless people. Generally these are met with more demanding policies, governance strategies and techniques, limiting their scope for self-determination, autonomy or choice. As part of this, claimants may be forced to undertake particular work tasks as a condition for continued receipt of social assistance ('workfare').

Recent activation reforms tend to rest on a fairly narrow understanding of relevant and socially useful activity, as they mainly recognise paid work and participation in the mainstream labour market. There seems to be a disregard for care responsibilities in the family, with such responsibilities not counting as socially and economically valuable. Yet we know surprisingly little about the degree to which activation demands and requirements are enforced differently according to the gender, ethnic background and/or age of the claimant. In some countries, however, there has been the possibility of taking other forms of activity into consideration: subsidised employment and other social economy jobs, activity in the grey zone between self-organised voluntary work and income-generating self-employment, or other citizen activity which aims less directly at bringing people closer to the mainstream labour market.

All in all, a turn towards active citizenship according to the socio-liberal understanding tends to involve a stronger emphasis on citizens' duty to fulfil obligations to society or community. More specifically, it can lead to some citizens – those who are defined as being in greatest need – being subjected to more paternalistic policies which reduce their personal autonomy and freedom of choice. This stands in sharp contrast to traditional liberal values, but also to republican ideas of self-determination and capability as conditions for equal participation and deliberation. The active–passive dynamics of socio-liberal citizenship are summarised in Figure 5.1. But it is important to emphasise that in practice, active and passive elements may be combined in uneven – and perhaps contradictory – ways.

The dynamics of libertarian citizenship

The liberal understanding of the relationship between state and citizen is of a limited, but also explicitly contractual, relationship (Nozick, 1974; Miller, 2000). People are viewed as citizens only to the extent that they demand goods that require public provision. As such, the citizen tends to be seen as a rational consumer of public goods and the state is modelled as an enterprise. Apart from its role in enforcing basic personal and property rights it is not obvious which services and goods the state needs to provide. According to a libertarian

Figure 5.1: The active–passive dynamic of socio-liberal citizenship

Passive dimension	Active dimension
Focus on receiving and claiming rights to benefits and services	Focus on fulfilment of duties, especially in return for entitlement to benefits and services – conditional rights

understanding of citizenship, people should take responsibility for their own well-being and protection against risks. Citizens are to enjoy consumer sovereignty and this is to be accomplished through choice and contract. The role of people as 'consumer-citizens' will be limited to exercising choice between a given set of providers or 'suppliers' of services, whether private or public, eventually expressing their dissatisfaction through complaints or demanding a change of provider. The instrument of contract means that consumers who feel that they have not been given the service to which they are entitled may take legal action against the provider or, equipped with vouchers, may approach an alternative provider. In this kind of mixed or semi-private welfare market, people's demand for a service may be regulated through user fees or charges covering at least part of the cost of providing it.

The political ideologies associated with a libertarian or neo-liberal understanding of citizenship had a remarkable renaissance in the 1970s and 1980s under New Right ideologies. The implications have differed across the western countries. It is questionable how far they actually have had an impact on welfare reform, apart from in countries traditionally associated with a liberal welfare regime, for example, the US, the UK and New Zealand. But neo-liberal ideas have contributed to the remaking of the relationship between state and market at the forefront of welfare restructuring. Attempts have been made to introduce elements of a market logic into the management of the welfare state, involving new forms of welfare governance. The delivery of health, social care and other services has been contracted out whenever feasible. This usually prioritises cost-effectiveness over considerations of quality or accountability.

In areas such as health, social care services and education, 'the right to choose' has been emphasised ideologically and pursued practically through policy reforms in many countries, both nationally and locally. Substantial reforms of pension provision have been introduced also, encouraged strongly by the EU, OECD and other international institutions. Even countries with a long history of solidaristic and redistributive systems of income security, such as Sweden, have introduced substantial pension reforms. These are based on the idea that there should be a closer link between people's earnings in paid employment and their future pensions and that existing elements of redistribution in pension schemes should be played down. People are expected to take a greater financial risk in protecting themselves against a major reduction of living standards in old age, for example, through retirement planning and the use of private fund-based pension schemes and other investments. This implies that people must take greater responsibility for their own risk management by exercising foresight and choice and by operating as rational and knowledgeable actors in private or semi-private financial markets. To be a consumer-citizen in the pension area requires citizens to collect and digest complex information and to be able to make choices between a wide array of pension providers or funds: that is, to have financial literacy. As this kind of competence will be unequally distributed in society, pension reforms are likely to reinforce or increase existing social and economic differences. On the one hand, pension reform provides citizens with greater opportunities to decide the time for retirement. On the other hand, pension reform means that most people will have to work longer to obtain a comparable level of economic security in retirement in order to compensate for reductions in the guaranteed public pension provision or the outcomes of unwise investment strategies.

To summarise, a libertarian understanding of the turn to active citizenship places a stronger emphasis on individual responsibility and self-sufficiency and allows greater scope for exercising freedom of choice. The active–passive dynamics of libertarian citizenship are summarised in Figure 5.2. Again, it is important to emphasise that in practice, active and passive elements will be combined in uneven – and perhaps contradictory – ways.

The dynamics of republican citizenship

Republican citizens are viewed as actively participating in discussions about decisions that influence the shaping of future society (Lister, 1997; Habermas, 1998; Miller, 2000; Siim, 2000). Ideally, citizens identify with the community to which they belong and seek to promote its common good. While the capacity or competence to participate may be unevenly distributed, there is a belief in its learning or empowering effect. The emphasis is very much on stimulating people's capability, that is, their ability to act or exercise agency (Sen,

Figure 5.2: The active–passive dynamic of libertarian citizenship

Passive dimension	Active dimension
Focus on consuming welfare provisions, regardless of whether delivery is public or private	Focus on fulfilment of individual self-responsibility and exercise of choice in the private market
Welfare consumerism on the basis of managed choice	

1992; Nussbaum, 2000; Raveaud and Salais, 2001).The enjoyment of basic civil, political and social rights is seen as an important condition for people's opportunity to participate. Participants may legitimately pursue their own views and interests but in their capacity as citizens they have to be able to convince others about the reasonableness and fairness of their claims.

Recently, the republican understanding of citizenship has experienced a small revival. Both socio-liberal and libertarian approaches have been criticised for being passive, based on a narrow conception of citizenship activities and a 'top-down' process.Arguments have been raised in favour of new and more elaborated visions of citizen activity, participation and self-governance (a theme developed in Chapter Six). In relation to welfare governance, active republican citizenship would mean that citizens were encouraged to participate in deliberation, decision-making and dialogue with relevant agencies, as well as in self-directed activity. People should not only have the theoretical possibility of participation in discussions and decision-making affecting their future well-being, but actually use these opportunities. Consequently, more active citizenship could mean that citizens were provided with improved possibilities for participation and co-determination in their relations with the welfare state. To a increasing extent, 'involvement' – on both an individual and collective level – has been seen as important in many social services, although often it has been linked to the narrower status of 'user' rather than to 'citizen'. Self-organised activity may be an alternative or complementary channel for participation in processes that can influence people's welfare and well-being, as well as serve as a 'training ground' for participation in broader public arenas, including confrontations and negotiations with public authorities.

The active–passive dynamics of republican citizenship in relation to welfare governance is summarised in Figure 5.3. Here the context is citizens' relation to welfare governance. Again, it is important to emphasise that in practice the relationship between active and passive elements will be uneven and contested.

Figure 5.3: The active–passive dynamic of republican citizenship

Passive dimension	Active dimension
Focus on managed participation in terms of user involvement, informed consent, agency-directed self-help	Focus on self-governed activity, combined with co-responsibility for and commitment to participating in deliberation and decision-making on common affairs

It is possible to identify different strands of these republican ideals:

- communitarian citizenship – this emphasises the importance of traditional values and virtues, mainly expressed through civil society or the family, defined in contrast to the state's activities. Generally, activities which conflict with the social norms of the family, community or the social group are defined as uncivic activities. To a certain extent, these arguments are compatible with active socio-liberal citizenship, as the communitarian argument has focused on work as the major form of citizen participation (Etzioni, 1997, 2000);
- deliberative citizenship – this rests on the mutual recognition of citizens as having an equal right to participate in public deliberation. Democratic participation takes place in the public sphere, so that giving, weighing, accepting or rejecting arguments is something that is open and transparent. The deliberative ideal has full trust in the competence of citizens: it assumes that, if they are given opportunity for dialogue, they will come to a conclusion jointly, with individual preferences being transformed through rational argument for the sake of the general will. Unlike the communitarian vision there is no given conception of 'the common good', rather agreement on this is emergent (Habermas, 1998);
- radical citizenship – here the deliberative approach is viewed as too limited, narrow or even naïve, since it is detached from the social and political context in which deliberation takes place. Radical views identify citizen participation as a complex process of identity building that takes place through everyday activities in local communities as people confront established power relations and structures (as in the 'everyday maker' discussed by Henrik Bang in Chapter Eight). Through participation citizens try to make their voices heard, get their positions accepted and gain influence within the general public debate. Citizenship and citizen participation is thereby a field of power, involving struggle and conflicting identities and cannot be reduced to acceptance of the traditional virtues of communitarianism or procedural visions of deliberative democracy (Mouffe, 1992).

These three strands have different implications for welfare governance. Communitarianism and deliberative democracy offer routes towards consensus while radical theories assume the possibility of contestation. Each stands in sharp contrast to the forms of activation inspired by the socio-liberal conception of citizenship. As discussed previously, most activation measures tend to limit the scope for voice, influence and dialogue about the kinds of activities that would be positive and constructive for particular groups of citizens.

New dynamics of welfare governance

Many countries are faced with the challenge of redefining state–citizen relationships; in some cases both the state and citizens are assuming a more active profile. But in most, the turn or return to active citizenship is associated with a withdrawal of state responsibilities. To analyse further the attempts to create new settlements around the notion of active citizenship, we need to address a set of questions about the different ways in which welfare governance may realise, be neutral to or impede the desired shift from passive to active citizenship.

First, there is a strong pressure on some nations to reform the traditional administration-led welfare state and to introduce more flexible and deregulated forms of welfare state and welfare governance (Peters, 1996). During the 1980s and 1990s the traditional administrative state was subjected to a process of reform to make it more responsive and effective (Clarke and Newman, 1997). Administration based on detailed rules and strict hierarchical lines of authority was claimed to be ineffective and power was devolved to a plurality of agencies operating within the framework of broad policy objectives and enabling legislation. Decisions about means, procedures and the best ways to solve problems were devolved to agencies whose heads were given greater autonomy and held more closely to account for operational management through an array of objectives and performance management techniques. At the same time, the 'enabling' frameworks of the state created more scope for innovation and experimentation.

Contemporary welfare governance focuses on means–ends relations (instrumentalism, management by objectives, enforcement of obligations, performance management, market intervention). Such measures stand in sharp contrast to earlier governance strategies based on rule-making, rule of law and rights-granting (often termed 'hierarchical governance'). These new mechanisms of governance proliferated at a European, as well as a national, level. Lately, the EU has played down previous ambitions to build a social Europe by means of harmonisation, lawmaking and legal governance and instead has emphasised 'soft' governance methods such as OMC (as described in Chapter Two).

Second, there is a shift to a more market-led welfare state and forms of welfare governance. The tendency towards a market-led welfare state is based on the assumption that financial incentives are more efficient in achieving objectives than detailed rules and administrative instructions. The actual delivery of services is contracted out where feasible, with state bodies specifying the standards and criteria to be fulfilled by contractors and monitoring their performance. Decisions about providers are based on the price and quality of the 'product', irrespective of whether they are public or private actors. These steps are presumed to promote greater responsiveness and flexibility, as well as reducing costs. Contemporary welfare governance, then, is inspired by new public management, creating incentive structures and private or semi-public welfare markets, outsourcing and contractualisation as ways to introduce market regulatory mechanisms into welfare provision. These principles produce more dynamic and diverse forms of welfare governance than the strict neo-liberal focus on the minimal state, but fit well with the libertarian view of active citizenship discussed previously.

Third, there have been some attempts to move in the direction of providing greater scope for a participatory welfare state. Contemporary welfare governance tends to encourage broad participation in decision-making, providing support to citizens' initiatives and associations and establishing dialogues with social partners in order to promote the more active involvement of citizens. To a greater extent than before, citizens are involved in negotiation and consultation about the future development and design of services. Individual users are encouraged to take part in dialogues with agency staff about the formulation of treatment or action plans or the arrangement of service packages. Organisations or groups may be granted financial assistance and practical support in order to facilitate participation. Yet such developments tend to fall short of the kind of broad popular participation in decision-making associated with models of deliberative or discursive democracy (Newman et al, 2004). (These themes are developed in Chapter Six.)

New governance strategies and techniques tend to transgress established social categories such as self-help groups and user associations. Rather, citizens and citizens' groups are invited as partners, in different forms of partnerships with public agencies. Such forms of welfare governance link up with republican citizenship ideals, at least on a rhetorical level. But this also demonstrates some of its weaknesses, as participation based upon this kind of welfare governance is highly ambiguous. As Rebekah Sterling shows in Chapter Seven, being in a partnership with public agencies means being drawn into new ways of being governed by the state as well as new forms of self-governance.

Conclusion: towards ambiguous forms of citizenship and governance

This chapter has argued that a new and more complex relationship between state and citizens has emerged, settled around the notion of active citizenship. A socio-liberal understanding of citizenship – admittedly, with a stronger emphasis on the social rights side than in Marshall's original codification – has tended to dominate the picture of the modern welfare state. This is most explicit in Esping-Andersen's (1990) regime typology and his discussion of the decommodifying aspect of social rights. This has been a strong theme in Nordic welfare states, but has also been a frame of reference for analyses of other welfare states' trajectories of change. In our view, recent changes have made it clear that Esping-Andersen's interpretation of the socio-liberal type of citizenship is insufficient and partly misleading. As we have noted, welfare reform across a number of different countries has reinforced the obligations side of welfare and income maintenance schemes as well as producing a stronger enforcement of already existing obligations. This Marshallian (socio-liberal) citizenship has been complemented by more emphasis on some aspects of libertarian and republican citizenship. In other words, recent reforms have not only involved a stronger emphasis on obligations, but also on notions of individual responsibility, freedom of choice and contract as well as the participation, dialogue and self-activity of citizens. This is a complex configuration which cannot be captured by one-dimensional notions of citizenship as involving extensive social rights and decommodification.

The dynamic interaction between different forms of citizen activation produces a field of tensions that is lived out in the everyday experience of citizens. The practical impact will be differentiated according to socio-economic status, gender, ethnicity and other dimensions of difference. Put sharply, one may ask whether active citizenship in the socio-liberal sense is mainly for the poor and socially excluded, while active citizenship in the libertarian and republican senses is for the well-integrated and more affluent sections of the population. Our answer is that there may be some tendencies in this direction, but that this is not the whole story. Even people who traditionally have been seen as socially and economically well-integrated may now be faced with activation demands. By contrast, people with disabilities may be benefiting from greater scope for choice, for example, with vouchers to engage personal assistance, home help and transport services. Even poor and excluded groups are able to achieve a voice in dialogue, consultation and negotiation with public authorities, partly as a result of the new opportunity structures created by the action programmes of the EU.

At the same time, the role of the state in welfare provision is changing. The state has become less dominant as a sole provider of protection against risks, while adopting more complex and dynamic structures of governance regarding welfare provision. In some respects the state has taken on more active roles, for example, in activating those without work and combating social exclusion and discrimination. In other respects, it is retreating from the tasks that it had previously taken on and instead expecting individuals and market actors to provide services and protection against risks. The new and more complex governance structures associated with these changes cannot be viewed simply as a consequence of the more multifaceted forms of active citizenship that we can see emerging in different countries. Neither are the new forms of citizenship simply brought about by the changes in the structures of welfare governance. The dynamic relationship between the two is probably better captured by Max Weber's concept of 'elective affinity' (Ringer, 1997).

These changes in the relationships between states and citizens have been brought about by the interplay of external and internal challenges with the contemporary welfare states, as these developed and matured during the greater part of the 20th century. However, as the 2005 rejection of the EU constitution shows, there has been an unfortunate tendency to view international regimes of law regulation, human rights and non-discrimination provisions as a threat to established arrangements between the (national) welfare state and citizens. We argue that it is equally important to address questions regarding the extent to which internationalisation creates new opportunities for citizens to exercise agency in relation to the welfare state. In particular, it is important to trace how it can strengthen the position and capability of minorities and others who have been marginalised or excluded by the policies of nation-states. Internationalisation has the potential to extend and enrich citizenship. It can contribute to creating the conditions for full citizenship for a larger proportion of the total population, in terms of rights and responsibilities, freedom of choice and participation. This is significant, not only because of concerns about equality of living conditions or economic efficiency, but also because of democratic considerations.

This chapter has sought to contribute to the development of a more dynamic analysis of the relationship between welfare governance and citizenship. Until recently, comparative research has tended to produce simplified and static pictures ('types', 'models' or 'regimes') of state welfare in individual countries or groups of countries, and has taken related notions of citizenship almost for granted as a kind of a sub-category. These pictures can easily become reified, being treated as substitutes for nuanced empirical description and analysis of these countries. We have outlined a more complex and diversified conception of citizenship, tracing three different dynamics of active citizenship, but also claiming that the trend towards denationalisation does not necessarily point in the direction of a contraction of national welfare provision. In some respects, the emerging transnational regime of human rights and protection against discrimination may even contribute to the development of new forms of welfare governance.

References

Beck, U. (2000) *What is globalization?*, Cambridge: Polity Press.

Beck, U. and Beck-Gernsheim, E. (2002) *Individualization*, London: Sage Publications.

Clarke, J. and Newman, J. (1997) *The managerial state: Power, politics and ideology in the remaking of social welfare*, London: Sage Publications.

de la Porte, C. and Pochet, P. (eds) (2002) *Building social Europe through the Open Method of Co-ordination*, Brussels: Peter Lang.

Esping-Andersen, G. (1990) *The three worlds of welfare capitalism*, Cambridge: Polity Press.

Etzioni, A. (1997) *The new golden rule*, New York, NY: Basic Books.

Etzioni, A. (2000) *The third way to a good society*, London: Demos.

European Union (1997) 'Consolidated version of the Treaty establishing the European Community', in *Consolidated treaties*, Luxembourg: Office for Official Publications of the European Communities.

Giddens, A. (1998) *The third way*, Cambridge: Polity Press.

Habermas, J. (1998) 'Three normative models of democracy', in *The inclusion of the other*, Cambridge, MA: MIT Press, pp 239-52.

Kjær, A.M. (2004) *Governance*, Cambridge: Polity Press.

Leibfried, S. and Pierson, P. (2000) 'Social policy. Left to courts and markets?', in H. Wallace and W. Wallace (eds) *Policy-making in the European Union* (4th edn), Oxford: Oxford University Press, pp 267-92.

Lister, R. (1997) *Citizenship: Feminist perspectives*, New York, NY: New York University Press.

Marshall, T.H. (1965[1950]) 'Citizenship and social class', in *Class, citizenship and social development*, New York, NY: Anchor Books, pp 71–134.

Miller, D. (2000) *Citizenship and national identity*, Cambridge: Polity Press.

Mouffe, C. (1992) 'Democratic citizenship and the political community', in C. Mouffe (ed) *Dimensions of radical democracy*, London: Verso, pp 225–39.

Newman, J., Barnes, M., Sullivan, H. and Knops, A. (2004) 'Public participation and collaborative governance', *Journal of Social Policy*, vol 33, no 2, pp 203–23.

Nozick, R. (1974) *Anarchy, state and utopia*, Oxford: Blackwell.

Nussbaum, M.C. (2000) *Women and development*, Cambridge: Cambridge University Press.

Peters, B.G. (1996) *The future of governing: Four emerging models*, Lawrence, KS: University Press of Kansas.

Pollack, M.A. (2003) 'The Court of Justice as an agent: delegation of judicial power in the European Union', in *The engines of European integration*, Oxford: Oxford University Press, pp 155–202.

Raveaud, G. and Salais, R. (2001) 'Fighting against social exclusion in a European knowledge based society: what principles of action?', in D. Mayes, J. Berghman and R. Salais (eds) *Social exclusion and European policy*, Cheltenham: Edward Elgar, pp 47–71.

Rieger, E. and Leibfried, S. (2003) *Limits to globalization*, Cambridge: Polity Press.

Ringer, F. (1997) *Max Weber's methodology*, Cambridge, MA: Harvard University Press.

Sen, A. (1992) 'Functionings and capability', in *Inequality reexamined*, Oxford: Clarendon Press, pp 39–55.

Siim, B. (2000) *Gender and citizenship*, Cambridge: Cambridge University Press.

Wincott, D. (2003) 'The idea of the European social model: limits and paradoxes of Europeanization', in K. Featherstone and C.M. Radealli (eds) *The politics of Europeanization*, Oxford: Oxford University Press, pp 279–302.

SIX

Participative governance and the remaking of the public sphere

Janet Newman

Introduction

> Democratic institutions and the representatives of the people, can and must try to connect Europe with its citizens. This is the starting point for more effective and relevant policies (European Union White Paper on Good Governance; European Commission, 2001, p 3).

Participative governance is important in terms of our focus in this book on 'remaking' governance because it apparently offers not only a response to the problem of the legitimacy of government institutions, but also the potential solution to a range of social problems. It is linked to a *decentred* form of governance in which the role of the state – and the institutions of representative democracy on which it rests – is viewed as unable to deal with the complexity of policy problems and to respond to the differentiated needs and identities of citizens (Kooiman, 1993, 2000). This chapter examines the turn towards participative governance, focusing on two related issues. The first is the constitution of the public sphere in which participation is enacted. As earlier chapters of this volume have argued, the boundaries between public and private are fluid and contested (see especially the Introduction and Chapter Four). As power flows to transnational bodies such as the European Union (EU), down to 'communities' as a newly significant site of governance and outwards to a multiplicity of service providers, how is the public sphere delineated? What issues are deemed to be the province of public deliberation as opposed to the privatised choices or voices of individual consumers?

The second issue focuses on the public itself: how the technologies of power associated with participative governance produce classifications and divisions that shape the forms of political and social imaginaries from which the public sphere is constituted. The interest here is in the ways in which, by drawing citizens into more direct and involved relationships with governance practice, collaboration and participation may serve to enable the production of new forms of governable subject; but also, how the spaces which are opened up may form points around which social identity and agency is mobilised.

Remaking the public sphere

The concept of a public sphere in which citizens openly engage in deliberation on policy issues and problems is most closely associated with the work of Habermas. Much of the literature on new forms of public participation looks back to *The structural transformation of the public sphere* (1989), in which Habermas set out a concept of the public sphere as a domain of rational discourse, a public form of deliberation and decision-making and a site of communicative action by participatory publics. Its meaning is formed through both its conceptual distinction from three other spheres (patriarchal family, state and market economy) and its role in linking these together. Habermas's analysis highlights what he views as the erosion of the public sphere through processes of commodification (the rise of the mass media) and feminisation (through a progressive interweaving of public and private realms). He argues that to overcome the resulting legitimacy crisis it is necessary to repoliticise the public sphere by providing opportunities for citizens to engage in what he terms 'communicative interaction'. He also lays down a set of ethical considerations associated with the 'ideal speech situation' in which such interactions could flourish.

Habermas has been widely debated and critiqued. Feminist writers have highlighted the privileging of rational forms of communication that bracket particularistic interests and identities in the orientation towards universality. The privileging of rationality serves to subordinate affective, expressive and experience-based forms of discourse. Finally, it fails to acknowledge that the identities of participants, rather than being 'fixed' embodiments of pre-formed patterns of interests, may be formed and transformed through public communicative practice (Young, 1990). I cannot hope to replicate the subtlety and richness of these debates here (see Warner, 2002; Barnett, 2004). Instead, I want to trace the ways in which Habermas's ideas have been influential in shaping political, policy and some academic discourses on the renewal of civil society and the overcoming of democratic deficits. Each has emphasised the importance of the public sphere as a domain of rational deliberation and debate beyond the formal institutions of government.

Habermas's work has been significant in part because of its intersection with other kinds of debate about a crisis of representative democracy. As governance theorists have noted, the 'hollowing-out' of the nation-state, the emergence of multilevel governance and the dispersal of power to multiple agencies and sectors have all challenged the centrality of representative institutions (see Chapter Nine of this volume). At the same time, sociologists have drawn attention to patterns of social change that have undermined the legitimacy of hierarchical or paternalistic relationships between state and citizen. Representative democracy, it is argued, is associated with a modern, Fordist, technical rationality, while deliberation is more attuned to 'reflexive modernity' (Beck et al, 1994; Giddens, 1994). The emergence of what Taylor-Gooby et al (2003) term 'querulous citizens', who are equipped to make choices rather than accept tradition or habit, "leads to demands for a more dialogic democracy, in which government, to retain its legitimacy, must win an active trust rather than simply presuming a habitual loyalty" (2003, p 2).

Social movement studies have also provided numerous critiques of the presumed universality of democratic practice. Here, the literature has highlighted the ways in which notions of universality and a formal politics of representation fail to encompass questions of difference based on a politics of identity (Benhabib, 1996). Feminist literature in particular has pointed to the gendered basis of citizenship rights and the poverty of a public sphere based on masculine models of citizenship and politics (Phillips, 1995). Social movement studies highlight the importance of forms of politics based on the experience of everyday practice around health care, domestic violence, mental health, disability and other struggles, while research on new forms of protest and dissent note the emerging significance of transnational political action (for example, environmental movements or anti-globalisation protests; Dryzek, 2000). Such literatures open up discussions on the extent to which deliberative or dialogic forms of participation can offer new modes of democratic engagement that are more capable of dealing with the new politics of identity and difference, both within and beyond the nation-state. Across these different literatures, representative democracy is viewed as a necessary but insufficient means of connecting citizens with governing institutions and processes:

> [C]ontrary to the classic form of 'government',
> contemporary governance is not imprisoned in closed
> institutions and is not the province of professional
> politicians. Though rarely defined with precision, it refers

to patterns of decision-making taking place in a larger set of institutions, with a broader range of actors and processes. One of the ambitions of those who defend this new concept is indeed to enlarge the accepted notion of civic participation beyond the well established and constantly declining procedures of representative democracy. (Magnette, 2003, p 144)

The political and social shifts outlined in this section have produced a new set of policy discourses about how best government and non-government institutions can open up the possibility of deliberative interactions with citizens. The result has been a proliferation of experiments in involving stakeholders in the policy process, devolving power to local citizens, promoting e-democracy, involving users in decisions about services, and so on. "The goal is to provide access and explanation of data to all parties, to empower the public to understand analyses, and to promote serious public discussion" (Fischer, 2003, p 15). However, underpinning the normative statements about the importance of public involvement and dialogue – including the EU statement with which this chapter opened – is a set of governmental concerns about policy legitimacy and effectiveness. Consent to policies is more possible where those who may have oppositional views are directly engaged in policy formation, and the delivery of policy is more likely to be effective where those responsible for, or affected by, its implementation are involved from the outset (see, for example, the rationales for more emphasis on participation in two UK documents: Cabinet Office, 1999; Social Exclusion Unit [SEU], 2001).

Thus participative governance plays a crucial part in a modernised policy process suited to the needs of complex societies, in which questions of legitimacy are at least as important as scientific, expert approaches to problem-solving. It opens up key issues concerning the remaking of the public sphere, in particular the models of citizenship that are produced.

Models of citizenship

The engagement of citizens in a re-energised public sphere through consultation exercises, community involvement strategies, deliberative forums, citizens' juries and other strategies appears to be closer to the 'republican' ideal discussed by Johansson and Hvinden (Chapter Five) than the neo-liberal forms of citizenship associated with the modernisation of welfare states. The aim is to respond "not only to common concerns about citizen apathy and mistrust of government but also to many positive opportunities which exist to revitalise local democracy" (Demos, 2003, cover). Participative governance is viewed as a strategy to address social exclusion, expanding the possibilities for state–citizen interaction into informal arenas, thus helping to broaden the base of participation by reaching so-called 'hard-to-reach' groups. It is viewed also as a means of engaging the public in taking responsibility for their own care and welfare: "In this model the state does not act upon society: it does not provide a service. Instead the state creates a platform or environment in which people take decisions about their lives in a different way" (Leadbetter, 2004, p 16). Here, the role of the state moves from (paternalistic) provider to (participative) enabler, with consequent reductions – it is hoped – in demands on the state for welfare. This implies a tighter intersection between (neo)liberal and republican models of citizenship than might have been initially supposed. Whereas the representative democracy of liberal governance offers a state-centred conception of the public domain in which citizenship is mobilised around conceptions of rights (afforded by the state) and duties (of citizens to the state), participative governance is associated with a form of advanced liberal governance that constitutes subjects as active, autonomous agents (Foucault, 1991; Rose, 1999).

Both liberal and republican models of citizenship are also implicated in the proliferation of participation initiatives linked to the modernisation of state services. Here, the figure of the 'citizen-consumer' is invited to be involved in, and comment, discuss and deliberate on, public policies and services. The citizen-consumer is constituted as a choice-making subject in a market place for public goods. The transformation of citizen into consumer is viewed by many commentators as diminishing the collective ethos and practices of the public domain (embodied in the figure of the citizen) and as privatising and individualising them (in the figure of the consumer). For Needham, this corrodes the public domain as the site of both collective solidarity and political choice and mobilisation:

> This process has profound implications for the relationship between government and citizen. It restricts citizens to a passive consumption of politics, excluding them from playing a creative and productive role in civic life. An individualised and commodified form of citizenship is taking hold in which communal and discursive elements are lost.

> [T]here is a more fundamental question to be asked about
> the extent to which people do in fact expect government
> and public services to relate to them in the same way as
> private sector businesses. The danger is that by encouraging
> this read-across, government may itself be eliding a crucial
> distinction between the public and private domains without
> which public engagement with democratic processes, and
> support for public provision, is ultimately bound to be
> undermined. (Needham, 2003, pp 8, 28)

The new strategies of participative governance, then, offer both an
expanded conception of the public sphere (as one with multiple points
of connection between state and citizen and new spaces of deliberation
and communicative action), and the potential for its diminution into
a series of marketised encounters between service users and service
providers (with deliberation and communication forming feedback
loops to providers and policymakers in their search for legitimacy and
competitive success). The notions of civic responsibility that were
discussed in Chapter Five open up the public to new discursive
categorisations: responsible residents versus nuisance neighbours;
responsible families versus truanting children (and feckless parents);
responsible communities versus antisocial youth, and so on. In each
case the state is attempting to act in 'partnership' with responsible
civic actors to solve the social problems associated with those deemed
irresponsible.

Putting people in their place: citizenship and the re-spatialisation of the public sphere

The remaking of governance means that the relationship between
citizenship and nation-states is brought into question. As Warner (2002,
2005), Barnett (2004) and others have noted, the public sphere cannot
be viewed as a fixed spatial entity, and the public cannot be imagined
as simply an assembly or series of groups. The role of the media and
other cultural institutions serve to produce multiple spatial and temporal
publics which are connected in a mobile and reflexive manner.
However, the participative governance practices discussed in this
chapter can be viewed as attempts to 'fix' such connections in particular
spatial and temporal configurations – the (monthly) community or
service-user forum, the (one-off) public meeting, the (temporally
bounded) consultation exercise, and so on. While each of these
contribute to the reflexive interactions of the wider public sphere,

they also help to shape new political and social imaginaries. Participative governance involves a re-imagination of space and place in which the traditional imagery of sociopolitical relations – based on hierarchical relationships between states and peoples – is displaced by a horizontal imagery of governance as a series of interconnected spheres.

I want to highlight two processes of re-spatialisation that touch on themes developed elsewhere in this volume. The first concerns Europe as an 'impoverished' public sphere in which policymaking is viewed by many commentators as taking place in the absence of a notion of the EU as a shared space of public communication or democratic involvement. The EU is viewed as suffering from democratic deficit for a number of reasons:

- the relative weakness of the European Parliament in relation to the European Commission;
- the reluctance of nation-states to cede political authority to the EU;
- the complexity of governance forms and structures that obscure where processes of influence or decision-making take place; and
- the absence of public involvement in a public sphere of deliberation or communication.

Where involvement takes place this is largely through expert bodies (non-governmental organisations – NGOs) drawn into formal and informal forms of participation in the policy process, a process which tends to have little impact on wider public discourse (analogies could be made here with Henrik Bang's discussion of 'expert citizens' in Chapter Eight of this volume). In one of the few examples of research on the EU as a public sphere, Peters et al (2005: forthcoming) comment that public discourse is:

> [T]he primary medium for the development of public knowledge, values, interpretations, and self under-standings, and for change and innovation as well as reproduction or transmission over time in the inventory of idea and arguments available in a given public sphere.

As such, it is an important source of cultural reproduction and change. However, drawing on empirical research on public discourse on Europe in major national newspapers across five countries, the authors highlight the continued weakness of a trans-European public sphere compared to the resilience of national public spheres.

However, notions of 'community' as a series of localised public spheres are much more intensely developed (Staeheli and Mitchell, 2004). Participative governance has tended to privilege communities of locality as the prime focus for public participation, and local municipal governments and local partnership bodies provide the institutional architecture for many initiatives. This is closely associated with what Sterling (in Chapter Seven of this volume) terms a "complex reterritorialisation of governance". It derives in part from the emphasis on active community as a response to the problems of social deprivation and exclusion. For example, the language of 'community' pervades the documents of the SEU in the UK, partly since its primary focus was on the regeneration of particularly 'deprived' or run-down estates and partly reflecting New Labour's conception of community as a source of social cohesion and belonging (Driver and Martell, 1998). As such, it tends to view the problems being experienced in specific localities in terms of local causes requiring local solutions. In the process, such problems are detached from the national and global processes that create structural patterns of inequality and poverty.

Locality forms the basis for imaginary constructions of 'community' as a symbol of local attachment and identification. Whereas representative democracy invokes the public domain as vertical, with local, regional, national and transnational tiers of government organised in a hierarchical way, participative governance offers a different political imaginary. As Walters notes in respect of initiatives oriented towards building social capital, it involves images of the public realm or polity as a horizontal space of multiple communities as sites of self-governing activity. As such, "Governance is much less centred, less hierarchical … but this rather benign image should not blind us to its power effects" (Walters, 2002, p 388). These 'power effects' are conceptualised by Rose (1999) in terms of an 'ethico-politics' in which the technologies of advanced liberal governance construct identities for subjects as citizens organised within communities, with community constructed as a site of civility and ethical conduct. This has close links with the politics of the 'Third Way', in which the idea of community is invoked as a means of fostering civic responsibility and as a source of solutions to social problems (Giddens, 1994). Such imaginary unities foster a communitarian ideal in which the production of social integration and cohesion are paramount goals. Thus disorder and dissent are not legitimate elements of participative governance. This is very different from the forms of participation associated with the community activism of the mid- to late 20th century, an activism based around calls for the democratisation and decentralisation of welfare services in order to address issues of poverty and inequality (Everingham, 2003).

This section has focused on the ways in which the spaces of governance are being constituted and reconstituted through forms of governmental power that 'puts people in their place', arguing that locality forms a dominant strategy. This offers a narrow social and political imaginary not only by restricting deliberation to 'local' or 'particular' agendas, but also by replicating the Habermasian image of the rationality of communicative action. The idea of the public sphere as a series of spatially or temporally fixed arenas of rational debate punctuated by decision-making is part of what Warner (2005) terms the 'parliamentary ideology' that produces a myth of agency. To develop this theme further, the next section analyses participative governance in terms of the new technologies of power through which participating subjects are constituted. The approach attempts to disrupt the normative gloss that tends to be associated with public participation as a form of 'good governance' through which states can be reconnected to citizens and the public sphere re-invigorated.

Participative governance: technologies of power

The critiques of Habermas, and of the normative policy imperatives linked to notions of a public sphere of active citizenship, draw extensively on what Fischer (2003) terms a 'post-empiricist' approach to studying policy and politics: one which moves beyond objectivist conceptions of reality in order to take account of social constructivist and discursive perspectives. This helps to overcome some of the limitations of the rational image of the public sphere noted earlier, of which I want to note two in particular here. The first is the assumption of a clear separation between politics (defined as the actions of elected representatives) and administration (defined as the exercise of bureaucratic and hierarchical power by government institutions). Work on policy networks has shown how policy is shaped by actors who cross such neat boundaries, and how such networks are held together by common ideas as well as mutual interests (Marsh and Rhodes, 1992). The second concerns the assumptions about identity and agency on which they are based: notably that citizens are rational actors in weighing and assessing arguments and putting forward their objective interests to policymakers and/or politicians. This ignores "the role of language, discourse, rhetorical argument, and stories in framing both policy questions and the contextual contours of argumentation, particularly the ways normative presuppositions operate below the surface to structure basic policy definitions and understandings" (Fischer, 2003, p 14). That is, understandings of interests – whether self-interest or a wider conception of a public interest – are discursively constituted. This does not mean that people are (necessarily) manipulated by governments; more that discourse may set the limits of what it is possible to think, and thus the understandings of the choices that can be made or the interests that can be legitimately expressed. As Fischer (2003, p 28) comments, "It is not that institutions cause political action; rather, it is their discursive practices that shape the behaviours of actors who do".

Here Fischer is drawing on post-structuralist understandings of policy discourse as a technology of power, and of participation initiatives as aspects of advanced neo-liberal governmental regimes that seek to constitute new forms of governmental subject. Such perspectives develop the Foucauldian conception of 'governmentality', focusing on the ways in which power operates beyond the state and drawing attention to the ways in which multiple organisations, groups and individuals have become implicated in the process of governing (Foucault, 1991). In particular, the work of Rose (1996, 1999) describes how apparently 'free' actors are subject to new discursive practices that seek to shape conduct through discourses of responsibility and ethical self-conduct. New forms of citizen participation, then, may not just *reflect* external changes in the public realm and the public itself but may be *constitutive* in their effects. That is, new governmental strategies may involve calling into being particular conceptions of the public realm and may define – or constitute – the public in particular ways. Here, participative governance can be understood as a new political rationality through which citizens, users or communities are constituted as governable subjects. It is important to note that the use of the term 'discourse' in post-structural theory is rather different from the focus on discourse as communicative acts in Habermas's work. Although language is implicated in each, Foucault's work alerts us to the ways in which language and communication are anchored in the social processes – discursive practices – through which knowledge is produced. Rather than viewing power as inscribed in the state and its institutions, power is associated with professional disciplines and other forms of expertise that produce new ways of knowing the self and others.

This opens up analysis of the forms of expertise mobilised by participative governance and its consequences for state practice. Participative governance rests on a panoply of strategies and technologies:

- deliberative forums;
- citizen panels;
- user empowerment;
- consumer consultation;
- user or citizen involvement on the governing boards of public institutions;
- participatory evaluation; and
- the production of 'games' designed to popularise public involvement in policy discussions[1].

Citizen, user and stakeholder engagement has become a taken-for-granted norm of economic development, poverty reduction, health improvement and social inclusion strategies. To support these developments, there has been a proliferation of good practice guides which establish participation in its many forms as a preferred way of relating to citizens and users and which introduce appropriate technologies. Such guides and handbooks set out how best to facilitate participation that is 'fit for purpose' depending on the aims of the body concerned, how to select citizens or users in a way that will be viewed as legitimate by the wider public, how to engage with 'hard-to-reach' groups, how to enable feedback and learning through ongoing communication, and so on. The World Bank, for example, has produced a range of toolkits and manuals which advise its own staff and external stakeholders on participative techniques, with separate manuals covering civic engagement, community-driven development, participatory monitoring and consultation with civil society organisations (see www.worldbank.org/participation/tools&methods/toolkitsmanuals/htm).

Many handbooks and policy documents invoke images of ladders or scales along which degrees of involvement can be mapped[2]. The ladder imagery masks deeper distinctions that can be made between different types of participative technology. Some rely on quasi-professional techniques for communicating with and empowering service users in order to involve them as collaborators in their own care and welfare. Others draw on quasi-managerial or marketing technologies: surveys, market research, customer satisfaction surveys, focus groups. Yet others focus on quasi-democratic techniques for establishing and managing deliberative forums as arenas in which citizens – as residents, tenants, service users or community stakeholders – engage in dialogue with public bodies, the state or transnational bodies. The 'quasi' in each case signifies the points of disjuncture between the new participative technologies and the established institutions and strategies of hierarchical governance: the disjuncture between professional power and the new orthodoxy of service users as 'co-producers' of their own care or well-being; the disjuncture between bureaucratic and managerial power; and the disjuncture between representative and deliberative democracy.

The extent of the displacement of embedded forms of power by new governance technologies can be overestimated. Beresford (2002) notes a number of fundamental contradictions in public participation, for example: enhanced political interest but public dissatisfaction; official priority but very limited achievements and resourcing. Magnette argues that, as a strand of EU governance, participatory mechanisms "constitute extensions of existing practices, and are underpinned by the same elitist and functionalist philosophy" (2003, p 144). Participative initiatives may fall short of the ideals of empowerment or co-production and become part of a fundamentally managerial rationality (Newman, 2001; see also Skelcher et al, 2004[3]).

Nevertheless, the new technologies of power should not be underestimated. They provide a normative framework that constitutes ideas of good practice in public bodies and national or transnational institutions. They set out a new range of communicative skills that managers, professionals and development staff must acquire: fostering networks, facilitating interactions and reconciling difference. It is through network management that participants are selected, that the mechanisms or technologies of deliberation or participation are established and through which disagreements are handled. Such skills are more relational and process-oriented than traditional management skills (Larner and Butler, 2004). They have entered the curricula of public service management training courses and Master of Business Administration (MBA)/Master of Public Administration (MPA) programmes and are the focus of an explosion of textbooks and guides. They may also involve an increase in the emotional labour required by state workers as they engage more directly with 'the public' and manage the tensions and stress points arising at the interface between policy and practice, resources and needs, national targets and local priorities (Newman and Mooney, 2004).

Constituting the public

As noted earlier, the technologies and strategies of participative governance are assumed to be more capable of dealing with questions of difference than traditional forms of governance. Public consultation is viewed as leading to services that are attuned to individual preferences, in contrast to what policy documents like to call the 'one size fits all' products of the post-war welfare state. Deliberative forums are viewed as more responsive to subtle differences of interest and identity than the aggregative electoral processes of representative democracy. But in order to deal with questions of difference, the public has to be constituted as a differentiated entity so that citizens or service users can be included from appropriate categories. This categorisation has at least three implications that are important to my analysis.

First, it assumes that people can neatly be divided up into mutually exclusive groups: young or old, black or white, employed or unemployed, rural or urban. This fails to take account of the complexity of lives in a neo-liberal world in which employment, residence and other factors are increasingly transient. More importantly, it assumes a stable, fixed and singular identity that condenses both experience and interest. This can be contrasted with a conception of identity as multi-dimensional, with different facets being performed in different contexts (for example, identifying and performing as a mother in relation to childcare services, as an embodied woman in relation to health services, as part of a neighbourhood in relation to the planning process, as a worker in relation to employment and benefit services, as a rights-bearing citizen in relation to the police, as a consumer in relation to leisure services, and perhaps as a powerless supplicant in relation to organising care services for an elderly relative). Gender, 'race', class, age and even attachments to place do not form mutually distinct population groups; they are ways of forming relational or performance understandings of self rather than being essentialist categories (Squires, 1998).

Second, the troubling question of representation and representativeness arises. People are invited to collaborate in participation or consultation exercises on the basis that they are somehow representative of a wider public defined by a specific set of characteristics. However (as Michael Saward argues in Chapter Nine), the idea of representation is fluid and unstable. While some participative initiatives draw on individuals who have been formally elected to represent the interests of a wider membership – for example, tenants' groups, residents' associations – more usually this is not the case. Individuals tend to be invited to participate on the basis of characteristics such as age, class or gender in order to secure a representative sample of a wider population. As such, more collective or politicised voices are excluded.

In addition, participative governance is strongly oriented towards the production of consensus. The 'partnership' model of participation is one which assumes that different interests can and should be subsumed by a common goal. This is particularly the case with deliberative processes. The focus of deliberative democracy is the transformation of individual preferences through the process of dialogue; as such, points of potential conflict are likely to be submerged in the search for consensus. This conception has been widely criticised by feminist scholars. Young (1990) talks of the value of heterogeneity within the deliberative process, arguing that citizenship may mean organising politically around group identities and then interacting with others, rather than seeking to arrive at a general perspective which transcends difference. Fraser (1997) notes the importance of 'counter-publics' as an essential element of the democratic process because of their capacity to formulate oppositional views. Such groups act as both spaces for withdrawal and regrouping and as the basis for engagement with the wider public domain. These arguments suggest the value of enabling, for example, women to meet and deliberate as women in order to add a gender perspective to public deliberation, rather than inviting them as individuals to contribute to forums in which gender issues are not widely acknowledged. Such an argument is forceful in a political context in which (as we have seen) participative governance is viewed as a means of addressing social problems. Inviting women as 'carers', 'mothers' or 'pregnant teenagers' to collaborate with government in addressing issues of care for the elderly, truanting behaviour or childcare may be viewed as constructive in social policy terms, but at the same time may involve the suppression of a more explicitly gender politics.

Finally, the process of constitution tends to assume a community of interests or identity among a particular group – travellers, the homeless, lone parents, and so on. But the process of categorisation tends to construct problems as the property of the group concerned rather than of the wider social or political system. 'Hard-to-reach' groups are constituted through a double taxonomy of assumed deficits (lack of skills or confidence, unwillingness to participate) and potential assets (in the form of social capital). As such, their participation is linked to a social inclusion agenda rather than a democratic one. One of the consequences of the emphasis on community noted in the previous section is that a cultural gloss is overlaid on structural problems; the forms of participation being fostered by the new technologies of power discussed in this chapter tend to focus on citizens as either the users of a specific service or as residents of a particular locality. This produces a fragmented array of multiple and overlapping initiatives that militate against the formation of wider collective identifications.

The limits of 'constitution'

The post-structuralist approach discussed above highlights the discursive constitution of actors into categories of governable subject. However, its critics have argued that a reliance on discourse-as-text is insufficient, and have called for more sociological or ethnographic studies of the working of governmental power (O'Malley, 1996; O'Malley et al, 1997; Li, 2004; Marston, 2004). One such study drew on an empirical study of deliberative forums to argue that it is not only official actors who are engaged in the process of constitution: "It is in the micro-politics of institutional engagement, rather than through officially espoused views or strategies, that the public is constituted as actors" (Barnes et al, 2003, p 396). Data from this study showed how governmental strategies are mediated through local public service managers who draw on a range of cultural resources – including backgrounds in trade union, feminist or community politics – rather than necessarily replicating the language of official discourse. Many citizens were highly skilled in the new participative techniques, often more so than many public officials, while others readily embraced traditional professional or bureaucratic norms that the process of 'empowerment' was supposed to eradicate. Yet others sought to subordinate participative practices to the formal norms and rules – and power bases – of the council chamber or trade union meeting. The boundaries of legitimate participation are permeable and may be disrupted by forms of political agency whose roots lie elsewhere.

The constitution of publics, then, is produced in the interaction between public officials and the public. General theories of the constitutive power of discourse may fail to capture the complexity and diversity of the ways in which conceptions of the public are negotiated and remade within the participative process itself. Nevertheless, power imbalances mean that public officials' 'claims to truth' tend to prevail over the experiences and knowledge that the collaborating publics bring to those interactions. The process of negotiating meanings and reconciling different claims to truth is not an equal one. While participative governance constitutes the public as active agents, it also constitutes the possibilities of their agency. It does so by controlling the places, norms and rules of participation – for example, by setting agendas, defining membership and delimiting the interests and identities that can be legitimately expressed.

However, while such strategies shape identity, they do not determine agency. While the proliferation of initiatives that seek to draw citizens and communities into participative governance subjects them to new regulatory strategies, it also creates the possibility of new subject positions and forms of identification which may not be 'tidy' or 'stable'. And the active citizen may not act in the way envisaged by government; the empowered service user may not use their power in an approved manner. The attempt by the state to construct inclusive, participating, responsible communities may be met by difficult questions of difference, dissent and conflict. Participative governance, then, can be viewed as a site where tensions over questions of power and legitimacy are played out. However, the process of categorisation and classification of publics and the models of citizenship at stake in new forms of collaborative governance delimits the kinds of political identity that are afforded legitimacy. Public participation can be viewed as one of an array of strategies oriented towards governing the boundaries between legitimate and illegitimate dissent (Cooper, 1998).

Conclusion: the dynamics of change

New and old regimes of power interact in complex ways and the tensions between hierarchical and network governance, managerial technologies and professional strategies produce a complex field of power. This chapter has highlighted the problematic overlaying of liberal and republican models of citizenship at stake in neo-liberal governance, and the complex interactions between the representative politics of nation-states and the complex re-territorialisations of the public sphere. But the notion of making the 'public' also opens up wider questions, so I want to end by returning to the concept of the public sphere as both a constructed and contested space. First, the modernisation of welfare states that was discussed in Chapters Four and Five produces a parallel contraction in the kinds of 'public' agendas on which the public is invited to participate. Public consultation is focused predominantly on changes at the margins of how public services are delivered, not on the consequences of the withdrawal of services or their shift to other sectors. There are some exceptions to this – for example, in the UK legislation has required public consultation about the transfer of local authority housing to voluntary trusts. But such forms of participation remain marginal. The public/ private distinction brings into view issues about *who* it is that is being invited to do the work of participation. As Chapter Four in this volume argued, the constitution of women as 'active citizens' invited to participate in the formal governance arrangements of schools, community organisations, partnership bodies, and so on, is in tension with the emphasis on the further commodification of women's labour.

Citizens are being constituted not only as active participants in the labour market and as responsible welfare users, but are also charged with sharing responsibility for civic and community well-being. Here, participation appears to be open and voluntaristic – anyone may participate, in contrast to the more coercive strategies associated with the reform of state benefits.

However, as we have seen, the active subject is a constituted subject: the process of categorisation and classification delimits the kinds of political identity that are given legitimacy in participative governance. The result may be a constrained, managed and consensus-oriented political imaginary that will do little to achieve the connection between government and people envisaged by the EU in its promulgation of 'good governance'.

Notes

[1] See, for example, the card game 'Democs' produced by the New Economics foundation: www.neweconomics.org/genn/participation_democs. See also Walker and Higginson (2003).

[2] Such images derive from Arnstein (1971).

[3] This study of partnership working found that of three possible models – elite, participative and managerial – a managerial model of partnership working was most dominant.

References

Arnstein, S.R. (1971) 'A ladder of participation in the USA', *Journal of the Royal Town Planning Institute*, April, pp 176-82.

Barnes, M., Newman, J., Sullivan, H. and Knops, A. (2003) 'Constituting "the public" in public participation', *Public Administration*, vol 81, no 8, pp 379-99.

Barnett, C. (2004) 'Media, democracy and representation: disembodying the public', in C. Barnett and M. Low (eds) *Spaces of democracy: Geographical perspectives on citizenship, participation and representation*, London: Sage Publications, pp 185-206.

Beck, U., Giddens, A. and Lash, S. (1994) *Reflexive modernisation: Politics, tradition and aesthetics in the modern social order*, Cambridge: Polity Press.

Benhabib, S. (ed) (1996) *Democracy and difference: Contesting the boundaries of the political*, Princeton, NJ: Princeton University Press.

Beresford, P. (2002) 'Participation and social policy: transformation, liberation or regulation?', in R. Sykes, C. Bochel and N. Ellison (eds) *Social Policy Review 14*, Bristol: The Policy Press/Social Policy Association, pp 265-87.

Cabinet Office (1999) *Professional policymaking in the twenty-first century*, London: The Stationery Office.

Cooper, D. (1998) *Governing out of order: Space, law and the politics of belonging*, London: Rivers Oram Press.

Demos (2003) *Demos project policy briefing no 4*, July, London: Demos.

Driver, S. and Martell, L. (1998) *New Labour: Politics after Thatcher*, Cambridge: Polity Press.

Dryzek, J.S. (2000) *Deliberative democracy and beyond: Liberals, critics, contestations*, Oxford: Oxford University Press.

European Commission (2001) *European governance: A White Paper*, Brussels: European Commission.

Everingham, C. (2003) *Social justice and the politics of community*, Aldershot: Ashgate.

Fischer, F. (2003) *Reframing public policy: Discursive politics and deliberative practices*, Oxford: Oxford University Press.

Foucault, M. (1991) 'Governmentality', in G. Burchell, C. Gordon and P. Miller (eds) *The Foucault effect: Studies in governmentality*, Hemel Hempstead: Harvester Wheatsheaf.

Fraser, N. (1997) *Justice interruptus: Critical reflections on the 'postsocialist' condition*, London: Routledge.

Giddens, A. (1994) *Beyond left and right: The future of radical politics*, Cambridge: Polity Press.

Habermas, J. (1989) *The structural transformation of the public sphere*, Cambridge, MA: MIT Press.

Kooiman, J. (ed) (1993) *Modern governance: Government–society interactions*, London: Sage Publications.

Kooiman, J. (2000) 'Societal governance: levels, models and orders of social–political interaction', in J. Pierre (ed) *Debating governance: Authority, steering and democracy*, London: Sage Publications, pp 138-64.

Larner, W. and Butler, M. (2004) 'Governmentalities of local partnerships', paper presented to the Contemporary Governance and the Question of the Social Conference, Alberta, Canada, June.

Leadbetter, C. (2004) *Personalisation through participation: A new script for public services*, London: Demos.

Li, T. (2004) 'Governmentality and its limits: Development, environment and the practice of politics', paper presented to the Canadian Anthropology Association Conference, University of Western Ontario, London, Ontario, May.

Magnette, P. (2003) 'European governance and civic participation: beyond elitist citizenship?', *Political Studies*, vol 51, no 1, pp 144-60.

Marsh, D. and Rhodes, R.A.W. (1992) *Policy networks in British government*, Oxford: Clarendon Press.

Marston, G. (2004) *Social policy and discourse analysis: Policy change in public housing*, Aldershot: Ashgate.

Needham, C. (2003) *Citizen-consumers: New Labour' market place democracy*, London: The Catalyst Forum.

Newman, J. (2001) *Modernising governance: New Labour, policy and society*, London: Sage Publications.

Newman, J. and Mooney, G. (2004) 'Managing personal lives: doing welfare work', in G. Mooney (ed) *Work: Personal lives and social policy*, Bristol: The Policy Press, pp 39-72.

O'Malley, P. (1996) 'Indigenous governance', *Economy and Society*, vol 25, no 3, pp 310-26.

O'Malley, P., Weir, L. and Shearing, C. (1997) 'Governmentality, criticism, politics', *Economy and Society*, vol 26, no 4, pp 501-17.

Peters, B., Sifft, S., Wimmel, A., Brüggmann, M. and Königslöw, K. (2005) 'National and transnational public spheres: the case of the EU', in S. Liebfried and M. Zürn (eds) *Transformations of the state*, Cambridge: Cambridge University Press.

Phillips, A. (1995) *The politics of presence*, Oxford: Clarendon Press.

Rose, N. (1996) 'The death of the social? Reconfiguring the territory of government', *Economy and Society*, vol 25, pp 327-56.

Rose, N. (1999) *Powers of freedom*, Cambridge: Cambridge University Press.

Social Exclusion Unit (SEU) (2001) *National strategy for neighbourhood renewal action plan*, London: The Stationery Office.

Skelcher, C., Mathur, N. and Smith, M. (2004) 'Public governance in the institutional void: discourse, democracy and collaborative design', paper presented to the Political Studies Association, Lincoln, April.

Squires, J. (1998) 'In different voices: deliberative democracy and aesthetic politics', in J. Good and I. Velody (eds) *The politics of postmodernity*, Cambridge: Polity Press, pp 126-46.

Staeheli, L. and Mitchell, D. (2004) 'Spaces of public and private: locating politics', in C. Barnett and M. Low (eds) *Spaces of democracy: Geographical perspectives on citizenship, participation and representation*, London: Sage Publications, pp 147-60.

Taylor-Gooby, P., Hastie, C. and Bromly, C. (2003) 'Querulous citizens: welfare knowledge and the limits to welfare reform', *Social Policy and Administration*, vol 37, no 1, pp 1-20.

Walker, P. and Higginson, S. (2003) *So you're using a card game to make policy recommendations? The evolution of Democs October 2001–January 2003*, London: New Economics Foundation.

Walters, W. (2002) 'Social capital and political sociology: reimagining politics?', *Sociology*, vol 36, no 2, pp 377-97.

Warner, M. (2002) *Publics and counterpublics*, New York, NY: Zone Books.

Warner, M. (2005) 'Making public', lecture at Tate Modern, London, 25 February.

Young, I.M. (1990) *Justice and the politics of difference*, Princeton, NJ: Princeton University Press.

SEVEN

Promoting democratic governance through partnerships?[1]

Rebekah Sterling

Introduction

Changing discourses and practices of governance sit uneasily with ideas of democracy. On the one hand, the much-debated move from *government* to *governance* is seen to represent an opening up of decision-making to a wider range of actors (Stoker, 1998). On the other hand, governance is also associated also with increased institutional fragmentation at all levels, so that much public decision-making has unclear lines of accountability to the public, and is linked only tenuously to structures of representative government. At the same time, governments and other organisations seem to be experimenting with new, innovative participatory practices (see Chapter Six of this volume and McLaverty, 2002), and many areas of policy now have an expectation of public or user involvement. These apparent contradictions raise questions about how democratic governance can be achieved within changing practices (Burns, 2000; Hirst, 2000). It is easy to be pessimistic about the prospects for democracy within governance, and to bemoan the 'democratic deficit' arising from unclear lines of accountability and legitimacy. But it is also possible that changing governance practices might open up new spaces and possibilities for democratic debate and public participation.

One of the most visible recent manifestations of changing governance practices is the growth of partnership arrangements for developing and delivering policy. As this chapter uses the term, partnerships denote a relatively formalised arrangement between two or more organisations in order to achieve a specific set of objectives, generally with a degree of independence from any one partner (Edwards et al, 2000; Painter and Clarence, 2001; Powell and Glendinning, 2002; Moseley, 2003).

Many, although not all, partnerships are multi-sector, involving organisations from both the public and private or voluntary sectors, and are area-based, focused on policy or development for a specific geographic area. The partnership phenomenon is not restricted to any single national context, but is taking shape across many policy areas throughout Europe and beyond (see Geddes and Benington, 2001; Kjaer et al, 2003; Moseley, 2003).

Partnerships are at once a tangible result of the changing patterns of governance – part of the range of new and often fragmented institutions – as well as an encapsulation of some of the central trends underlying those changes. As such, they also illustrate some of the paradoxical relationships between governance and democracy. Often, the rise of partnership arrangements has coincided with demands for greater public participation within them, such that the language of partnership is often 'coupled' (Lowndes and Sullivan, 2004), arguably even conflated, with the language of participation. Thus partnerships are sometimes (and, arguably, erroneously) portrayed as one mechanism of participation, or as a uniquely 'participative' arrangement for decision-making. However, like other elements of new governance practice, partnerships largely tend to bypass traditional mechanisms of representative democracy, and some authors have argued that partnerships thus represent a form of elite, non-accountable governance (see Elander and Blanc, 2001).

Given these paradoxes, what contribution might partnerships make to a more democratic governance? The answer to this question depends, of course, on how 'democratic governance' is defined. This chapter does not set out to offer a single or prescriptive model of democratic governance against which one could measure partnerships. Ideals of democratic governance will always be contested (Saward, 2003; see also Chapter Nine of this volume), and whether certain practices of governance are seen as good or bad for democracy depends on which ideals are prioritised (Sehested, 2003). Furthermore, the complexity of both the institutional landscape of contemporary governance and the societies that they are meant to 'steer' or 'manage', creates new challenges for democratic practice and for conceptualising issues such as democratic accountability (Papadopoulos, 2003). As Elander and Blanc (2001, p 108) point out: "Traditional mechanisms of accountability in representative democracy were never designed to cope with multi-organisational, fragmented policy systems." This complexity may require, in turn, the development of new practices and the adoption of a pluralistic approach using a range of different mechanisms in different contexts (Warren, 2002; Saward, 2003). This chapter seeks to interrogate the possible ways in which partnerships might contribute to more democratic governance in that pluralistic sense: how they might promote greater influence by members of the public on decisions that affect their lives, but without prejudging the mechanisms or forms of participation that might be appropriate in different contexts.

In assessing the democratic potential of partnerships, it is important to recognise that the partnerships phenomenon is a complex one. This author has argued elsewhere (Sterling, 2002) that the analysis of partnerships is hampered by a lack of conceptual clarity, so that discussions of them often confuse rhetoric with practice and institutional forms with wider processes of governance. So, the next section of this chapter will introduce an analytic framework for understanding partnerships as institutional arrangements in which various trends and processes of governance may play out. The following section builds on that analytic framework to discuss three possible roles for partnerships in promoting democratic governance: as democratic spaces; as catalysts for wider democratisation; and as part of the political opportunity structure. While Chapter Six conceptualised participation as a constitutive process, this chapter considers partnership arrangements as empirical phenomena, and tries to understand how certain governance trends interact within them to influence partnerships' potential contribution to democratic practice.

Institutional form, collaboration, territory and participation: towards an analytic framework for understanding partnerships

The analytic framework adopted here understands partnerships as institutional arrangements in which various trends and processes of governance may play out. Accordingly, to understand the constraints and opportunities for collective action within partnerships – including action towards changing governance cultures or democratisation of governance – it is necessary to examine partnerships in two dimensions. The first dimension relates to the organisational or institutional features of specific partnership arrangements. This may seem of less interest to students of changing governance cultures, but it is important since it is through particular institutions and partnership arrangements that wider processes and changes are mediated. This dimension of partnerships encompasses a range of contextual and internal organisational factors that inevitably have considerable influence on how partnerships operate and what they can achieve. Often, these factors are specific to a particular partnership arrangement and contingent on time, place, policy framework, and the people and organisations involved. Important internal factors include, for example, the availability and quality of staff to support the partnership's work (Moseley, 2003), methods of monitoring and evaluating progress, the partnership's legal status or constitutional form (Sullivan and Skelcher, 2002), as well as the style of implementation (focused on project delivery or strategic policy; concerned with pooling financial resources or with securing external funding, and so on). External and contextual factors also frequently determine how partnerships organise themselves and their work; particularly important are the availability, amount and duration of funding, externally-imposed demands for reporting and performance management and the wider parameters of welfare governance described by Håkan Johansson and Bjørn Hvinden in Chapter Five of this volume. Studies of partnerships need to be able to distinguish analytically between such contingent, organisational features and the broader processes of governance that may be evident in partnerships, and to explore the interaction between organisational features and those wider governance trends.

The second dimension concerns wider governance processes and trends which are not unique to partnership arrangements but often find expression within them. Here I want to identify three wider trends that, arguably, often converge in current forms of partnerships (although sometimes uneasily): a drive toward integration and collaboration; a reconfiguration of governance around 'territory'; and a renewed emphasis on 'bottom-up' processes, stressing 'participation' and 'community'. Each of these trends could be said to derive from the strategies for 'governing the social' explored in earlier chapters of this volume. The rest of this section considers these three trends of governance in more detail, with special attention to how their internal tensions and problems might have an impact on partnerships.

The collaborative governance trend

Of the three governance trends considered here, perhaps the most central is the drive toward integration across policy and functional areas and collaboration among organisations within and outside the public sector. This trend is evident in many areas of policy (Balloch and Taylor, 2001; Sullivan and Skelcher, 2002), and arguably underpins much of the rhetoric of 'joined-up' working, 'holistic' solutions and 'partnership working'. The literature provides various competing and complementary explanations for this drive toward collaboration:

- the existence of cross-cutting problems;
- a dissatisfaction with hierarchical, sectorally-organised policy-making structures (Healey et al, 2002) that ignore the interactions across policy areas;
- the fragmentation of public services and governing institutions;
- the declining ability of the state to exert direct control over services and policy.

And for those theories of governance that see 'new governance' as characterised by a shift towards networks and a broadening out of the actors involved in public decision-making (for example, Rhodes, 1996), this move towards collaboration is integral to the idea of governance.

This collaborative trend has an obvious connection with partnerships, which are essentially formalised arrangements for collaboration[2]. Just because partnerships are established *for* collaboration, however, does not necessarily mean that they succeed at working collaboratively. The processes and rhetorics that make up 'the collaborative trend' may be realised only imperfectly in actual partnership arrangements and it is important to distinguish between partnerships as institutional arrangements or structures and the principles (for example, of 'partnership working'; Edwards et al, 2000) and 'modes of governance' (Lowndes and Skelcher, 1998) which they may or may not exhibit.

Further, there are several tensions and challenges within this wider trend that may also manifest within partnerships. First, some of the governance literature seems to portray collaborative and network-based processes as supplanting or displacing other modes of governance, such as hierarchical/sectoral or market-based approaches, but several authors have argued instead that these approaches continue to exist alongside each other and are sometimes in tension (Newman, 2001). Partnerships, too, may be subject to competing and conflicting approaches to governance, as Lowndes and Skelcher (1998) have illustrated in relation to network, market and hierarchy modes of governance. Second, collaborative governance is sometimes associated with a more participatory style of governance, because decision-making is open to more actors – sometimes even members of the public or civic organisations. However, there are good reasons not to conflate collaborative and participatory governance. Many of the demands for collaboration have nothing to do with a goal of 'opening up' decision-making to greater public influence, but arise instead from more functionalist or managerial imperatives (Papadopoulos, 2003). Although some collaborative arrangements (notably regeneration partnerships) do indeed seek to include 'communities' or the public as 'partners', public participation is not intrinsic to collaboration, which might involve only public agencies or public agencies alongside business interests without any involvement from the public or 'third-sector' organisations. Similarly, while the words partnership and participation are often 'coupled' (Lowndes and Sullivan, 2004), not all partnerships involve public participation or voluntary sector–statutory sector collaboration. Third, while collaboration is thought to provide certain advantages, such as synergy, avoiding duplication, resource pooling or transformation of other partners' ways of acting (Mackintosh, 1992; see also Hastings, 1996; Sullivan and Skelcher, 2002), there are difficulties inherent to collaboration which may apply also to particular partnership arrangements. Some of these include unequal power among partners, differing institutional objectives and cultures and, above all, the costs in time and other resources required to work in collaborative settings (Huxham and Vangen, 2000; Stewart, 2000). Fourth, collaborative arrangements are established for many different purposes, some very specific or project-focused, some more strategic. It is important to consider the types of public decisions that can be taken within a given collaborative arrangement and how much autonomy and wider influence such arrangements have. Finally, it is important to remember that these collaborative processes are mediated through the institutional arrangements established for particular partnerships, which may set their own constraints on the degree of local autonomy, the level of resources available to support collaborative working and the availability of skills required.

The territorial governance trend

The second governance trend implicated in the rise of partnerships is a reconfiguration of governance around territory. This general trend captures several processes. First, a new 'territorialisation' of policymaking (Geddes and Le Galès, 2001), in which territories below the level of the central state become increasingly important sites of decision-making. This new territorialisation does not represent a simple or straightforward process of decentralisation of governance, but rather a complex realignment of governing responsibilities at different territorial scales. Second, Healey et al (2002) have argued that increasingly, place and territory are becoming a focus around which collective action (and governance) will integrate: they suggest that issues of place identity and place quality, in particular, prove cogent for mobilising interests and integrating the activities of different organisations and institutions. Third, some authors have turned attention to the way that territorial identity is created deliberately through governance (Ray, 1998) or (in the language of the Foucauldian governmentality literature) the way that territory is 'rendered visible' so as to be acted upon (Ward and McNicholas, 1998).

Many partnerships illustrate this changing and complex repositioning of governance in relation to territory. Often (although not always), partnerships are area-based, focused on policy or development within specific territorial boundaries, which can range from a neighbourhood or village to a local authority area, or to even larger regions. As such, they are implicated also in the shifting of responsibilities within multilevel governance.

There are several tensions and unresolved questions within this trend, which in turn can have an impact on partnerships. What degree of decentralisation of governance is appropriate, for what types of decisions or policies and to what territories or levels? How useful is a focus on place for addressing particular problems or integrating collective efforts, and what trade-offs might such a focus entail? Finally, to what extent does a territorialisation of policy and governance result in differential results across territories? Edwards et al (2000), for example, note a growing gap between 'partnership- poor' and 'partnership-rich' areas, those where prior experience of partnership leads to further success at securing development resources and establishing new partnerships.

The participatory governance trend

The third trend often evident in partnerships takes the form of a renewed emphasis on participation, the role of 'community' and 'bottom-up' processes within governance. First, this trend encapsulates a resurgence of interest in participation across a range of institutions in society and the public sphere, through agendas such as democratic renewal, user involvement in services and active citizenship (Kearns, 1992; Leach and Wingfield, 1999; Wilson, 1999). Second, it embraces the discourse of community, with its emphasis on empowerment, capacity building and the responsibilities of communities, as well as on related concepts such as social capital. Often, partnerships – at least certain kinds – are expected to involve the public or 'community' and many also aim to contribute towards 'empowerment', 'capacity building' or 'social capital'.

Again, however, there are a number of tensions within this trend.

First, calls for greater public or community participation often skirt around the issue of *who* is to participate. As many have pointed out, the concept of community is problematic (Frazer, 1999; Liepins, 2000) and the idea that a community, as a single homogenous entity, can participate or build its capacity seems to be a fallacy (Shucksmith, 2000); questions arise concerning which sections of a 'community' are actually involved in governance and what power relations exist within so-called communities. Contemporary democratic theory raises further questions about how to integrate difference and diversity into democratic structures (Young, 1990, 2000; Benhabib, 1996; Fraser, 1997).

Second, despite the general emphasis on participation and community involvement, several different roles might be envisaged for communities or the public. For example, Richardson and Mumford (2002, p 210) suggest a distinction between self-help or community action, where members of the public act as "organisers of their own projects, providing services and tackling problems directly themselves", and involvement in decision-making, referring to participation in more formal governance mechanisms. Similarly, Sharp and Connelly (2002, cited in Luckin and Sharp, 2004) categorise different types of participation along a 'policy–action continuum': individual action, communal action (for example, volunteering in collective activities), community organising (involvement in more formalised organisations) and policy participation. All of these possible roles involve some degree of public involvement in governing or managing aspects of society, but the nature of that involvement, and the decisions in which it is allowed, can differ substantially among those roles.

Third, given the focus on the role of 'communities', questions arise about the role of associations, such as community and voluntary organisations, in processes of participation (Fung, 2003; Luckin and Sharp, 2004). Can – and should (Williams, 2003) – such organisations serve as intermediaries between state and citizen for the purposes of public participation? Do associations have a cultivating role in developing the skills and virtues that people need to be 'active citizens' or to participate in formal decision-making?

Finally, the widespread endorsement of the idea of participation tends to be vague about the kinds of participation envisaged and the ideals of democracy which underpin different styles of participation. For example, there are tensions between participation based on representative and deliberative models of democracy (see Burns, 2000; Young, 2000; Fishkin and Laslett, 2003); each of these models is problematic in itself. Within a representative model, there are tensions between different forms and interpretations of 'representation' (Barnes et al, 2003), for example, between traditional partisan (and aggregative) forms and new forms using community activists and parallel community representation structures (Hughes and Carmichael, 1998). Further, some authors query the assumption of rational, reasoned discussion and deliberation behind many models of deliberative democracy, an assumption that seems to sideline the role of conflict, disagreement, the emotions and other non-rational styles of communication within politics (Young, 1996; Thompson and Hoggett, 2001). Moreover, whatever the underlying model of democracy, participation may entail varying degrees of empowerment and influence. Building on Fung and Wright's (2001, 2003) notion of participatory governance, Somerville (2003) draws a distinction between 'empowered' and 'disciplined' participatory governance, where the former is "concerned with transforming our political institutions so that ordinary citizens have equal say in all key decision-making processes" (2003, p 16) and the latter refers to a situation where "citizens sign up to a governance regime over which they have no real influence – a form of 'productive subjection' (Foucault) in which the participants become disciplined by the rules and norms of the regime itself" (2003, p 12). This distinction is related to one made by Newman (2001) between managerial and political models for public engagement. Partnerships' successes and failures in participation and envisaging roles for the 'community' must be viewed at least partly in light of these tensions within the wider participatory trend, which influence the constraints and opportunities for action within particular partnership arrangements.

This analytic framework provides a way of understanding partnerships as institutions in which different trends of governance play out and interact. The governance trends identified here each have their own internal tensions and as they converge within particular partnerships, they might produce either synergics or conflicts. Also, the institutional characteristics of particular partnership arrangements may further constrain or enable the realisation and interplay of these wider governance processes. The interaction between institutional structure and wider governance processes in partnerships creates a unique set of possibilities and tensions for partnerships in developing democratic governance. The next section attempts to reflect on some of these possibilities in the light of this analytic framework.

The role of partnerships in democratic governance

What opportunities does this interplay between participatory, territorial and collaborative governance trends create for partnerships to promote more democratic forms of governance? This section proposes three sets of questions which might serve as the basis for investigating the democratic contributions of partnerships. First, to what extent do partnerships themselves, in their own work, represent 'democratic spaces'? Second, to what extent might partnerships promote democracy and participation more widely, beyond their own operation to other parts of society? Third, what role do partnerships play within the 'political opportunity structure' for action by citizens and civil society – in other words, to what extent does the existence of partnership arrangements create opportunities and/or constraints for citizens wishing to articulate their interests, influence decision-making and engage in collective action?

Partnerships as democratic spaces?

Might partnerships contribute toward a democratisation of governance through themselves operating in a democratic way, acting as 'spaces' in which democratic decision-making can occur? Certainly, there is a preoccupation with public – or community – participation in much of the literature on partnerships, with a widespread (although not ubiquitous) expectation that partnerships should involve members of the public and local communities in their work (see, for example, Anastacio et al, 2000; Osborne et al, 2002). Existing research, however, suggests that partnerships vary considerably in the mechanisms, purposes, extent and inclusiveness of participation (Sterling, 2005, forthcoming). The mechanisms which partnerships use range from 'community representation' through individual activists or community organisations (very common), to public meetings, consultations or surveys (fairly common), to more 'innovative' mechanisms such as citizens' juries or participatory appraisals (less common). In general, however, research consistently finds that most partnerships involve participation by only a small number of people and, with a few isolated exceptions, issues of community diversity, 'race', gender, disability and class still receive little attention in partnership practice (Anastacio et al, 2000; Edwards, 2002). Further, participation is sought for a range of different purposes at different stages of partnerships' work: for identifying needs, implementing projects or delivering services, allocating funding (for example, regeneration or rural development funding streams), planning and strategy development, providing feedback on decisions made by others or some or all of these purposes. Thus democratic practice within partnerships is imperfect and uneven, both in the degree of influence that the public can have over decisions (and what kinds of decisions the public can influence), and the extent to which different sections of the public can have access to, and have influence on, partnerships' decision-making processes.

These criticisms of participation within partnerships are familiar and well documented. However, beyond these obvious shortcomings there may be a number of tensions and synergies that arise from the interaction between collaborative, territorial and participatory trends of governance. On the one hand, the consensual style of decision-making which tends to characterise collaborative governance would appear, at first glance, to favour equal participation by all participants, thus being somewhat democratic in spirit; but this veneer of consensus can mask power relations between the 'partners' that could work to silence some voices and bolster others. On the other hand, the 'integrated' and holistic nature of discussions in collaborations, if achieved, could be more 'user-friendly' than 'sectoral' approaches, since sectoral divisions may seem somewhat artificial and ill-matched to people's lived experiences. While not guaranteeing participation, holistic discussions might ease it at times. Similarly, the territorial focus, as it plays out in partnerships, could have mixed implications for creating democratic spaces. Where the territory is local, the immediate nature of issues may help to foster the public's interest in participation. But there are several caveats. First, a focus on territory within governance might lead to a tendency to view territories as homogenous and seek participation on a territorial basis rather than exploring different interests and perspectives within the population. Also, might a focus on place and territory run the risk of alienating those who lack a strong identification with place, such as some young people (see, for example, Jamieson, 2000)? Second, within the complex territorialisation of governance, there is a need to attend to the decisions that are taken at what levels or territories. Evidence from the literature on partnerships suggests that direct public influence tends to be limited to the 'lowest' levels or smallest territories and is focused largely on implementation rather than strategic decision-making (Edwards et al, 2000; Osborne et al, 2002); democratising partnerships surely involves querying what decisions, and at what territorial scales, citizens are permitted or enabled to influence and how to broaden citizen influence to wider-reaching areas of policy and governance. Finally, organisational features such as the willingness and ability of staff to promote democratic engagement, as well as the constraints of resources and operation styles, might influence also the degree to which partnerships could implement more democratic practices.

Partnerships as a catalyst for wider democratic governance?

Another way in which partnerships might contribute towards more democratic governance is by acting as a catalyst or stimulus for participation and democratic practice in other institutions and parts of society, beyond the partnership arrangement itself. The collaborative element of partnerships' work does appear favourable for encouraging other institutions and organisations to engage with the public in a more democratic way. Collaboration is widely seen to require the development of new ways of working and a culture change in the way that organisations work internally and with each other (although these changes may be difficult and slow). This transformative quality of collaborative working has the potential to help democratise other 'partner' institutions: if democratic ideals about the value of participation are endorsed by the partnership, the partnership may be in a position to influence the way that partner organisations engage with the public. Also, where partnerships have been involved in developing community infrastructure and networks to facilitate participation within the partnership itself, this infrastructure may have wider benefits for facilitating citizens' engagement in policymaking and other agencies' links with citizens, if those agencies also make use of that infrastructure (evidence suggests this is happening in some places – Sterling, 2005: forthcoming).

Of course, whether either of these possibilities can be achieved depends on many factors. For both, the commitment of staff is essential, whether to promote active citizenship or a culture of better engagement with the public. And while the 'transformation' of partners' cultures and ways of working is one potential advantage of collaboration, whether this occurs depends on the partner organisations' willingness and ability to be influenced and the degree of power that these organisations have to resist change. Any investigation of partnerships' attempts to stimulate wider 'democracy' through either of these ways would need to be attentive to the ideological context and thus to what kind of participation or engagement was being promoted, whose participation, in what activities and for what goal.

Partnerships as part of the 'political opportunity structure'?

What role might partnerships play as part of the political opportunity structure for citizens' action? The concept of the political opportunity structure is drawn from social movement theory and recently has been applied to discussions of local governance (Maloney et al, 2000; Taylor et al, 2003; Newman et al, 2004). Tarrow defines political opportunity structures as

> consistent – but not necessarily formal or permanent – dimensions of the political environment that provide incentives for people to undertake collective action by affecting their expectations of success or failure ... [including] the opening up of access to power, shifting alignments, the availability of influential allies and cleavages within and among elites. (1994, pp 85–6)

In their work on social capital, Maloney et al (2000) argue that the concept helps to focus attention on the institutional frameworks that provide the context – and constraints and opportunities – for the use of social capital and collective action by civil society (or, by extension, other groups). It may be fruitful also to apply this concept to a consideration of the role of partnerships in democratic governance, in order to examine the constraints and opportunities that partnerships present for citizens who are trying to influence decision-making and governance. In this case, the concept also helps to turn attention away from an exclusive focus on institutional frameworks (and the workings of partnerships themselves) and towards questions about independent action by citizens and how they utilise and work around local institutions of governance. To what extent does the presence of partnerships in an area facilitate or hinder citizens' attempts to promote their interests through collective action or engage with decision-making and governing institutions?

Synergies and tensions with the other trends evident in partnerships – and their organisational characteristics – may be important in considering this role. Does the collaborative, integrated nature of partnerships mean that the partnership eases citizens' access to information and contact points, at least within 'partner' organisations? Or might the presence of the partnership simply constitute another layer of institutional complexity and confusion for citizens seeking to influence decisions in their area? Does the degree of independence of partnerships as collaborative arrangements influence how accessible partnerships are for citizens to negotiate? Does a partnership's focus by territory rather than sector help or hinder the ability of citizens to utilise any political opportunities opened up through partnerships? Finally, do specific aspects of partnerships' practices, relating to communication, staff accessibility, and so on, make partnerships easier or harder for citizens to negotiate?

Conclusion

This chapter has sought to consider the potential within partnerships for promoting democratic governance. In order to understand better some of the tensions and possibilities for democratic practice, it introduced an analytic framework interpreting partnerships as institutional arrangements in which three broader trends of governance converge: a collaborative and integrative trend, a reconfiguration of governance in relation to territory and an emphasis on participation, community and 'bottom-up' governance processes. It has been argued that tensions within and between each of these trends create both opportunities and constraints on what partnerships can achieve in relation to more democratic governance practices. The chapter then considered several possible roles for partnership: as democratic spaces themselves, as a catalyst for wider democratic practice and culture and as an aspect of the political opportunity structure for independent action by citizens.

It must be acknowledged that partnerships are not intrinsically democratic institutional arrangements. Indeed, as many critics have pointed out (Elander and Blanc, 2001; see also the discussion in Sullivan and Skelcher, 2002), partnerships can take the form of particularly undemocratic arrangements, characterised by elite participation and an acute 'democratic deficit'. Certainly, there are examples of partnerships with little or no involvement by the public. And while both collaboration and territorialisation in governance may be conducive in some ways to greater or better participation, neither requires it.

Participation in partnerships is evident most often where community participation is a central theme of the policy framework for which partnerships are established (as in much urban regeneration, social exclusion and rural development policy). The current emphasis on participation within many areas of policy may then provide a fertile environment for extending and deepening democratic practice within partnerships. Inevitably, practice is imperfect, and further research is needed to explore the ways that partnerships might perform the 'democratising' roles proposed in this chapter and what enables or hinders partnerships from taking stronger roles in promoting democracy.

A final caveat is necessary. While partnerships may be able to contribute as (a small) part of a complex and pluralistic democratic system, their ability to engender widespread democratic transformation (for example, of the type that Somerville [2003] seeks) is hampered by the highly circumscribed remit within which most partnerships are allowed to make decisions.

Notes

[1] An earlier version of this chapter was prepared for the 2003 Conference of ESPANet: Changing European Societies – The Role for Social Policy, Copenhagen, 13–15 November 2003, which contributed to the paper session on 'Governance, Democracy and Citizenship'.

[2] Although not the only kind: Sullivan and Skelcher (2002), for example, distinguish partnerships from both contractual and network arrangements.

References

Anastacio, J., Gidley, B., Hart, L., Keith, M., Mayo, M. and Kowarzik, U. (2000) *Reflecting realities: Participants' perspectives on integrated communities and sustainable development*, Bristol/York: The Policy Press/ Joseph Rowntree Foundation.

Balloch, S. and Taylor, M. (2001) *Partnership working: Policy and practice*, Bristol: The Policy Press.

Barnes, M., Newman, J., Knops, A. and Sullivan, H. (2003) 'Constituting "the public" in public participation', *Public Administration*, vol 81, no 2, pp 379-99.

Benhabib, S. (ed) (1996) *Democracy and difference: Contesting the boundaries of the political*, Princeton, NJ and Chichester: Princeton University Press.

Burns, D. (2000) 'Can local democracy survive governance?', *Urban Studies*, vol 37, nos 5-6, pp 963-73.

Edwards, B., Goodwin, M., Pemberton, S. and Woods, M. (2000) *Partnership working in rural regeneration: Governance and empowerment?*, Bristol/York: The Policy Press/Joseph Rowntree Foundation.

Edwards, C. (2002) 'Barriers to involvement: the disconnected worlds of disability and regeneration', *Local Economy*, vol 17, no 2, pp 123-35.

Elander, I. and Blanc, M. (2001) 'Partnerships and democracy: a happy couple in urban governance?', in H.T. Andersen and R. van Kempen (eds) *Governing European cities: Social fragmentation and governance*, Aldershot: Ashgate, pp 93-124.

Fishkin, J.S. and Laslett, P. (eds) (2003) *Debating deliberative democracy*, Oxford: Blackwell.

Fraser, N. (1997) 'Rethinking the public sphere: a contribution to the critique of actually existing democracy', in *Justice interruptus: Critical reflections on the 'postsocialist' condition*, London: Routledge, pp 69-98.

Frazer, E. (1999) *The problems of communitarian politics: Unity and conflict*, Oxford: Oxford University Press.

Fung, A. (2003) 'Associations and democracy: between theories, hopes and realities', *Annual Review of Sociology*, vol 29, pp 515-39.

Fung, A. and Wright, E.O. (2001) 'Deepening democracy: innovations in empowered participatory governance', *Politics and Society*, vol 29, no 1, pp 5-41.

Fung, A. and Wright, E.O. (eds) (2003) *Deepening democracy: Institutional innovations in empowered participatory governance*, New York, NY and London: Verso.

Geddes, M. and Benington, J. (eds) (2001) *Local partnerships and social exclusion in the European Union: New forms of local social governance?*, London: Routledge.

Geddes, M. and Le Galès, P. (2001) 'Local partnerships, welfare regimes and local governance', in M. Geddes and J. Benington (eds) *Local partnerships and social exclusion in the European Union: New forms of local social governance?*, London: Routledge, pp 220-41.

Hastings, A. (1996) 'Unravelling the process of "partnership" in urban regeneration policy', *Urban Studies*, vol 33, no 2, pp 253-68.

Healey, P., Cars, G., Madanipour, A. and Magalhães, C.D. (2002) 'Transforming governance, institutionalist analysis and institutional capacity', in G. Cars, P. Healey, A. Madanipour and C.D. Magalhães (eds) *Urban governance, institutional capacity and social milieux*, Aldershot: Ashgate, pp 6-28.

Hirst, P. (2000) 'Democracy and governance', in J. Pierre (ed) *Debating governance: Authority, steering and democracy*, Oxford: Oxford University Press, pp 13-35.

Hughes, J. and Carmichael, P. (1998) 'Building partnerships in urban regeneration: a case study from Belfast', *Community Development Journal*, vol 33, no 3, pp 205-25.

Huxham, C. and Vangen, S. (2000) 'The New Public Management: an action research approach', paper presented to the ESRC Seminar Series on the New Public Management, Imperial College, London.

Jamieson, L. (2000) 'Migration, place and class: youth in a rural area', *Sociological Review*, vol 48, no 2, pp 203-23.

Kearns, A. (1992) 'Active citizenship and urban governance', *Transactions of the Institute of British Geographers*, vol 17, no 1, pp 20-34.

Kjaer, L., Abrahamson, P. and Raynard, P. (eds) (2003) *Local partnerships in Europe: An action research project*, Copenhagen: The Copenhagen Centre.

Leach, S. and Wingfield, M. (1999) 'Public participation and the democratic renewal agenda: prioritisation or marginalisation?', *Local Government Studies*, vol 25, no 4, pp 46-59.

Liepins, R. (2000) 'New energies for an old idea: reworking approaches to "community" in contemporary rural studies', *Journal of Rural Studies*, vol 16, no 1, pp 23-35.

Lowndes, V. and Skelcher, C. (1998) 'The dynamics of multi-organisational partnerships: an analysis of changing modes of governance', *Public Administration*, vol 76, no 2, pp 313-33.

Lowndes, V. and Sullivan, H. (2004) 'Like a horse and carriage or a fish on a bicycle: how well do local partnerships and public participation go together?', *Local Government Studies*, vol 30, no 1, pp 51-73.

Luckin, D. and Sharp, L. (2004) 'Remaking local governance through community participation? The case of the UK community waste sector', *Urban Studies*, vol 41, no 8, pp 1485-505.

Mackintosh, M. (1992) 'Partnership: issues of policy and negotiation', *Local Economy*, vol 7, no 3, pp 211-24.

McLaverty, P. (ed) (2002) *Public participation and innovations in community governance*, Aldershot: Ashgate.

Maloney, W., Smith, G. and Stoker, G. (2000) 'Social capital and urban governance: adding a more contextualised "top-down" perspective', *Political Studies*, vol 48, no 4, pp 802-20.

Moseley, M.J. (ed) (2003) *Local partnerships for rural development: The European experience*, Walingford: CABI Publishing.

Newman, J. (2001) *Modernising governance: New Labour, policy and society*, London: Sage Publications.

Newman, J., Barnes, M., Sullivan, H. and Knops, A. (2004) 'Public participation and collaborative governance', *Journal of Social Policy*, vol 33, no 2, pp 203-23.

Osborne, S.P., Beattie, R.S. and Williamson, A.P. (2002) *Community involvement in rural regeneration partnerships in the UK: Evidence from England, Northern Ireland and Scotland*, Bristol: The Policy Press.

Painter, C. and Clarence, E. (2001) 'UK local action zones and changing urban governance', *Urban Studies*, vol 38, no 8, pp 1215-32.

Papadopoulos, Y. (2003) 'Cooperative forms of governance: problems of democratic accountability in complex environments', *European Journal of Political Research*, vol 42, no 4, pp 473-501.

Powell, M. and Glendinning, C. (2002) 'Introduction', in C. Glendinning, M. Powell and K. Rummery (eds) *Partnerships, New Labour and the governance of welfare*, Bristol: The Policy Press, pp 1-14.

Ray, C. (1998) 'Territory, structures and interpretation – two case studies of the European Union's LEADER I programme', *Journal of Rural Studies*, vol 14, no 1, pp 79-87.

Rhodes, R.A.W. (1996) 'The new governance: governing without government', *Political Studies*, vol 44, no 4, pp 652-67.

Richardson, L. and Mumford, K. (2002) 'Community, neighbourhood and social infrastructure', in J. Hills, J. Le Grand and D. Piachaud (eds) *Understanding social exclusion*, Oxford: Oxford University Press, pp 202-25.

Saward, M. (2003) 'Enacting democracy', *Political Studies*, vol 51, no 1, pp 161-79.

Sehested, K. (2003) 'Cross-sector partnerships as a new form of local governance', in L. Kjaer, P. Abrahamson and P. Raynard (eds) *Local partnerships in Europe: An action research project*, Copenhagen: The Copenhagen Centre, pp 89-95.

Sharp, L. and Connelly, S. (2002) 'Theorising participation: pulling down the ladder', in Y. Rydin and A. Thornley (eds) *Planning in the UK: Agendas for the new millennium*, Aldershot: Ashgate, pp 33-64.

Shucksmith, M. (2000) 'Endogenous development, social capital and social inclusion: perspectives from LEADER in the UK', *Sociologia Ruralis*, vol 40, no 2, pp 208-18.

Somerville, P. (2003) 'Governance and democratic transformation', paper presented to the *Policy & Politics* International Conference: Policy and Politics in a Globalising World, Bristol, 24-26 July.

Sterling, R. (2002) 'Unpacking the role of partnerships in addressing social exclusion in urban and rural areas', draft paper presented to the Second Warwick Seminar on Social Exclusion and Inequality, University of Warwick, Coventry, 20 November.

Sterling, R. (2005, forthcoming) '*Support for community governance in urban and rural partnerships*', final research report, Glasgow: University of Glasgow.

Stewart, M. (2000) 'Local action to counter exclusion', in Department of the Environment, Transport and Regions (DETR) (ed) *Policy Action Team 17: Joining it up locally – The evidence base*, London: DETR, pp 13-77.

Stoker, G. (1998) 'Governance as theory: five propositions', *International Social Science Journal*, vol 50, no 155, pp 17-28.

Sullivan, H. and Skelcher, C. (2002) *Working across boundaries: Collaboration in the public services*, Basingstoke: Palgrave Macmillan.

Tarrow, S. (1994) *Power in movement*, Cambridge: Cambridge University Press.

Taylor, M., Craig, G., Warburton, D., Parkes, T. and Wilkinson, M. (2003) '*Willing partners? Voluntary and community organisations in the democratic process*', full report on research activities and results (ESRC grant no L215252049), available at: www.esrcsocietytoday.ac.uk/ESRC/InfoCentre/

Thompson, S. and Hoggett, P. (2001) 'The emotional dynamics of deliberative democracy', *Policy & Politics*, vol 29, no 3, pp 351-64.

Ward, N. and McNicholas, K. (1998) 'Reconfiguring rural development in the UK: objective 5b and the new rural governance', *Journal of Rural Studies*, vol 14, no 1, pp 27-39.

Warren, M.E. (2002) 'What can democratic participation mean today?', *Political Theory*, vol 30, no 5, pp 677-701.

Williams, C.C. (2003) 'Developing community involvement: contrasting local and regional participatory cultures in Britain and their implications for policy', *Regional Studies*, vol 37, no 5, pp 531-41.

Wilson, D. (1999) 'Exploring the limits of public participation in local government', *Parliamentary Affairs: A Journal of Comparative Politics*, vol 52, no 2, pp 246-59.

Young, I.M. (1990) *Justice and the politics of difference*, Princeton, NJ: Princeton University Press.

Young, I.M. (1996) 'Communication and the other: beyond deliberative democracy', in S. Benhabib (ed) *Democracy and difference: Contesting the boundaries of the political*, Princeton, NJ: Princeton University Press, pp 120-36.

Young, I.M. (2000) *Inclusion and democracy*, Oxford: Oxford University Press.

EIGHT

Among everyday makers and expert citizens

Henrik Bang

Introduction

All over the western world we have long been witnessing an individualisation of politics and a decline in the active support and membership of conventional modes of collective political organising through political parties, interest organisations, and (big) voluntary associations (Norris, 1999). Many stories have been written about the decline of civic engagement and the increasing numbers of individuals who are 'bowling alone' (Putnam, 1995; Boggs, 1997). Most stories describe how political participation as a collective activity has fallen prey to globalising market forces, transforming virtuous citizens into atomised individuals who are exploiting the state as a means to realise their own interests and values (Putnam, 1993; Braitwaite and Levis, 1998; Mouffe, 2000). Democratic governance, it is said, is undermined by consumer politics and other market-driven oddities such as 'spin doctors', fan democracy and celebrity politics (Bennett and Entman, 2001; Corner and Pels, 2003; van Zoonen, 2005). Democracy is making concessions to the market view of citizens as self-interested consumers and customers, who will punish government if it does not deliver the goods that they demand from it. In politics, we are witnessing a profound 'thinning' of social and political community, showing "the limitations of the deracinated solitary – he is alone" (Barber, 1998, p 49).

In the modern normative equation of individualisation, more market autonomy-less social solidarity, the many new, more individualised forms of citizenship appear (and must appear) to create a problem of free-riding. This threatens the exercise of 'strong' democracy in a normatively well-integrated state and civil society. This idea of common norms as the 'glue' of democracy still looms large in most participatory and deliberative approaches to citizenship. The worry is over the ongoing marketisation or individualisation of people in civil society that is said to undermine the pillars of virtuous citizenship, namely that:

(1) citizen activism expresses a collective enterprise for keeping the state accountable to the needs of civil society;
(2) citizen identity is essentially about the creation of strong, affective moral ties to the (national) social community, committing citizens to act normatively, responsibly and in the name of the common will.

This chapter will challenge both of these presumptions (Habermas, 1998).

Today, many – and probably most – new forms of citizen activism do not occur outside the political system in civil society. Rather, they take shape inside this system in various governance networks and partnerships between private, public and voluntary organisations, striving to make the production of political outcomes more effective through more heterarchical, communicative, participatory and deliberative modes of interaction and production (Zadek, 2001; McIntosh et al, 2004). I see this relocation of republican discourse into the exercise of political authority and leadership as evidence of a new expert citizenship, which we will call 'republican elitism', uncoupling republican values from democracy as we have come to know it. We have been studying new tendencies towards elite uncoupling among expert citizens in the neighbourhood of Inner Noerrebro in Copenhagen (Bang et al, 2000[1]). Of course, this neighbourhood is not representative, but it can give important insights as to where the new forms of citizenship may be leading us.

The challenge that republican elitism raises for democracy is the classical one of access and recognition (see Rawls, 1993). It requires certain professional skills and competences on behalf of individuals and groups, if they are to make a difference to the communication between elites. Hence, all those who either cannot, will not, or do not understand how to engage themselves in such a professionalised kind of citizenship between leaders or managers from public, private and voluntary organisations, will be excluded from it (Etzioni-Halevy, 1993, 1997). As Rebekah Sterling argued in Chapter Seven of this volume, this is a tendency which is characteristic of many governance networks and partnerships. The new republican elitism speaks the old words of democracy – deliberation, participation, common will, and so on – but it puts them only in the service of acquiring success or influence. I am highly sceptical of those who celebrate the growing influence of non-governmental organisations (NGOs) in governance as the victory of autonomous civil society. Of course, it does sound wonderful when Keane speaks of the expansion of new forms of voluntary organising in civil society at the global level, as revealing how

> global civil society is a haven of difference and identity – a space of many different, overlapping and conflicting moralities. Those who dwell within it have at least one basic thing in common: they have an ethical aversion to grandiose, pompous, power hungry actions of those who suppose, falsely that they are God, and try to act like God. The ethics of pluralism is not negotiable. (Keane, 2003, p 208; see Dower, 2003)

Nevertheless, the fact remains that the new partnerships between expert citizens reveal a new form of political authority at play in various fields or domains, ranging from the local to the global. Expert citizens manifest an intrusion of political authority into civil society, not something that is socially autonomous from that authority. Indeed, expert citizenship does reveal an ethics of pluralism that is neither hierarchical nor uniform. But this ethic is put to use by NGOs in order to govern more effectively by cooperating with other expert citizens.

I see the occurrence of the expert citizen as a functional necessity for a new kind of more pluralist, interactive, communicative and flatly-organised political authority of the emerging information society (Bang, 2003, 2004). However, the tendency of expert citizens to adopt a new republican elitism raises many new challenges for democracy that go well beyond the problem of free-riding. These have to do with the uncoupling of everyday political experiences from strategic communication among experts. Republican elitism shows a neglect of the 'small' political tactics of ordinary citizens and thereby of the difference that a self-reflexive politics of the ordinary can (and ought to) play for 'testing' and expanding the democratic imagination (Bang and Dyrberg, 2000, 2003).

The problem is not that expert activists are suppressing the 'weak' or reifying or distorting political communication. Rather, the problem is in their strategic communication they exclude certain conventional democratic values and practices in favour of those of success or influence.

Expert citizenship is probably a necessary political response to growing complexity and reflexivity in society. But one can recognise the importance of expert citizenship as a new kind of creative political rule and at the same time criticise it for not contributing sufficiently to political solidarity, which is something quite distinct from social solidarity. Political solidarity identifies an imagined discursive practice where everybody enjoys the right and possibility to make a difference.

Political solidarity does not rely on any kind of normative agreement on a common good. What it seeks is simply that that no one individual or group is excluded from being heard and from engaging in deliberation, precisely because everybody shares the same creative political potential for decision and action in the democratic imagination. Political solidarity means accepting and recognising that everybody has such creative capacity by virtue of their involvement in an authority relationship, as either senders or receivers of its politically communicated messages (Easton, 1947; see Benhabib, 1996). Therefore, governments, states, governance networks and political communities should concentrate not only on stopping free-riding, but also on overcoming the uncoupling that results from a self-appointed 'creative class' which hinders ordinary people from exercising their creative political capacities and thus from enjoying their rights and practising their freedoms.

First, this chapter will sketch the profile of the expert activist, then it will trace the ways in which what we termed the 'everyday maker' presents a new kind of political challenge. The everyday maker is a form of lay citizenship shaped by everyday experience. It is their experience which is being sought in a range of partnerships and governance networks in neighbourhoods, and it is they whom elites seek to 'empower' in new forms of collaborative governance. The everyday makers are a direct response to the development of elite attitudes among those who have replaced their old grass roots identity with a new professional expert activist identity. They consider knowing as doing, refusing to take on a professional, full-time or strategic citizen identity. They want to do things in their own way, right where they are, when they have the time or feel like it. Their engagement is more 'on and off' and 'hit and run' than that of the expert activist (Bang and Sørenson, 1997, 1999, 2001). Everyday makers do not shy away from being enrolled in strategic civil governance projects, but do so only if these give them the opportunity to also pursue their own 'small' tactics and exercise their creative capacities as 'ordinary' citizens. In what follows, the consequences of these two new political identities for studying political participation are discussed, then the chapter concludes by outlining how they might be interconnected in order to bring democracy back in.

Among expert citizens and everyday makers

Political decision-making in Copenhagen, as elsewhere in Denmark, is decentralised to local public institutions that enjoy relative autonomy (Bang et al, 2000). Voluntary organisations play a central part in the governing of a whole range of areas in the locality: they cooperate closely with institutions, the municipality and various street-level authorities in areas such as education, social problem-solving, immigrant integration, retraining of the unemployed, infrastructural planning and housing maintenance. Traditionally, the Inner Noerrebro is a stronghold of left-wing parties and grass roots movements fighting the system, but today this kind of collective and oppositional participation has been replaced partly by a new project-oriented kind of participation, indicating how:

- the political is growing increasingly personal and self-reflexive;
- civil engagement is couched increasingly in political networks rather than positioned against a hierarchy;
- participation is becoming structured around the choice of whether and when one will 'engage' in, and 'disengage' from, a given context;
- the desire and perception of necessity together drive the sense of engagement;
- ethics, personal integrity and mutual confidence appear as central elements in political life (see de Certeau, 1984; Beck et al, 1994).

Let us now look in more detail at the two new identities connected with this new kind of citizenship attitude towards participation in a late-modern society.

The expert citizen

Expert citizens are those who Hirst (1994, 2002) describes as the new professionals in voluntary associations, who feel they can do politics and make and implement policies quite as competently as the 'old' politicians and the corporatist systems. In Inner Noerrebro, expert citizens appear as a new (sub-)elite cooperating regularly with elites from both private and public organisations in the area. Their professionalism and cooperative attitude distinguish them from the old grass roots, which – more than anything else – drew their political identity from their antagonistic relationship to the authorities (Castells, 1997). As a major study from the 1980s phrased it:

> [T]he participants in the grassroots are angry. They feel
> that they are being stepped on by the authorities.... For a
> lot of them, it is as though the scales are falling from their
> eyes. Suddenly they see how the system hangs together
> and that, in reality, the politicians do not maintain the
> population's interests. Their level of engagement in the
> conflict is therefore very high. A sharp distinction between
> friends and enemies is made, where the friend is the one
> that contests the foundation of the organisation. (Gundelach,
> 1980, p 13)

However, in the 1990s a new kind of activist appeared that began to make a break with the oppositional identity of the older grass roots movements. As one activist notes: "Things also change. Just like I did twenty years ago." Like many other activists, Maria (as we shall call her) has experienced a decline in her ideological 'spirit of '68'. She no longer considers public authorities to be the self-given enemy. In relation to her own contributions to anti-racist struggles for integrating immigrants in the light of a comprehensive doctrine of social solidarity, she notes: "If you want to do anything today – if you really want to get something done – then it's not enough just to talk politics. The big challenge is to get things done."

The expert activist experiences, or interrogates, events and people less in regard to their rational meaning in an old oppositional identity than in relation to their existential meaning. They possess a project identity, comprising a cooperative attitude towards the local authorities, but not a legitimating one. Maria was one of the first examples of an expert citizen that we met who engaged in a variety of partnerships and governance networks at Inner Noerrebro. For her, voluntary political work is a matter of:

- having a wide conception of the political as a discursive construct;
- adopting a full-time, overlapping project identity as one's overall lifestyle;
- possessing the necessary expertise for exercising influence in cooperation with other elites;
- placing negotiation and dialogue before antagonism and opposition;
- considering oneself a part of 'the system' rather than external to it.

Another former grass roots activist had previously had a narrow notion of the political as focused on government and the state, but she was convinced now that being an activist in contemporary society meant being connected to the exercise of political power-knowledge at every level of the social. For her, 'the political' was less a matter of mirroring, representing or acting in the name of certain 'objective' interests than of discursive knowledge and power to create what counts as political reality for others:

> Often – if you choose to do so, in any case – it can have a political angle. That is the perspective I usually assume ... because I think politically. I often speak together with people who might not understand what is going on, but if I can give them a political definition of why things appear as they do, then the world suddenly appears differently for them.

Politics for the expert activist is a fusion of representation and participation in and through a strategic form of communication, where it is necessary to make one's expertise felt discursively upon the conduct of others. For them, success becomes a matter of being able to communicate strategically, reforming and utilising individual and collective conduct so that it might be amenable to one's influence. This discursive strategic capacity is developed in the various governance networks and partnerships in which they engage in cooperation with politicians, administrators, interest groups and the media.

Thus the expert citizen possesses a 'networking consciousness' about how in context A they have competence X, while in context B they have competence Y. They also feel that these couplings between contexts and competencies give them a more differentiated and precise image of their own role. Furthermore, the goal of their new role and identity as an expert citizen is no longer social solidarity, but political influence. What is of concern to them is no longer fighting the system as a 'constitutive other', but rather gaining access to the bargaining processes which go on between public authorities and various experts from private and voluntary organisations. To do so, the expert citizen knows that one must be as professional as the others, rather than meet them with some abstract ideology. As one of them phrases it:

> You've gotta be damned competent if you're going to be able to make them [the local authorities] budge. You've gotta be damned good, and you've gotta know what you're talking about before they're going to take the trouble to talk to you at all.

The critical potential still exists for the expert citizen, but it has different directions. The weakening of the antagonism between the political system and society does not mean that antagonism has disappeared. But the primary element is not, as was the case with the grass roots activists, to oppose 'the system' and keep it outside of the sphere of the social. New adversarial images crossing the state–civil society divide are emerging, and the criticism of the system becomes geared to making it an effective partner in day-to-day life, rather than an opponent (Heffen et al, 2000; Newman, 2001).

No doubt, expert citizens are a resource for the political governance of the social by providing a fund of knowledge about how to deal systematically with complex everyday problems of exclusion based on 'race', gender, sickness, poverty, and so on. However, the dilemma that the expert citizens constitutes for democracy is also obvious. It comes out clearly in this statement from one of them:

> One can achieve democracy only for those who are willing to engage themselves in it. And that is, then, where things will be made to happen, for those who can exercise it, who choose to exercise it. They will have frames within which they can act. For the others there will not be these opportunities.

'Democracy' becomes confined to those who possess the strategic faculties that the exercise of expert citizenship requires. However, this republican elitism, in which participation, deliberation and public reason become the prerogative of a new 'creative class', is challenged by another new political identity that we found at Inner Noerrebro: that of the 'everyday maker'.

The everyday maker

Civic engagement in Inner Noerrebro has become politicised to the extent that the dividing line is no longer between voluntary networks and the coercive state. Instead, a new tension has developed between expert citizens and everyday makers – a tension that the expert citizens were themselves the first to discover:

> The way I look at it, the young aren't any more egoistic than before. Rather, my experience is that the way you engage yourself and the way in which you show your solidarity are different. I've seen how young people over

the course of the last decade organise and involve themselves differently. The fact of the matter is that young people are actually very engaged. The thing is that they are engaged in ways that the older generations consider unconventional. It's often a matter of getting involved in a concrete project, and then engaging oneself 100% in it for a short period, and then they stop. They don't participate in the long term. People fail to take note of this fact concerning the engagement of young people today. I believe this is why they have a problem in the labour unions: they can't activate the young because the opportunities that they provide to get involved are ongoing – they last forever. And this feeling that 'there's no end to it' prevents the young people of today from getting involved.

Like expert citizens, everyday makers are project-oriented and want to deal with common concerns concretely and personally rather than abstractly and ideologically. Everyday makers do not feel defined by the state; neither do they see themselves as apathetic or opposed to it. They simply do not want to spend their precious time participating in formal political institutions. Those studying 'big' politics in the parliamentarian and corporatist arenas or 'big' oppositional social movements would simply assume that many everyday makers are 'apathetic'. Indeed, they often are in relation to 'big' politics. But just writing them off as apathetic would be to miss their crucial political argument, which is that "it's important that you're active where you are; and this is very political. I'm not too crazy about the big lines. In reality, I don't think they're particularly significant".

Everyday makers are by no means apathetic when it comes to their 'small' politics (see Marsh et al, 2003a, 2003b; Norris, 2004; Norris et al, 2004). One big challenge today concerns the issue of how to make formal institutions significant and relevant to everyday makers. However, their lack of interest in 'big' politics does not mean that they possess a narrow local identity. Typically, they think globally but want to act locally, because they want to do things by themselves, where they are, on their own terms and for their own purposes. Unlike the old grass roots activists, they show no interest in producing a new form of interest representation in advanced industrial democracies (Dalton and Kuechler, 1990, p 10). Their interest in party politics is minimal. As one of them states: "I vote for a party because that's the way the system is set up when I go to the ballot box when there's an election." Everyday makers consider it "natural to deal with things differently [than party politics]. It's more of a personal thing – I find that I become more engaged and more active when dealing with concrete things".

Everyday makers are highly sceptical of the organisational life of political parties. One of our respondents tried it for a short while, but found that politicians "praised dogmas rather than ideas. There was no debate. And I think that every tentative effort [to discuss ideas] only generated more of the same.... Generally, I don't like politicians very much".

Everyday makers are not happy with the old grass roots organisations either:

> As soon as we're dealing with bigger associations, then I don't believe [that they can sustain their internal democracy]. Associations reveal a tendency to pursue their own politics, and then we have little influence on what it is.

However, everyday makers do not wish to become expert activists. They draw a clear distinction within the realm of politics between elite networks and their own politics of the ordinary in the locality. They believe that lay involvement is valuable in itself as a way to develop oneself as a reflective being with a sense of commonality (Beck et al, 1994). As one of them said about his engagement in a parental board in his child's daycare institution, he is there "not to gain control of things but to feel engaged – also in the life of one's children". Furthermore, unlike the old grass roots activists, everyday makers are not afraid of mixing the more pleasurable and personal with the more serious and societal. As a young woman told us about her voluntary engagement in a local journal:

> I have tried to choose some things that combined that which I think is fun and that which I think is necessary. For example, I chose to get involved with layout work because I feel that it is something I would really like to learn. I think that could be exciting and relevant in relation to my education. And then I chose to get involved with the place I did because I think that it was a good magazine. A good cause. So I kind of tried to combine it, you know? And I think that is very good, so that you don't become self-righteous and so that you also feel that you get something out of it yourself.

The everyday maker is "not one of these full-time grass roots activists who are always going on weekend trips somewhere to discuss something". Sometimes they do not "think about anything else but how to cope with the normal run of things". Their engagement is of a much more 'roll on–roll off' nature than can be captured by Turner's (1990) old model for studying active and passive citizenship (see Figure 8.1). Here, participation is either active and society-driven or passive and state-driven. Furthermore, such participation is connected with a normatively derived identity which is either legitimating (consenting to state domination) or oppositional (struggling against state domination). But the everyday maker has a project identity, not a legitimating or oppositional one, and neither wants to be a full-time activist nor sees themselves as either a minimally involved or alienated citizen.

Thus everyday making is much more fluid, opaque, non-planned and impulsive than the old models of participation and strategic communications of expert citizens. Everyday makers consider their lay knowledge embodied in their activities. They do not separate knowledge and practice, which is why they insist on deciding themselves where to 'hit' and when to 'run', whether alone or in cooperation with others. Summing up, one can say that the credo of everyday making is:

- do it yourself;
- do it where you are;
- do it for fun, but also because you find it necessary;
- do it ad hoc or part time;
- do it concretely, instead of ideologically;
- do it self-confidently and show trust in yourself;
- do it with the system, if need be.

Figure 8.1: Active and passive participation

	PARTICIPATION	
	Active	Passive
IDENTITY	Society-driven, collective action	State-driven, individual behaviour
Legitimating	Representation groups	Minimal participants
Oppositional	Grass roots, social movements	Alienated non-participants

Source: Turner (1990, p 189)

The critical question for democracy then is: can this new credo be employed to overcome free-riding and stop the uncoupling of elites from laypeople by helping to create more viable and balanced relations of autonomy and dependence, and a mutual acceptance and recognition of difference?

Free-riding and uncoupling

Modern participation studies speak of the individualisation and project orientation of the new citizens operating outside the formal institutions as atomised citizenship (Pattie et al, 2004). The story of atomised citizenship comes in two versions. One is Putnam's by-now almost classical narrative about the undermining of social capital in the US. Putnam (1995, p 668) speaks about a "mysterious disengagement" which has "afflicted all echelons of our society". He sees a serious "downward trend in joining, trusting, voting, and newspaper reading". Social networking is in the process of being replaced by individuals who "bowl alone" (1995, p 674). The putative consequences of this development are many. Democracy is threatened by a situation where "[d]efection, distrust, shirking, exploitation, isolation, disorder, and stagnation intensify one another in a suffocating miasma of vicious circles" (Putnam, 1993, p 177). A decline in collective political involvement in state affairs will "powerfully affect the prospects for effective, responsive government" (1993, p 16). Weaker civic engagement in civil society leads to weaker governments that are less effective and responsive than they would have been otherwise. All in all, in Putnam's framework, we witness an era of great decay of both social and political trust and in normative commitment to sharing in collective concerns. We also see a direct fall in social engagement and political participation (see Boggs, 1997).

However, there is a more optimistic version of the story of atomised citizenship which is created in the aftermath of the social capital debate and is influenced by new studies of civic engagement and political participation. This version does not identify politics solely with what is going on in, or is directed at, democratic government; neither does it focus exclusively on orientations and activities that are oppositional and antagonistic to 'the system'. Such authors consider Putnam to be wrong in his description of individualised politics as involving a decline in political interest and involvement as such. In this vein, Norris et al identify:

[A] growing channel of political expression used for the legitimate articulation of demands in a democratic state, and a form of activism that has evolved and expanded over the years to supplement and complement existing organizations in civil society. (2004, p 20; see Norris, 2004)

Similarly, Pattie et al point to new modes of

micro-political participation [as] actions designed to influence indirect agents of the state in the day-to-day world. For parents this means trying to influence their children's education in school, for patients it means trying to influence their medical treatment, or for the employed it means trying to influence their working conditions. Given that the state is becoming less and less a direct service provider and more of an overseer and regulator, this is an aspect of politics which is growing in importance. (2004, p 266)

Yet, even though many today would disagree with Putnam's description of a decline in participation, most would still agree that citizens have become increasingly atomised and behave increasingly according to market logic, voting more with their feet than on the basis of public deliberation and dialogue with one another. Here, everyday makers appear as atomised political consumers, the only positive quality of which is that they allow for the exercise of political power through the plebiscite of the pocketbook and, in so doing, bring more efficiency and quality to policy (Chambers and Costain, 2000, p 70). The negative aspect of this increasingly market-wise citizenship is that it fragments and trivialises the public sphere, turning democratic debate and opinion-making into a spectacle performed by competing political celebrities from state, market and civil society (McKee, 2005). Hence, modernity is increasingly emptied of its normative content. Egoism is triumphing over solidarity. The struggle for 'our' good life is being replaced by a quest for 'my' good life. Individuals no longer feel obliged to their social and political communities but simply want to consume and be entertained.

Given this modern view of political participation as stretched between 'economic man' and 'normative society' the problem that atomised citizenship raises for democracy is, above all, one of free-riding on the collective efforts of others to solve common concerns. Now, one does not doubt that free-riding, which must result if the gap between individual calculation and social morality becomes too large, is an important problem requiring serious consideration in contemporary society. However, as we have seen, the new forms of political participation unfolding outside the established boundaries of modern society do not only (or even primarily) manifest this tension between an individualising market and a socialising civil society.

Neither expert citizens nor everyday makers fit into the old participatory schemes. They do not believe that representative democracy can be rescued, either by strengthening steering from above, or by accumulating more and more social capital from below. Their strategies and tactics of involvement reveal a practical alternative to Putnam's conceptual strategy for combining 'strong government' and 'thick community'. Although they do vote and keep themselves informed about 'big politics', primarily they do not gain their political identities from being citizens of the state or of an autonomous civil society, but from being ordinarily engaged in the construction of networks and locales for the political governance of the social. Both expert citizens and everyday makers are much more interested in enhancing their personal and common capacities for self-governance and co-governance, right where they are, than in submitting themselves to an abstract social norm or mode of state citizenship. They prefer a 'thin' form of democratic political community that allows for the reciprocal acceptance and recognition of difference (Dryzek, 2000). They also consider 'strong', effective and responsive government from above to be a permanent threat.

Both everyday makers and expert activists would reject the view that politics is the prerogative of 'strong' politicians and virtuous citizens. Further, they would reject the idea that dislocation, disagreement, struggle, and so on, automatically signify that we are "cursed with vertically structured politics, a social life of fragmentation and isolation, and a culture of distrust" (Putnam, 1993, p 15). Rather, they would insist that a political culture of trust involves acceptance of profound disagreements and struggle.

Hence, to call expert citizens and everyday makers either market or civil society-driven forces, fighting against the state or seeking to keep it responsive to their needs, is merely to neglect:

(1) how citizenship is becoming uncoupled from state, market and civil society as an increasingly professional kind of political networking or partnering between elites from the private, public and voluntary domain;
(2) how this uncoupling of citizenship from traditional conceptions of democracy establishes a problem of exclusion.

Such exclusion applies to all those who cannot, or will not, participate in the professional political discourses of the new republican elitism. What expert citizens really do is to envelop old notions of democracy in a new form of elite political governance of the social, and what everyday makers react against is not the state, but this new communicative steering authority that they meet in various governance networks and partnerships.

Conclusion: connecting culture governance and everyday making

Free-riding is neither *the* core problem of democracy nor *the* key to studying citizenship in the emerging information society of reflexive modernity. There is another core problem of exclusion at play here: how increasingly professional political deliberation, participation and cooperation uncouples citizenship from the politics of the ordinary, which is also at the heart of democracy. It is argued that the result is an erosion of political capital, in terms of both a declining trust in representative political institutions and a lack of recognition of the creative potentials of laypeople in their ordinary political practices.

Democratic language has been taken over by the new republican elitism's steering ideology of effectiveness through ongoing dialogue, pluralisation and empowerment (Zadek, 2001; Dower, 2003; Fischer, 2003; McIntosh et al, 2004). One intriguing feature of political citizenship today is exactly that it reveals how strategically communicating elites 'above', 'below' or 'within' the nation-state systematically employ the old democratic values in their efforts to rule various politics of scales from the global to the local more successfully. These elites do not replace in any way the old representative institutions and administrative apparatus of the nation-state, but they do contribute to their qualitative transformation through various rescaling processes, complementing representative democracy and bureaucracy with a new discursive aspect.

Leaders and managers from all kinds of organisations have found out that, in order to succeed in the emerging information society, their systems must be more open, dialogical, interactive and flatly organised within their strategic communication than was the case in the industrialist society. They recognise that they can no longer control themselves and their environments directly from the 'top-down' as a unified steering centre (Newman, 2001). They must govern much more indirectly by getting more and more of their members to assume an active and independent co-responsibility for their effective rule

(Bang, 2003). I call this new kind of political rule 'culture governance' (Bang, 2004), because it operates at close range in the culture, communicating that it wants to talk openly and share with people rather than to talk down to them or preach for them (Bang and Dyrberg, 2003). Culture governance operates as an open and non-coercive form of strategic communication that enters into cooperation and dialogue with people in their different 'lifeworlds', in order to enable them to help in governance by governing themselves.

Culture governance is intrinsic to the political conception of the expert activist. It is a kind of political rule which is based on constructing political identities rather than seeking legitimation from them (see also Michael Saward in Chapter Nine of this volume). It gains its successes (and failures) from empowering and educating ever more individuals and groups to engage freely in its networks. It presents itself as providing a new discursive arena, alongside the parliamentarian and corporatist arenas, for making firms more socially responsible, administration less bureaucratic and voluntary organising more politically effective. Culture governance is politicising both the private, the administrative and the voluntary and as such stands out in sharp contrast to the 'old' democratic logics of market, state and civil society.

As has been argued, today there is a tendency for culture governance to contribute to political exclusion. The spread of the logic of strategic communication to 'big' politics, mediatising and professionalising the official public sphere as an expert 'spectacle' between top politicians, media gurus, spin doctors and other political celebrities (Bennett and Entman, 2001) removes laypeople even further from exercising their creative political capacities *as* laypeople. Even in their most 'strong' and self-reliant versions, laypeople are excluded in growing numbers from partaking, even indirectly, in the constitution of 'big' politics and policy except at election times. Thus western political systems are experiencing a serious coupling problem, which in the long run may threaten not only their legitimacy but also their ability to handle complexity in an efficient and democratic manner (Etzioni-Halevy, 1993).

Does the uncoupling of participation and deliberation from democracy suggest that democratic and competitive elitists have always been right in assuming that the idea of public democracy is no more than a utopian fiction? Or, by focusing on the day-to-day experiences and actions of laypeople (see Marsh et al, 2003a, 2003b), can we find political spaces of potential public relevance which refute the elitist hypothesis as one-sided and neglecting the necessary role of laypeople in any authority relationship? To answer such questions means recognising that the relation between political authorities and laypeople can no longer be described exclusively as a relationship between elites and masses. Everyday makers are not masses, and expert citizens do not treat them as masses but as reflexive individuals (Beck et al, 1994; Lash et al, 1996). As such they indicate that the conventional governing models of hierarchy ('state'), solidarity ('civil society') and 'anarchy' ('market') are no longer sufficient to provide political systems with the wholeness, coherence and efficiency that they need (Bang, 2003). What is needed is discursive cooperation and networking across old boundaries in order to negotiate around common concerns through a common democratic imagination. Furthermore, despite their free-riding tendencies in relation to 'big' politics, everyday makers do challenge elitist rule, by proclaiming that they can do something for the solving of common concerns.

However, if everyday makers are to become a political resource for democracy, the new expert activists must be convinced that their culture governance could become more effective if they committed themselves to listening and learning from laypeople. They must recognise the potential democratic value of enrolling laypeople in networks and partnerships on their own terms rather than submitting them to elite goals of influence or success. March and Olsen (1995) suggest that a revitalisation of popular democracy would require a new kind of political leadership, which would systematically:

- contribute to the development of democratic identities for both citizens, politicians and administrators;
- add to the development of political resources and political competencies for both citizens and other political actors;
- be democratically responsible;
- create possibilities for democratic learning and democratic experiments.

These values constitute a minimal set of rules for the democratic interaction between elites and non-elites in the context of new forms of culture governance. However, they rely on the appearance of new political identities and new arenas for negotiating, discussing and practising common concerns. A commitment to participation, public dialogue and deliberation does not make, ipso facto, the practice of social governance democratic in nature.

Note

[1] Based on the project 'Democracy from Below' (see Bang and Sørensen, 1999, 2001).

References

Bang, H.P. (ed) (2003) *Governance as social and political communication*, Manchester: Manchester University Press.

Bang, H.P. (2004) 'Culture governance: governing reflexive modernity', *Public Administration*, vol 82, no 1, pp 159-90.

Bang, H.P and Dyrberg, T.B. (2000) 'Governance, self-representation and democratic imagination', in M. Saward (2000) *The democratic imagination*, London: Routledge, pp 146-61.

Bang, H.P and Dyrberg, T.B. (2003) 'Governing at close range', in H.P. Bang (ed) *Governance as social and political communication*, Manchester: Manchester University Press, pp 222-41.

Bang, H.P. and Sørensen, E. (1997) *Fra Græsrødder til hverdagsmagere* (*From grass roots to everyday maker*), Copenhagen: Department of Political Science.

Bang, H.P. and Sørensen, E. (1999) 'The EM: a new challenge to democratic governance', *Administrative Theory and Praxis*, vol 21, no 3, pp 325-42.

Bang, H.P. and Sørensen, E. (2001) 'The everyday maker: building political rather than social capital', in P. Dekker and E.M. Uslaner (eds) *Social capital and participation in everyday life*, London: Routledge, pp 148-61.

Bang, H.P., Hansen, A.D. and Hoff, J. (2000) *Demokrati Fra Neden* (*Democracy from below*), Copenhagen: Djoef.

Barber, B.R. (1998) *A place for us*, New York, NY: Hill and Wang.

Beck, U., Giddens, A. and Lash, S. (1994) *Reflexive modernisation*, Cambridge: Polity Press.

Benhabib, S. (ed) (1996) *Democracy and difference: Contesting the boundaries of the political*, Princeton, NJ: Princeton University Press.

Bennett, W.L. and Entman, R.M. (eds) (2001) *Mediated politics*, Cambridge: Cambridge University Press.

Boggs, C. (1997) 'The great retreat: decline of the public sphere in late twentieth-century America', *Theory and Society*, vol 21, no 26, pp 741-80.

Braitwaite, V. and Levis, M. (eds) (1998) *Trust and governance*, New York, NY: Russell Sage Foundation.

Castells, M. (1997) *The power of identity*, Oxford: Blackwell.

Chambers, S. and Costain, A. (2000) *Deliberation, democracy, and the media*, London: Rowman & Littlefield.

Corner, J. and Pels, D. (2003) *Media and the restyling of politics*, London: Sage Publications.

Dalton, R.J. and Kuechler, M. (eds) (1990) *Challenging the political order*, Cambridge: Polity Press.

de Certeau, M. (1984) *The practice of everyday life*, Berkeley, CA: University of California Press.

Dower, N. (2003) *An introduction to global citizenship*, Edinburgh: Edinburgh University Press.

Dryzek, J.S. (2000) 'Discursive democracy vs. liberal constitutional-ism', in M. Saward (ed) *The democratic imagination*, London: Routledge, pp 66-78.

Easton, D. (1947) 'The theory of the elite', unpublished doctoral dissertation, Harvard University.

Etzioni-Halevy, E. (1993) *The elite connection*, Cambridge: Polity Press.

Etzioni-Halevy, E. (1997) *Classes and elites in democracy and democratiza-tion: A collection of readings*, New York, NY and London: Garland Publishing.

Fischer, F. (2003) *Reframing public policy: Discursive politics and deliberative practices*, Oxford: Oxford University Press.

Gundelach, P. (1980) *Græsrødder er seje* (*Grass roots are cool*), Aarhus: Forlaget Politica.

Habermas, J. (1998) *The inclusion of the other*, Cambridge: Polity Press.

Heffen, O., Kickert, W.J.M. and Thomassen, J.A. (2000) *Governance in modern societies*, Dordrecht: Kluwer Academic Publishers.

Hirst, P. (1994) *Associative democracy*, Cambridge: Polity Press.

Hirst, P. (2002) *Renewing democracy through associations*, ECPR Joint Sessions.

Keane, J. (2003) *Global civil society?*, Cambridge: Cambridge University Press.

Lash, S., Szerszynski, B. and Wynne, B. (eds) (1996) *Risk, environment and modernity*, London: Sage Publications.

McIntosh, M., Waddock, S. and Kell, G. (2004) *Learning to talk*, Sheffield: Greenleaf Publishing.

McKee, A. (2005) *The public sphere: An introduction*, Cambridge: Cambridge University Press.

March, J.G. and Olsen, J.P. (1995) *Democratic governance*, New York, NY: The Free Press.

Marsh, D., O'Toole, T. and Jones, S. (2003a) 'Tuning out or left out? Participation and non-participation among young people', *Contemporary Politics*, vol 9, no 1, pp 45-61.

Marsh, D., O'Toole, T. and Jones, S. (2003b) *Political liberty cuts both ways: The politics of non-participation among young people*, London: The Political Quarterly Publishing.

Mouffe, C. (2000) *The democratic paradox*, London: Verso.

Newman, J. (2001) *Modernising governance: New Labour, policy and society*, London: Sage Publications.

Norris, P. (1999) *Critical citizens*, Oxford: Oxford University Press.

Norris, P. (2004) *Young people and political activism*, Cambridge, MA: John F. Kennedy School of Government, Harvard University.

Norris, P. et al (2004) *Who demonstrates? Anti-state rebels, conventional participants or everyone?*, Cambridge, MA: John F. Kennedy School of Government, Harvard University.

Pattie, C., Seyd, P. and Whiteley, P. (2004) *Citizenship, democracy and participation in contemporary Britain*, Cambridge: Cambridge University Press.

Putnam, R.D. (1993) *Making democracy work*, Princeton, NJ: Princeton University Press.

Putnam, R.D. (1995) 'Tuning in, tuning out: the strange disappearance of social capital in America', *Political Science and Politics*, vol 6, no 1, pp 664-83.

Rawls, J. (1993) *Political liberalism*, New York, NY: Columbia University Press.

Turner, B.S. (1990) 'Outline of a theory of citizenship', *Sociology*, vol 24, no 2, pp 189-217.

van Zoonen, L. (2005) *Entertaining the citizen*, New York, NY: Rowman & Littlefield.

Zadek, S. (2001) *The civil corporation*, London: Earthscan.

NINE

Governance and the transformation of political representation

Michael Saward

Introduction

As Janet Newman points out in the Introduction to this volume, the shift in styles of politics in western countries from the more formal and hierarchical to the more informal and network-based – from government to governance – brings with it the need to question many of our received assumptions about politics and the state. This chapter sketches some of the traces of new kinds of political imaginary which change the meaning of political representation. Rules and practices of representation are fundamental to democratic politics. The legitimacy of policies and actors primarily rests on the extent to which they legitimately represent, or can successfully claim to represent, some group or larger set of social interests. The shifts in styles of governance from state-centric and more formal modes to plural and often informal modes of engagement with citizens at local, national and supranational levels raise important new questions about the scope and legitimacy of traditional notions of political representation. In the spaces of public–private partnerships, stakeholder involvement and new, more direct forms of citizen engagement, is there a transformed notion of political representation emerging? Can more groups, people and styles of activity count as 'representative' and, if so, what does this mean for the way in which we understand the term and more broadly for the legitimating role that representation plays in democracy?

The chapter will proceed as follows. First, it will critically appraise conventional approaches to political representation, suggesting in particular that they have ignored the process of constituting the represented which is so critical to political practice. In this sense, conventional approaches have overlooked the aesthetic and cultural aspects of representation, and the ways in which these are them-selves deeply political. Second, accepting the constitutive role of representative practices for the sense of identity that political actors bring to the political process adds impetus to the need to look at a range of would-be representatives beyond the conventional electoral arena. What claims can appointed local or other officials, local activists or participants in public–private partnerships make to be representative, and how might we appraise and evaluate them?

Finally, this takes us to the heart of the challenge that modern governance poses for political representation. As other chapters have documented, processes of governance seep into a wider array of contexts and embrace a wider array of actors. We are not dealing here with a simple transfer of 'representative' politics from one type or domain to another, but rather a significant shift in the primary political sense of representation as a practice and concept.

Traditional thinking about political representation

If Pierre (2000) is right in arguing that the most important shift expressed by the notion of a change in focus from 'government' to 'governance' involves a move from more state-centric, formal steering to more hybrid, informal and (would-be) cooperative strategies and perspectives, then traditional notions of political representation face a double challenge. The first is to the strongly electoral focus of much of the writing and attention that is paid to representation, as both an idea and a practice. The second is a challenge which was already there in the traditional literature but which becomes more critical within a governance framework: how to acknowledge and to take more seriously the role of representation in actually constituting identities and issues, rather than merely reflecting pre-existing ones.

Let us deal with the second of these issues and return to the issue of electoral focus in a moment. In political science there is an enormous literature on political representation, which can be traced back over many decades. In some ways it is unfair to generalise on such a complex and multifaceted set of arguments, but there is one key limiting factor in most discussions which seems to me to be so strong that we might almost call it a persistent blind spot. That factor is the strong focus in this larger literature on the make-up and character of the representative, and the closely-related overlooking of the make-up and character (and ultimately the constitution) of the represented.

The nature of this blind spot can be illustrated effectively if we look briefly at the single most influential text on the theory of political representation in Anglo–American work at least over the past 30 years, the classic *The concept of representation* by Hanna Pitkin (1968). Pitkin's book is complex and dense, and I cannot even begin to explore it in depth here. However, the relevant single point – because it defines the basic approach to political representation in recent decades – is that the approach that Pitkin adopts is unidirectional and electoral, and on both counts it has real limitations when it comes to understanding political representation in the more complex and differentiated processes of contemporary governance.

In essence, Pitkin places the focus on the character and composition of the representative, not the represented. For example, representatives could be conceived of as being authorised by the represented, or as being accountable to them or acting in their substantive interests. Less often (and for Pitkin, less centrally and interestingly), they could stand for the represented symbolically, as a monarch might stand for or symbolise a nation. Her own preference – in the normative political philosophy vein in which she was writing – was for a conception of the representative as acting in the substantive interests of the citizen. Two points in particular stand out for our purposes. The first is that Pitkin gives virtually no time to the idea that the represented might be something other than known, given, transparent in composition, meaning and interest. Her theory is unidirectional – all the flows of interest are from the known represented to the question of how to understand and to constitute the representative. What does such unidirectional analysis miss? In a nutshell, it can miss (or underestimate, and therefore fail to pay due attention to) the ways in which the represented are not pre-given in composition in character: the extent to which the represented needs to be constituted and defined and understood *within* the process of political representation itself, and not somehow apart from or prior to it. There is a point to be made about the analysis of electoral representation: traditional geographical constituencies do not have characteristics, faultlines or policy preferences which can be simply (or even not so simply) read-off by would-be elected representatives. The latter, and their parties and advisers, need to and do play an active part in selecting the aspects of their constituencies about which they talk and on which they focus. They will seek to shift and change preferences structures in constituencies by highlighting some aspects of the lives of voters – moral issues connected to family life, for example, or the tax burden – rather than others. They will seek to show or tell constituents what they (the constituents) think, or should think, about the issues that are selected for focus. In short, an electoral constituency is, and needs to be, constituted, constructed out of the raw materials of peoples and places.

Why does this matter? The main reason is that in principle, the search for who or what type of individual (or party) may be an appropriate – one might say more strongly, an authentic – representative of a given constituency can have a definite answer if the character of who is to be represented is assumed to be fixed, or at least knowable. But if we do not make such a 'transparency assumption' and take on board fully the view that constituencies can reasonably be conceived, interpreted and constructed in different ways for different political purposes, then the issue of who is the real, or appropriate, or indeed authentic, representative becomes more problematic (and in some ways more interesting). There is no essence of the represented that we can trace directly to the character of the would-be representative. We are left, in the end, with a variety of *claims* to be representative, but each of the claims will be partial and contestable.

On one level, this is merely to pose a challenge to the traditional electoral notion of political representation. But overlooking the constitution of the represented exposes an even greater and more distinctive gap in the theory, as the emphasis shifts from the traditional notion of a fixed, territorial and formal electoral 'constituency' to new, more fluid and sporadic conceptions and invocations of political constituencies. New modes of non-electoral citizen engagement and interaction with policymakers and managers (such as those discussed in the previous three chapters of the volume) challenge received notions of public and private in terms of who the makers and recipients of policy are. This opens up new domains in which representation happens, or is claimed, by actors and groups which seek legitimacy and access in these new governance arrangements. Like elected councillors in many local authorities in the UK, 'public' actors offer themselves as enablers rather than providers of policy, and in so doing they co-opt 'private' actors, for example, from voluntary associations and community groups, to play formal and informal roles as policy participants. In such contexts, the 'private' actors can lay claim to being representatives too, although not of the traditional electoral variety. Further, often these new domains of representative politics are characterised by a flexibility and looseness of identity; for example, class is no longer the primary political faultline and repository of political identity. Age, lifestyle, ethnicity, culture and religion are competing bases of political identity, and are therefore also competing grounds for claims to be legitimately representative of wider social interests. So, in sum, not only are there grounds to emphasise much more than traditional approaches to the constitutive character of representation, we need also to extend the scope and spaces of that insight to contexts which are non-electoral and to plural perspectives and identities.

Electoral representation, in its varied permutations, remains rightly at the core of a discussion of political representation. But claims to be representative, the pressing of new political issues and concerns, and the constitution and presentation of new combinations of people and interests (new 'constituencies'), occur more often and insistently. Such claims demand attention beyond as well as within the electoral context. It has become desirable to consider a wide array of claims to be representative, both electoral and non-electoral; but doing so involves moving beyond the boundaries of the categories and assumptions about representation that were set for the contemporary era by Pitkin's analysis.

Even radical recent attempts to rethink representation assume that the architecture of conventional electoral democracy remains the representative baseline. Jane Mansbridge (2003), for example, has recently advocated a shift in perspective from 'singular, aggregatively-oriented, and district-based' criteria for representation, to what she calls plural, deliberatively-oriented and systemic criteria. However, her valuable effort remains within an orthodox framework. For example, even when writing of how some citizens regard elected representatives from other constituencies as *their* representatives because of their 'race', sexual orientation or opinions, she speaks the language of 'surrogacy', implying that the 'real' electoral constituency representative remains the baseline and that legitimate representatives are always elected. Mansbridge's impressive account is more realistic than many conventional political science accounts of representation with regards to how difficult achieving formal accountability really is in systems of representation, and recognises accordingly how important deliberation among legislators and their constituents is with respect to the quality of political representation. On these grounds, her arguments take the debates forward; representation and accountability need to be seen as a matter of constant exchange, dialogue, education and adjustment between the representative and the represented. But for all this, her argument remains confined within an electoral paradigm, at a time when representative politics – the politics of making, and attempting to substantiate, representative claims – encompasses but also transcends electoral politics.

Political representation is a process that involves the constitution of the identity of the representative *and* of the represented. In the context of new styles of governance, it is misguided to overlook the claims and instances of political representation that are not based in an immediate way on the mechanism of election. If the new governance is about government happening in ways and places that are not contained within formal, hierarchical and bounded conceptions of representative politics, then these are the directions that theories of representation need to take in order that they might keep up with the realities of contemporary governance. The following sections will look briefly at the questions of the new spaces, identities and styles of governance, respectively.

The currency of political representation

What is political representation? The literature on the subject dissects different types and roles in some detail. Generally, a representative is regarded as one who stands for or acts for an (absent) other. They may do so by being a delegate – acting on the express wishes of the represented – or a trustee, acting in the perceived best interests of the represented. Further debates about legitimate representation also revolve around whether a representative needs to share social characteristics with the represented, or whether representation is a matter of representing attitudes and ideas rather than identities.

In my work a different perspective is adopted that problematises the whole notion of representation. At the most general level, it is argued that representation is not a fact, but rather a process that involves the making of *claims* to be representative. One does not act or stand for another, but rather claims to do these things. And, for example, that claim may be based on prioritising a delegate or trustee role (or some combination of the two).

A representative claim is a claim to represent, or to know what represents, the interests of someone or something. Representative claims can be accepted or rejected, implicit or explicit, electoral or non-electoral, and so on. Seeing representation as an economy of claim-making provides a frame through which to examine how representative politics is practised and reshaped within a context of contemporary governance. It also facilitates efforts to tap into the sense in which representative politics is ubiquitous: there is no place beyond representation (Prendergast, 2000). This does not mean that there is nothing 'real'. Rather, it means that people and things are not invested with meaning without representation. It also does not mean that the word does not have meanings, but rather that those meanings have complex genealogies. As makers and receivers of representative claims of varied sorts, we are simultaneously inside and outside of representation: if someone claims to represent me, they necessarily portray both themself as an actor with particular characteristics and abilities, and myself as a different character with interests which need to be spoken for. Both of us are caught up in depictions, portraits or representations. As the philosopher Jacques Derrida has written, 'man' is now "not only someone who has representations, who represents himself, but also someone who himself represents something or someone" (1982, p 316). Men and women are "interpreted throughout according to the structure of representation.... Structured by representation, the represented subject is also a representing subject" (1982, p 315).

Contemporary governance is about many things. One of them is how a range of actors and institutions that are not elected exercise political power. Indeed, many non-elected actors, inside and outside the state, make claims to be representative. Getting such claims accepted may involve a different sort of process from standing for election, but in polities where so much negotiation about, participation in and administration of policy is conducted beyond clearly electoral arenas, they deserve serious attention.

New spaces of governance and representation

Public–private partnerships, new consultative mechanisms, new participative forums such as citizens' juries, marketisation and stakeholder engagement are among the key mechanisms at stake in the remaking of governance. One thread that runs through such developments is that more 'unconventional' political actors take their places within decisional or implementational processes, at local, national and supranational levels of governance: pressure groups, individual citizens, businesses, and so on. Complexity increases with the wider array of actors, the varied roles set for them and which they play, and the range of new and hybrid forums in which participation occurs. Against this background there is a wide variety of actors who may be representative or, rather, who may make claims to be representative, and who may do so on grounds that differ substantially from traditional formal and hierarchical conceptions of electoral representative relationships.

As Janet Newman suggests in the Introduction to this volume, narratives of globalisation have been central to accounts of governance change. A range of actors and organisations operating across and above national boundaries claim to be representative of different global and local interests, and in ways that differ markedly from the types of claims that traditional state representatives make. The point will be illustrated briefly through the example of stakeholder representation – a relatively new form of non-electoral representation of interests at the global and other levels which has risen to prominence because the governance of international problems, not least environmental ones, required new actors and processes in complex new spaces (for a fuller account, see Backstrand and Saward, 2004).

Processes of stakeholder representation, such as those at the 2002 World Summit for Sustainable Development in Johannesburg, can be seen as instances of creative rethinking of what representation is, and who can do it. The purpose is not to "replace states but rather find more effective and more legitimate ways of addressing the shortcomings of exclusive territorial governance" (Eckersley, 2004, p 193). This space can lead to a renewal and reinvention of democratic governance: new devices, sequences, decision rules, procedures and modes of representation. Of course, because there is no 'world state', one might anticipate a complex array of hybrid multipolar processes, which are more or less institutionalised, to operate at regional and global levels even more than at national and local levels.

The model of stakeholder representation is a creative set of possibilities rather than a fixed model; as such it is a set of practices that constitute constituencies. It does so within a context where the topography of governance is changing, with new emerging spaces of politics (institutional void) without any predetermined rules. In the governance process in which people deliberate, political community and meaningful participation is created (Hajer, 2003, p 89). Depending on the devices and their sequencing, policymaking procedures create a sense of a 'community of fate' among people who had never (or only dimly) conceived of themselves to be part of the same community (Hajer, 2003, p 97; Saward, 2003). Stakeholding is suitable in the context of governance with overlapping 'communities of fate' that do not respect territorial boundaries. Global environmental threats highlight the need for those affected to have a say in defining and addressing them – bringing what has been called the 'all-affected principle' to bear on deliberative and decisional procedures (Saward, 2000).

We commonly think of democratic mechanisms as governmental and permanent. There is a strong case, not least an environmental and global one, for shifting our attention to non-governmental and temporary or sporadic mechanisms (Saward, 2000). This is not the most influential perspective in new models of global governance; Held's (1995) influential model of cosmopolitan democracy, for example, is a proposal for replication of governmental permanence at the global level, an approach that seems at once both utopian and over-familiar. The familiar ways of thinking of democratic mechanisms are familiar because we are used to thinking in relatively fixed and territorial terms. Interesting alternatives emerge when we begin to think of new mechanisms which might help us to address issues which are changeable, perhaps temporary, sporadic in their manifestations and which constitute and define new political communities (of fate) across national boundaries. The Rio and Johannesburg summits of 1992 and 2002, for example, and especially the stakeholder practices at their core, represent a shift from the permanent to the temporary and more flexible. The complex and pressing nature of the issues discussed arguably requires more extensive grounds or bases for political representation than merely involving delegates of various states and United Nations (UN) agencies. The difficulty of obtaining agreement on how to address issues of global environmental governance and how to follow through on actions perhaps demands involvement from varied groups beyond states. On these and other counts, formal and informal stakeholder representation comes to the fore as a governance mechanism within the larger sporadic structures. Both the definition of the problems and the formulation and implementation of 'solutions' pose such a degree of difficulty that wider inclusion of interests, inclusion that 'digs down' more into functional and other civil society and cross-national affected groups, becomes desirable and even necessary.

Stakeholder governance is one example of new spaces of political representation. Sometimes the delegates of business, indigenous people, farmers, women and others taking part in the stakeholder forums at the World Summit were elected, but mostly were not. They stood mostly for functional interests rather than territorial ones. The style of legitimacy that they could claim arose more from the fact of their official participation in the UN-sponsored process than formal accountability to a specified group membership (or constituency). Their legitimacy – such as it was, and certainly it was subject to contestation – also had a pragmatic basis: these were broad social interests whose participation was seen by the UN agencies and many state participants as essential to the practical workability of any agreed outcomes. In that sense, their participation was an acknowledgment of the limits of the writ of states and of the power of state actors whose legitimacy rested on more traditional electoral foundations. Are the so-called major groups co-opted, or do they have real influence? Are stakeholders really representative of the interests for which they (claim to) speak? There is room for argument on these and a range of other points. But the key factor for our present purposes is this: a shift towards a more multipolar and participative process of governance opens up spaces for new types of representative claim, and in turn the process serves to legitimise those claims, partly by formalising them.

The stakeholder model resonates with deliberative models of democracy. It is worth noting that examples such as the World Summit stakeholder forums are built around the notion of deliberation, carrying a democratic legitimacy in its own right. This has been a major theme in democratic theory for nearly two decades now (Dryzek, 2000; Saward, 2000). The principle of stakeholding is central to the idea of a transnational democracy: those affected by, causing or having stake in the issue at hand should have a voice in its resolution (McGrew, 2002, p 223). Stakeholding is suitable to governance with overlapping 'communities of fate' that do not respect territorial boundaries.

The deliberative account of democratisation of the world order is based on the premise that democracy is more about deliberation, reasoned argument and public reflection as much as (and on some accounts, more than) voting and aggregation. The deliberative governance model moves beyond the conventional language of representational politics. The key is to encourage vital transnational public spheres rather than institutional reform or democratic constitution of the world polity. This means relaxing the necessity for a homogenous global constituency or 'demos', and assuming that legitimacy can be enhanced through deliberation rather than an international equivalent of constituency-based national elections. The argument is that stakeholder democracy taps into the strengths of a deliberative emphasis, in that the latter is more deeply compatible with the structures and processes of global governance as compared to an aggregative or conventional electoral politics.

New identities in governance and representation

As suggested above, in representative politics, portrayals of constituencies, the nation or voters' interests are just that: portrayals (Spivak, 1988, p 276). There is no self-presenting subject whose essential character, desires and interests are transparent, beyond representation, evident enough to be 'read-off' from their appearance or behaviour. Politicians often claim to be able to read-off constituency and national interests, to have a unique 'hotline' to voters' real wants and needs. But the fact is that they can only do so after first deploying an interpretative frame containing an imaginative construct or portrait of their constituents. To speak for others – as elected representatives do, of course – is to construct portraits of the represented that bring selected character traits and the interests of the latter into some focus. Linda Alcoff puts the point well:

> In both the practice of speaking for as well as the practice of speaking about others, I am engaging in the act of representing the other's needs, goals, situation, and in fact, *who they are*. I am representing them as such and such … I am participating in the construction of their subject-positions. This act of representation cannot be understood as founded on an act of discovery wherein I discover their true selves and then simply relate my discovery. (1991, p 9; emphasis in original)

The view presented here suggests that the political science sense of representation – someone standing for or acting for someone else – requires that attention be paid also to representation in the cultural studies sense: the making of depictions or portrayals of others. To act for someone is unavoidably to portray them in a certain way as well.

If a portrait or a representation of constituency is a precondition for representative action, then we can see that that portrait has to be constructed – it is a key ingredient in the construction of the constituency. Nobody – critics, political representatives, academics – can just 'report' on external events and phenomena as if the latter are reliably knowable, transparent. Elected politicians construct verbal and visual images of their constituencies and their countries (among other things). Constituencies are 'hard-working', 'good, honest folk', 'family-oriented', 'patriots'. At least, one might want to insist on the 'mutual constitution' of representative and constituents (see Young, 2000). Both are, in Seitz's words, "the effect of a practice" (1995, p 144), the practice of representation itself: "Representation fills in the blank spaces of possibility reserved for representatives, but it also fills in what gets represented" (1995, p 134). From a slightly different angle, note Ankersmit's comment that "without political representation we are without a conception of what political reality – the represented – is like; without it, political reality has neither face nor contours. Without representation there is no represented" (2002, p 115). To represent is to do much more than see just what a constituency wants and to replicate that want. Invariably, there will not be a clear 'want', but rather a mixed and shifting set of preferences, half-preferences and apathy that a would-be representative must shape, mould, quite possibly 'create' and try to sell back to the relevant constituency.

It is all the more important to attend to this feature of political representation in the context of contemporary governance, because politics operates increasingly across boundaries between formal and informal, state and civil society, national and supranational, and so on, involves increasingly complex efforts to mould, press and establish new conceptions of functional and territorial interests and constituencies. Consider, for example, five types of non-electoral representative claim that are found within varied, new, hybrid forms of governance. These claims are based on the idea that there is a 'constituency' that needs its interests to be identified, shaped and spoken for within consultative, participative or implementational processes alongside elective governmental institutions. 'Stakeholders' are those individuals or groups whose participation is needed to make a process or a policy 'work'. 'Marginalised interests' involve (as it is claimed by would-be spokespersons or representatives) voices that have been excluded previously or downgraded in importance. 'Intense' interests are those that are not catered for (again, it is argued) within more formal or electoral arenas, where one person–one vote procedures explicitly do not take into account intensities of preference with regards to public policy proposals. And 'emergent interests' are those that constitute new actors on the political scene. Such interests are encouraged to emerge as authorities seek to engage and consult citizens in new ways, and often assert themselves to be the result of new or hybrid or neglected conceptions of constituency identity which are not captured by – indeed, cannot be captured by – traditional electoral notions of representation.

New styles of governance and representation

Governance processes may well encompass a wider array of actors and interests, and involve a wider array of groups and individuals in politics, than more traditional conceptions of politics and government. But they do not guarantee the empowerment of this array of actors. Techniques of governance are suspected just as reasonably as being new or revamped techniques of social and political control as they are of empowerment or inclusion (see Chapter Six of this volume). In this respect, it would be a mistake to imagine that the making of a wider range of claims to be politically representative, by a wider range of actors, necessarily implies the strengthening of those actors. Relative political silence may be a reflection of political strength or contentment. Representative claim-making may reflect political insecurity in the complexities and uncertainties of the new processes of governance –

a sign of weakness and of a desire for reconnection or belonging as much as a sign of participation or strength.

With that caveat in mind, let us consider some of the key new styles of representative claim that the remaking of governance prompts and offers to us. Mostly these are examples of non-elective representative claims, and they encompass some of the examples mentioned at the end of the last section. First, there are claims which we might call 'wider interest' claims. The core idea here is that a representative claim may be based on the notion that larger and deeper human interests and needs need to be represented or voiced, but are too wide to receive sufficient voice in a national electoral political system. One might consider, for example, the rock stars Sir Bob Geldof and Bono and their advocacy of Third World debt relief, famine relief and poverty alleviation. This style of claim taps into the notion of rethinking governance, and the need to deal with a reconfigured social imaginary, in that such claims highlight the practices and consequences of governance that political systems may not have found adequate ways to recognise or with which to cope.

Second, claims to be a 'surrogate' representative suggest that formal electoral processes are not sufficiently subtle or encompassing in fast-changing social and cultural contexts, and that new and sporadic modes of representation, which bring into relief marginalised perspectives or emergent communities, are necessary. Mansbridge (2003) cites the example of Barney Frank, a gay congressman in the US who explicitly takes on the task of representing gay and lesbian interests well beyond the territorial boundaries of his own constituency. One thing that a focus on the remaking of governance does is to draw our attention to the existence of important perspectives which, by their nature, do not readily find voice in party and electoral politics. A representative claim might be based on the idea that one is a surrogate spokesperson for a group which, because of its cultural nature and consequent geographical dispersion, has no formal elected representative to speak for it. Young (2000) argues that in highly differentiated contemporary societies the representation of perspect-ives – points of view that arise from how people are differently positioned within a social field – is different from the representation of interests and opinions. Marginalised groups, for example, are not united or cohesive in their political opinions, but their perspectives condition their interests and opinions. Representing perspectives can involve claims that go beyond electoral forums:

> A more democratic representative government would have
> various layers and sites of elected, appointed, and volunteer

bodies that discuss policy options, make policy decisions, or review policy effectiveness. In such bodies it is possible and desirable to give specific representation to particular social group perspectives which might not otherwise be present. (Young, 2000, pp 152-3)

Third, as discussed in the previous section, stakeholder forums amount to a new style of representative claim, based on the notion that one stands for or speaks for a group which has a material or other 'stake' in a process or a decision, and therefore has a right to have its interests included in the process. Certainly, these examples involve a radical deconstruction of our received ideas of what a 'constituency' is. 'Constituencies', arguably, can be short-lived, non-territorial and spontaneously-formed, yet still form the basis of competing demands for political representation.

Conclusion

Wider interests, surrogates, stakeholder representatives – these are just a small handful of examples of new styles and forms of representation which are prompting a rethink of what representation can mean, and what it can contribute to our understanding of governance. As governance is rethought and remade, and new and complex arrangements cut across older boundaries between public and private, state and non-state, so new spaces are opened up for new representative claims to be made.

Given that they are non-elective, what legitimating arguments do these sorts of claims tap into in the attempt to justify themselves and, in turn, what do these arguments tell us about transformations of governance? Traditionally, representative claims from non-elective actors would be accompanied by, or imply, a further claim that there is a link with the formal line of democratic delegation, legitimating the claim. For example, an unelected government adviser, official or appointee might be in a position to claim representativeness of a larger group or interest on the basis of their formal connection to elected figures within a traditional set of line-hierarchy relationships. Interestingly, some of the newer and more challenging claims do not move in that direction when attempting to justify themselves (or when others attempt to justify them). Rather, they tend to try to break the bounds of a traditional, hierarchical model of democratic accountability. Given the importance of informal network governance to the broader idea of the remaking of governance, it is important to note that a key claim is that an actor is 'locked into' networks, and thus restricted or limited in what they can do by being embedded within a chain of mutually dependent relationships. So, a representative claim might be based on the actor being locked into a tight or dense network of organisational or other similar ties, such that alternative forms of accountability become exercised. For example, one might think in terms of the thickness of the "cobweb of connections in the ecology of communities" (March and Olsen, 1995, p 177). There are various mechanisms for achieving accountability of organisations which do not require election. As Giandomenico Majone writes:

> What is required to reconcile independence and accountability are richer and more flexible forms of control than the traditional methods of political and administrative oversight. Statutory objectives, procedural requirements, judicial review, budgetary discipline, professionalism, expertise, monitoring by interest groups, even inter-agency rivalry can all be elements of a pervasive system of control which only needs to be activated. When the system works properly no one controls an independent agency, yet the agency is 'under control'. (Majone, 1995, p 118)

Dense networks can foster legitimacy in part because they constrain actors in ways that are analogous to electoral constraints, although drawing that analogy need not be central to such claims.

Even more interesting are arguments that seek to establish the authenticity of new claims precisely by tapping into their very newness, their very separation from conventional electoral and related justifications and arguments. We might refer to these as the 'untainted' style of argument or claim: 'I can speak for or represent these marginalised interests because no one is paying me to do so, because I have no other axe to grind as all elected officials do, because I am the real thing, authentic.' I am not suggesting for one moment that we have some mysterious means by which claims to authenticity can be upheld – far from it – merely that this is a style of representative claim that one hears more often, perhaps in response to the ever-wider reach of governance and the counter-effort to retain and assert a sense of independence or authenticity.

In some respects, arguments which rest upon notions of the formal connectedness of a representative claimant to elective office appear to have reached a limit in terms of how much legitimacy their invocation can garner. Occupying or being connected to a position in a formal hierarchy or chain of delegation appears increasingly insufficient as the basis of a convincing representative claim in the more complex, public–private boundary crossing of contemporary governance. It still matters to us that politicians and other decision-makers and managers are formally accountable, and that there is a direct or indirect electoral component to that accountability. But the political–cultural resonance of the claim seems to be accompanied by greater scepticism, or cynicism, concerning the disengagement and unresponsiveness of formal governmental institutions.

So, although formal accountability still matters, other criteria seem to be on the rise. In particular, criteria which stress the role of claimants being locked into wider governance networks – and which appeal to underlying values of accountability and control, but which tap into different constructions or interpretations of 'accountability' and 'control'. Here, connectedness as a criterion is still invoked, but it is less formal, less clearly linked to elections and more to do with networks than hierarchies.

Further, surprisingly perhaps, there has been an apparent increase in the salience of criteria of untaintedness – that is, a rise in the perceived value of disconnection from formal hierarchies or lines of delegation centring on traditional governmental and elected actors. Criteria of untaintedness enact – or at least would like to enact – values of authenticity, a relatively new arrival in the pantheon of familiar democratic principles. Not all arguments that tap into this view would share the terminology – Iris Young's account, for example, would stress grounds of inclusion rather than untaintedness – but I believe that the term captures something crucial of the underlying thrust of such arguments. Besides, we are less concerned here with actual untaintedness (whatever that may mean), and more concerned with the claims to representation that seek to tap into an idea of untaintedness.

I want to argue that these subtle but important shifts in the types of argument that are made by would-be representatives tap into the notion of remaking governance, in that they reflect shifts in the ways that governance operates. If networks count more than hierarchies, then representative claims which base themselves precisely in network forms of organisation will rise in salience. And if the remaking of governance involves the reaching of governance processes into ever-wider social domains, then the urge to assert independent authenticity – 'untaintedness' – will be all the stronger.

References

Alcoff, L. (1991) 'The problem of speaking for others', *Cultural Critique*, winter, pp 5-32.

Ankersmit, F.R. (2002) *Political representation*, Stanford, CA: Stanford University Press.

Backstrand, K. and Saward, M. (2004) 'Democratizing global governance? Stakeholder democracy at the World Summit for sustainable development', paper presented at the Annual Meeting of the American Political Science Association, Chicago.

Derrida, J. (1982) 'Sending: on representation', *Social Research*, summer, pp 294-326.

Dryzek, J.S. (2000) *Deliberative democracy and beyond*, Oxford: Oxford University Press.

Eckersley, R. (2004) *Green state: Rethinking democracy and sovereignty*, Cambridge, MA: MIT Press.

Hajer, M. (2003) 'A frame in the fields: policy-making and the reinvention of politics', in M. Hajer et al (eds) *Deliberative policy analysis: Understanding governance in a network society*, Cambridge: Cambridge University Press.

Held, D. (1995) *Democracy and the global order*, Cambridge: Polity Press.

McGrew, A. (2002) 'From global governance to good governance: theories and prospects of democratizing the global polity', in M. Ougaard et al (eds) *Towards a global polity*, London and New York: Routledge.

Majone, G. (1995) 'Independence versus accountability? Non-majoritarian institutions and democratic government in Europe', in J.J. Hesse and T.A.J. Toonen (eds) *The European yearbook of comparative government and public administration* (vol 1, 1994), Baden-Baden: Nomos Verlagsgesellschaft, and Boulder, CO: Westview Press.

Mansbridge, J.J. (2003) 'Rethinking representation', *American Political Science Review*, vol 97, pp 515-28.

March, J.G. and Olsen, J.P. (1995) *Democratic governance*, New York, NY: The Free Press.

Pierre, J. (2000) 'Introduction: understanding governance', in J. Pierre (ed) *Debating governance*, Oxford: Oxford University Press, pp 1-10.

Pitkin, H.F. (1968) *The concept of representation*, Berkeley and Los Angeles, CA: University of California Press.

Prendergast, C. (2000) *The triangle of representation*, New York, NY: Columbia University Press.

Saward, M. (2000) 'A critique of Held', in B. Holden (ed) *Global democracy: A debate*, London: Routledge.

Saward, M. (2003) 'Enacting democracy', *Political Studies*, vol 51, p 1.

Seitz, B. (1995) *The trace of political representation*, New York, NY: SUNY Press.

Spivak, G.C. (1988) 'Can the subaltern speak?', in C. Nelson and L. Grossberg (eds) *Marxism and the interpretation of culture*, London: Macmillan.

Young, I.M. (2000) *Inclusion and democracy*, Oxford: Oxford University Press.

Conclusion

Janet Newman

In the Introduction to this volume it was claimed that governance theory tends to work with a 'thin' conception of the social. Here, I return to the three themes set out in the Introduction: the remaking of peoples, publics and politics. In doing so I debate the contribution of this volume to conceptualising how peoples and publics are constituted as both the object of governance and as the locus of new forms of social and political agency. Such an understanding, I argue, means rethinking governance as social and cultural, as well as institutional, practices.

Rethinking governance: the constitution of spaces and peoples

This book has been concerned with the multiple spaces of European governance: how these are constituted through governmental practices and how such practices are implicated in the production of cultural imaginaries of peoples and publics. The book began with John Clarke's chapter on European governance as a political–cultural project and the images of 'managed diversity' on which it rests. This chapter explored both the limits and possibilities of diversity in the construction of ideas of a European people, and the ways in which European governance attempts to contain that diversity through the construction and policing of its borders. Emma Carmel took up the theme of borders in Chapter Two, noting how the governance of a particular space or territory is achieved in two ways: first, by the institution of boundaries and borders; and second, by the institution of categories, institutions, rules, procedures and strategies which serve to define and organise the population to be governed. In Chapter Three, Noémi Lendvai then explored the dynamics of European accession and integration from the perspective of one of the Central Eastern European Accession Countries, noting how these dynamics are produced through meaning-making as well as institutional reform. Across these three chapters we can trace the ways in which governance practices attempt to shape new territorialised imaginaries of people, not only through the delineation and policing of borders, but also through the strategies and practices that serve to constitute a people as an imaginary unity. These ideas were taken up later in the book in relation to the construction of populations into categories based on presumed unities of identity or community (Chapters Six and Seven).

Across *Remaking governance* we have argued that the spaces of governance are not formed out of pre-given geographical entities. In Chapter One, John Clarke – following Balibar – argued that the borders of Europe as a governable space were institutionalised and policed not just at its 'edges' but also within its interior. The choices made through governance processes actively *constitute* both a space to be governed and the objects to be governed within that space. And as Emma Carmel argued in Chapter Two, changes in governance may take place along either or both of these dimensions. This produces wider questions about how the social is territorialised through the construction of imaginary unities of people, whether those of a common European people (Chapters One, Two and Three), of citizenship (Chapters Four and Five), of identity (Chapters Six and Seven) or political constituency (Chapters Eight and Nine). Such unities seek to mask or displace the social differences and divisions formed through historical and spatial processes that are organised around, and are constitutive of, representations of 'race' and ethnicity. Such questions tend not to be addressed in the governance literature but have been opened up in several chapters of this volume, which have debated how the remaking of governance embraces attempts to create a series of imaginary unities. This volume has attempted to 'put difference back in' by noting how the remaking of governance rests on gendered and racialised practices. For example, Chapter One noted how the social space of European governance is multiply constituted – as a geographic space, a multinational space and a racialised space. The European people who inhabit this space are the subject of 'splitting' – the subject of inclusion and exclusion on the basis of national citizenship rights and racialised classifications, but also the subject of inclusion strategies and the civilising ethos of tolerance.

This has profound implications for how we understand governance. First, it situates 'the people' in an historical context that goes beyond the usual narrative of a shift from liberalism to neo-liberalism or advanced liberalism. The peoples of Europe are formed through the contested discourses of multiculturalism and social diversity (Lewis, 2000). Yet older discourses remain – of minorities as subordinate, or as a danger to or polluter of the social body. Notions of racial difference produced through colonial discourses produce particular representations of 'the people' that are inscribed with notions of superiority and inferiority, with ideas about civilised or uncivilised practices, and with the cultural norms of what it means to conform to a particular culture or way of life. For example, in its period of colonial expansion, certain family forms and gender relations were used to establish the boundaries of what it meant to be 'British', and the patterns of inclusion and exclusion that flowed from this (Hall, 2002). Brah (1996) saw the formation of the European Union (EU) as producing a process of transformation in which a variety of different racisms were constituted into new configurations. Similar processes are taking place today as EU enlargement produces both new flows of people and new articulations between the racisms directed against people of colour and those against Eastern European migrants and asylum-seekers. And the debates around the proposed inclusion of Turkey as an Accession Country have surfaced new racial antagonisms. European integration and enlargement, then, can be understood as a complex process of confronting the legacies of multiple European colonialisms. These legacies are made material in the attempt by nation-states – and the EU itself – to exercise control over their borders and to govern access to social and economic goods by defining and redefining 'the people' into multiple categories of citizenship – nationals, asylum-seekers, economic migrants, denizens, visitors and so on – producing a differentiated structuring of economic, political and social rights.

Racialised minorities are subject to a double process of constitution in the new images of personhood and citizenship. The discourses of diversity and multiculturalism construct the person who is 'Other' as precariously positioned as both insider (as a source of richness, a richness constituted out of strangeness or difference from an unstated and unproblematised white norm) and outsider (the Muslim 'activist' or Eastern European asylum-seeker constituted as a threat to the order of the social body). They are both the saviour of the welfare state (as a low-waged and flexible workforce, and as taxpayers) and a threat to its very existence (by stretching resources and 'swamping' services). However, the policies of inclusion and exclusion are only one dimension of understanding governance as a racialised practice. A thick – or rich – conception of the social will view 'the people' not (just) as an entity to be governed or to be drawn into the process of governing, but as an unstable formation in which questions of difference refuse to be settled beyond very temporary points of apparent equilibrium. The contributions to this volume have highlighted ways in which imaginary unities of 'the people' are likely to be partial, incomplete and contested. Nevertheless, they have very material consequences in terms of access to, or exclusion from, a public sphere of citizenship rights and welfare entitlements.

Rethinking governance: constituting 'publics' and the public sphere

Marquand defines the public sphere as "the domain of citizenship, equality and service whose integrity is essential to democratic governance and social well being" (2004, p 1). The forms of citizenship and equality to which Marquand refers were embedded in the social, political and organisational settlements of the post-war welfare states of north-west Europe. The social policy narrative of welfare state transformation (discussed in the Introduction to this volume) is based on the idea that the economic imperatives of neo-liberal governance produce the need for wholesale welfare reform in order to 'recouple' economic and welfare systems (Palier, 2003). But for us it is more than a question of exploring the dynamics of recoupling. Imaginary unities of peoples – and the exclusions from them – are associated with welfare practices that foster collective forms of solidarity and identity. These are expressed "through systems of cultural representation and signifying practice, together with an assemblage of rights and duties" (Fink et al, 2001, p 3). These cultural representations circumscribe a domain of public responsibility, the boundary of which is shifting as a result of the restructuring of state welfare in neo-liberal regimes.

The chapters in this volume have explored, in different ways, the attempt to renegotiate the settlements between government and peoples, and between economy and society, that were formed in European welfare states (although as Fink, Lewis and Clarke argue, these settlements were always conditional and fragile). Such attempts destabilised the myriad conceptions of the public – the public sector, public safety, public health, public services, the public interest – that were inscribed in welfare provision. Although the public sphere, in Marquand's sense, is broader and deeper than the public sector, nevertheless the public sector stood as a marker of the institutional guarantors of equality and the symbolic representations of the collective and mutual responsibilities of citizenship. As has been widely noted, the series of restructurings and reforms associated with neo-liberal governance led to an assault on the institutions of the public sector, supported by the (partial) displacement of a general public service ethos by business values and managerial ideology (Clarke and Newman, 1997; and Chapter Five of this volume). These transformations served to dissolve partially social-democratic representations of the relationship between public and state, and to replace them with the idea of public provision as a series of provider–consumer transactions (Clarke et al, 2005; Newman and Vidler, 2005: forthcoming). They open up the possibility of the dismantling of collective forms of identification and the extension of the individualised ethos of the market place into the public sphere (Needham, 2003).

I do not want to deny the political importance of these shifts or to underestimate their political and cultural impact. Nevertheless, I want to argue for a more dynamic conception of change in which the dispersal of power associated with the remaking of governance opens up new forms of citizen activation and engagement. This requires paying attention to the particular ways in which 'the public' is being rearticulated with other discourses in specific sites of governance. Several chapters have highlighted the *different* conceptions of active citizenship which are called into being in the process of reform. As Johansson and Hvinden argue in Chapter Five, these are articulated in complex – and often uncomfortable – ways, and the dynamic interaction between different forms of activation produces a field of tensions that is lived out in the everyday experience of citizens. And in Chapter Four it was noted how this field of tensions is very specifically gendered, exploring, for example, the tension between women's activation in the labour force and their constitution as active citizens, coinciding with the reconfiguration of public and private welfare responsibilities.

Other chapters traced the constitution of new 'publics' through strategies of engagement and involvement. Alongside the withdrawal of publicly provided goods has been a new focus on incorporating groups that are involved in voluntary or self-help activities into new forms of contractual and partnership-based relationships, and on drawing citizens into new fields of power through public participation initiatives. This theme is treated in different ways by myself, Rebekah Sterling and Henrik Bang, but each notes the complex dynamics at stake in the process of shaping new identifications and allegiances. Each suggests how public policy discourse is constitutive of new categories of public (Chapter Six), of community (Chapter Seven) and of citizenship (Chapter Eight). But each also raises problems about the 'public-ness' of the domain of involvement and its democratic anchorage in a wider polity. We can trace contradictory processes at stake in the remaking of the public. First, as the boundaries of the public sphere of collective provision by the state contracts, so new publics are being brought into being as governments attempt to enhance their legitimacy through the consumerist, participative and partnership-based strategies discussed in Chapters Six, Seven and Eight. It might be argued that the expansive – but elusive – publics invoked by the latter serves to mask further the contraction of the more material embodiments of public-ness of the public sector or welfare state. Second, while some of the array of new governmental strategies may serve to strengthen *particular* links between public services and their publics by ensuring greater responsiveness and accountability to service users or local communities, those same strategies may weaken further the *general* imaginary of a solidaristic public sphere. This may have important and potentially damaging implications for the willingness of citizens to invest in public goods and public infrastructure. Third, while the policies and strategies of the EU and national governments are concerned increasingly with governing the social – constituting new conceptions of citizen responsibility, developing policies on social inclusion and public involvement – those same policies and strategies are characterised increasingly by forms of instrumental rationality that subordinate the social to economic imperatives.

The diminishing of the public sphere has very material consequences. While new forms of governing are viewed as unlocking 'old' forms of power and authority, opening up the political system to new forms of participation and collaboration, nevertheless they may produce new patterns of incorporation, new hierarchies of expertise and new forms of potential exclusion. The policies associated with the Open Method of Coordination discussed in Chapter Two, or the modernisation of welfare governance outlined in Chapters Four and Five, result in an intensification of the practices through which particular groups are marginalised or excluded alongside – and are in interaction with – new policies that aim to enhance social inclusion. Johansson and Hvinden argue that it is the poor and the excluded who are targeted as the subjects of those socio-liberal forms of citizenship that are associated with welfare-to-work activation policies, while the liberal or republican versions are directed towards the well-integrated and more affluent. The effects of the new activation policies, then, will be differentiated by economic status, gender, ethnicity and other dimensions of difference. But they also suggest that this is an incomplete picture – poor and excluded groups now have more opportunities for a voice and disabled people more capacity for choice, while the more affluent also may be subject to activation demands. So, in exploring how the remaking of governance reshapes our understanding of politics we need to explore who is brought into new fields of power as a result of institutional change, and with what consequences.

Although we can identify the contemporary remaking of governance with an assault on the public sphere, its effects are uneven and unfinished. As John Clarke has argued elsewhere: "The public realm ... remains selective, unequal, differentiating, constraining and oppressive in many ways. But it is also the site of political–cultural investment, attachments, identifications as well as old and new solidarities" (2004a, p 44). The public sphere, then – as a site of collective identification, state responsibility or service values – is both socially constituted and politically contested. However, new forms of governance serve both to obscure and depoliticise its boundaries. They mask the problem of who is providing services: the focus shifts to the nature of the transaction rather than its location in the public, private or not-for-profit sector. The more complex the mix of public and private financing, the more diverse the array of types of organisation providing services; the more entangled the field of multiple and interlocking partnerships, the more difficult it is to trace the boundaries of the public sphere and to discern whether it is (or is not) being dismantled. Further, the privileging of the ideas of network and collaborative governance conceals the extension of coercive and regulatory strategies that reach beyond the formal boundaries of the public sphere and into the governance of households, family and individuals. The ethos of consumerism masks the increasingly blurred boundary between public and private sectors, state and market. And the apparent pruning or rolling-back of the state dislocates collective notions of the public and the public interest and squeezes the public domain of political struggle or contestation.

Finally – and most critically – while offering a narrowed and constrained conception of public-ness, the modernisation of welfare governance produces greater intervention into the 'private' domains of personal lives by seeking to regulate conduct as well as produce new forms of governable subject. We can trace a double dynamic here. An array of policy shifts associated with the neo-liberal assault on the welfare state is producing a 'privatisation' of welfare in which individuals, households and communities are expected to provide for themselves (Clarke, 2004b). But at the same time, public policy shifts are increasingly oriented towards constituting the private as a governable domain through new forms of public intervention. Areas that were once regarded as the province of personal or private decision-making (how to raise children, how far to take care of one's own health, whether, if a parent of young children or a person with disabilities, to go out to work, how far to develop one's skills and capacities through training) are being 'publicised' – that is, made the focus of policy debates and governmental intervention. But as Warner (2005) argues, the public domain that is invoked here is one that has been remoralised and depoliticised.

These contradictions remind us that the definitions of publics and publicness are defined against *different* conceptions of the private: the closed decision-making of elites or clubs, the private sector, the privacy of household or family, the privacy of personhood. Each of these different boundaries must be conceptualised as fluid and the focus of struggles and contestation. Here I want to depart from Marquand, who argues for the analytical distinctiveness of the public and private domains; the former viewed as the province of politics and the latter as apolitical: "[I]f the personal is politicised, or the political personalised, the public and private domains are both likely to be twisted out of shape" (2004, p 80). What this misses is not only the feminist conception of the personal (private) as political but also the profoundly political nature of the ways in which the boundary between private and public is drawn and redrawn, made transparent and obscured, policed and traversed. Feminist perspectives have consistently highlighted the problems resulting from the sharp separation between notions of 'public' and 'private', with many of the concerns or agendas of significance to women being excluded from, or marginalised in, the public sphere (Phillips, 1995). The feminist social policy literature has drawn attention to the ways in which the welfare state, the symbolic embodiment of public provision, was always buttressed by the 'private' resource of informal, unpaid and predominantly female labour. Policies on care are now being brought into the public domain of political debate and policy development to an unprecedented extent as a result of women's increased presence in the labour market, yet women's disproportionate contribution to informal community provision and social action may remain unrecognised in policy debates about social inclusion and social capital (Chapter Four). The governance literature is typically silent on the gendered dynamics at stake in the remaking of governance. Yet, as with the questions of 'race' noted in the previous section, they are of central importance to the development of a politics of governance.

The remaking of politics?

As has been argued in the preceding sections, the remaking of governance opens up important political issues, not least the politics of gender and 'race' involved in the redefinition of the public sphere and the reconstitution of peoples as imaginary unities. Here, I want to trace questions about the new spaces and territories in which political agency might take place. It is widely recognised that new forms of governance imply a challenge to the centrality of representative democracy as a means of connecting citizens to a polity:

> The rise of a vocabulary of governance indicates a shift away from well established notions of politics and brings in new sites, new actors and new themes.... Their efforts to find solutions acceptable to all who are involved (and to expand the circle of involvement) nibble and gnaw on the constitutional system of territorially based representative democracy. (Hajer and Wagenaar, 2003, p 3)

Network governance, in particular, opens up the possibility of new political spaces that cut across traditional boundaries, including those of nation-states (Dryzek, 2000). Deliberative or discursive democracy is viewed as having the potential to give voice to more diverse identities and interests and to enhance social justice (Young, 1990). The processes of remaking and rescaling governance, then, produces new possibilities of collective identifications and social action.

This volume has touched on a diversity of practices which might be viewed in such terms. The remaking of governance both broadens and narrows the imaginaries of place, expanding the scale of political engagement (linked to the politics of the EU or to global movements) and narrowing it as communities of locality gain importance as discursively produced sites of political participation and social action. But the remaking of governance is not just about scale. It suggests new *imaginaries of identification*, with the active citizen, the consumer citizen, the responsible citizen emerging as key figures in the policy landscapes of modernising states. And it forms new *imaginaries of representation* as political attachments are formed in the new spaces of deliberative, participative and community politics which were discussed in Chapters Six to Nine. Each of these offers ways of imagining the self in relation to the polity which are rather different from liberal conceptions of the political rights and duties of citizenship. They may draw citizens into new – and potentially politicising – forms of engagement with policymakers and service organisations. However, rather than assuming that such processes produce an expanded form of democracy, it is important to explore their implications for patterns of inclusion and exclusion, voicing and silence and for the reconstitution of identities and interests. As was argued in Chapter Six, while interactive and dialogic forms of governing can be viewed as unlocking 'old' forms of power and authority, opening up the political system to new and more diverse voices, they also open up questions about who participates and what topics are made available for collaborative decision-making and action.

One way of addressing such questions is by tracing the reconfigurations of the 'political opportunity structures' (Tarrow, 1994) through which citizens engage with the public realm. However, as its name suggests, political opportunity structure is concerned with the degree of openness or closure of the *structures* that allow or enable access and participation. Here, I want to draw on the concept 'political imaginary' to denote the *cultural* dimensions of access and participation (see also Walters, 2002). New forms of governance enable a more differentiated conception of the public sphere, recognising that not all identities and interests can be expressed in formal political participation through elections and offering a panoply of informal arenas in which they can be articulated. They expand the opportunities for marginalised and disadvantaged groups to have a public voice and to influence the ways in which policy is shaped and delivered, and offer the possibility of a more open, differentiated and active political imaginary as well as new forms of representative claim (see Chapter Nine). However, they can also be understood as oriented towards securing a more consensual form of politics, one in which it is assumed that the class and gender conflicts of the past have been resolved and the more recent resurgence of 'race' as a locus of dissent and struggle can be contained by the production of a harmonious multiculturalism.

Such strategies can be viewed as part of an attempt to form a new settlement between state and people, a settlement more attuned to the modernisation of welfare states. However, a post-structuralist reading of this account might suggest that the active citizen becomes enmeshed in an intensification, rather than a diminution, of governmental power by being subjected to the (highly managerial) technologies of network management and collaborative governance. And, as Chapters Four and Six argue, the remaking of governance also changes the ways in which the boundaries of the public realm itself are imagined, obscuring the boundary between the issues that are considered to be the domain of collective public responsibility and the responsibility of the individual, family or household. That is, it redefines the boundaries of what is a matter for 'politics' and what is a purely 'private' matter. Many issues – for example, those concerned with environmental or social risk – fail to settle (or be settled) in either domain, being shunted back and forth in complicated and unpredictable ways.

While acknowledging the importance of the possibility of new spaces and opportunities for participating in the public sphere, several chapters of this book have been relatively pessimistic about the constrained political imaginary offered by the new strategies of involvement and participation. As John Clarke argued: "The people of Europe might be encouraged to speak, and they may be listened to respectfully, but the multiplicity of voices creates a precise space in which decisional power can be exercised centrally." Rebekah Sterling highlighted the limitations of partnership working, arguing that: "Thus democratic practice within partnerships is imperfect and uneven, both in the degree of influence that the public can have over decisions (and what kinds of decisions the public can influence)." Participative or partnership-based strategies can be understood as both 'empowering' and as a way of suturing publics into new forms of regulation and control. Chapter Six concludes by arguing that they may produce "a constrained, managed and consensus-oriented political imaginary that will do little to achieve the connection between governments and people envisaged by the EU in its promulgation of 'good governance'". Henrik Bang in Chapter Eight is more optimistic. He notes the ways in which participative governance practices result in the emergence of a new elite of 'expert citizens' and so fail in their attempt to reconnect government and laypeople. However, he also highlights the importance of studying the informal political activity characteristic of what he terms 'everyday makers'. This argues for an expansion of how 'politics' is defined, an issue taken up in Chapter Nine by Michael Saward as he traces a range of different forms of claim-making that intersect with representative democracy, often in uncomfortable ways.

The tension between more or less optimistic assessments of the political potential of new forms of governance cannot be resolved by means of abstract judgement, not least because they draw on very different theoretical traditions: for example, the normative emphasis of much of the collaborative governance literature or the critical perspectives of post-structuralism. However, we should be aware of the contradictory possibilities inherent in the governmental shifts of the kind we have been discussing. Perhaps this is illustrated best by looking back at the ways in which supposedly 'new' governmental strategies tend to draw on the older – and often quite radical – forms of political imagination and engagement that flourished in the 1970s and 1980s. The community activism of that period produced a new sensibility in its calls for the decentralisation of power and greater self-determination for deprived or disadvantaged populations. The 'new social movements' – feminism, gay liberation, civil rights and disability activism – challenged professional power bases and introduced new equality agendas which problematised the universalist ethos of the post-war welfare states. User movements opened up new demands as well as (in some cases) producing alternative models of practice outside the state in an expansion of non-profit and self-help organisations. Each helped to shape the ways in which 'peoples' and 'publics' were imagined in the policies and practices of welfare states. Each influenced the development of radical professional and occupational discourses, for example, in youth work, social work and education, producing shifts in mainstream state policy and practice. These influences have had a profound impact on the mainstream of state policies and practices.

However, the critical political challenges that they embodied are now being weakened as states and other governmental actors draw on this rich array of alternative discourses and reinterpret or recombine them in modernisation or transformation projects. The calls for de-bureaucratisation and the critiques of the paternalistic or authoritarian state can be viewed as opening up the space for the neo-liberal challenges that heralded the dismantling and disembedding of state institutions. The user movements created one of the conditions for the rise of the individuated citizen-consumer. The growth of the not-for profit sector and informal provision enabled governments to develop new models of service provision outside the state, a process subjecting community-based and advocacy organisations to what Everingham (2004) terms a process of corporatisation and managerialisation that neutralised their critical and radical potential. The discourses of community activism were readily appropriated into policy innovations concerned with overcoming disadvantage and social exclusion, reappearing in more conservative alignments of social capital and communitarianism. This depoliticisation of community was accomplished in part by its double constitution as both a resource for, and a partner with, government, producing a hegemonic conception of 'community' as a static location rather than a contestable domain. But this depoliticisation forms part of a much wider redefinition of the political terrain. As Walters comments:

> [G]overnance discourse seeks to redefine the political field in terms of a game of assimilation and integration. It displaces talk of politics as struggle or conflict. It resonates with 'end of class' and 'end of history' narratives in that it imagines a politics of multi-level collective self management, a politics without enemies.... Perhaps we can say that governance pertains to a political culture that no longer sees itself as at risk from fundamental class or geo-political divisions, where instead of threatening social order, social conflicts can now be harnessed to serve political ends. (2004, pp 36-7)

Nevertheless, the processes of change we have been describing in this book also open up questions about where new sites of struggle may be emerging. This is not just a matter of tracing points of global or local political struggle, from transnational environmental or anti-globalisation movements to protests against the closure of local hospitals or care homes. It also means tracing how, and in what ways, the remaking of governance involves the recasting of what we mean by politics itself, and how such meanings themselves are open to contestation. In Chapter Two, Emma Carmel suggests that:

> Processes of contestation are partly symbolic struggles about defining what *might be* contested. That is, they are about defining what is public and political, as opposed to what is domestic or privatised, in the sense of being removed to the economic sphere.

The struggle to define what is political and what is simply a matter of 'good governance' takes place across the range of transformations described in this volume.

Conclusion

Janine Brodie highlights the importance of analysing shifting philosophies of governance:

> The fact that these seemingly universal and timeless understandings of the world shift precipitously from one era to another occupies little space in the public imagination. The universal, the timeless, the commonsensical, by definition, resist public debate and the exploration of alternative ways of thinking. (2002, p 91)

Such 'philosophies of governance' inform assumptions about policy problems, policymaking and the processes of policy delivery. They also shape the patterns of political contestation and mobilisation to which governments must respond, and which sometimes produce counter-discourses and alternative ways of envisaging the public realm.

Remaking governance has traced the growing significance of 'the social' as both an object of governance strategies and a resource to be mobilised in the process of governing. In addition, it has noted the productivist and instrumental characterisations of the social implicated in the reforms of welfare governance taking place in the EU and in specific nation-states. But I want to highlight some qualifications and caveats to the idea that governing the social is becoming the hegemonic philosophy of neo-liberal governance. The first concerns the relationship between the symbolic and the material. We have tried to contribute to the analysis of governance as social and cultural practice, tracing the symbolic constructions through which particular common sense understandings of governance problems are produced, and particular kinds of solution to those problems are legitimated. For example, the ways in which the boundary between 'public' and 'private' is conceptualised produces the problematic of what role the state might play in regulating private activities (reproduction, drug use) or providing public goods (health services, care for the elderly, housing). Common sense images – the nanny state, bureaucratic red tape, consumer-oriented public services – are produced precisely through the ways in which public and private are reconfigured, contested and enacted through governance practice. And academic concepts – including the triptych of market, hierarchy and network critiqued in Chapter Four – themselves derive from a traditional (and ungendered) conflation of 'public' and 'state'.

This kind of approach has enabled us to challenge the narratives of change that are constructed symbolically in the stories of neo-liberalism, globalisation and the rise of the network society. Each tends to collapse history into a neat series of dualities of past and present, dualities in which the past tends to be misremembered and the present or future to be too resolved and tidy. They also tend to view macro processes as merely contextual: the external forces that produce change in conceptions of personhood, the reconstitution of peoples and the redrawing of the boundaries of the public domain. However, these external forces can be viewed as inside the processes being studied, as both generative of social formations and generated through them (Clarke and Newman, 1998). So, the conception of the person as a rational, instrumental actor itself legitimates neo-liberal forms of economics. The idea of the people as an imaginary unity is generative of policies of inclusion and exclusion. The conception of the household or family as a personal, private domain supports and legitimates policies that promote a limited conception of state responsibility and power. However, this form of analysis tends to mask the significance of material and coercive forms of governance. Governmental power may be engaged increasingly in what Steinberg and Johnson (2004), discussing the UK New Labour governments, term a 'war of persuasion'. Policies on criminal justice, asylum and immigration, welfare-to-work and other areas of public policy may rest on a great deal of discursive work that situates 'external' forces as a legitimating rationale for new forms of governance. But they also have very material consequences both for individual subjects and for the character of the social that they inhabit.

Finally, I want to argue for a form of analysis that is attentive to potential points of instability in the emerging governance regime. As was discussed in the Introduction, the idea of social governance is associated often with a social systems approach that strips it of concepts of instability or contestation (see also Newman, 2001). However, the contributions to this volume trace the attempts to fix the composition of the social in new forms – whether in the form of a consumerist, participative or activated citizenry. These attempts may be resisted, refused or challenged. The 'new' discourses may be coupled with older forms of social imaginary in complex articulations. While the 'hard' form of activation – linking labour market activation strategies to changes in access to welfare benefits – may be coercive in its effects, the subjects that are the focus of 'softer' activation strategies of participation or collaboration may not hear the messages, or may refuse to listen. The social, then, can be understood as a domain in flux that may not be 'fixed' in the form to which new governmental strategies are directed. New discursive alignments and articulations are not necessarily successful. Discourses are the product of ongoing work that seeks to hold them together in the face of other possible social and political imaginaries. What is important is the way in which some discourses are amplified through the political process, how they are coupled with others in new discursive articulations and how they become part of a new 'common sense' about the best way to govern.

Rather than assuming the effectiveness of new strategies for governing the social, *Remaking governance* has attempted to offer a conception of the social as richer, more complex, more differentiated and more contested. We have explored how new governance forms are being enacted in specific sites and how these may be the focus of practices of containment, contestation and negotiation. Taking this forward means paying attention to the struggles that are taking place over the meaning of cultural and social practices in areas beyond the scope of this volume, from parenting to work to sexuality. It means exploring the world of images and representations, from the 'spin' of politicians to the communication practices opened up by new-media technologies. It means theorising the ways in which the big narratives of governance, from welfare-state restructuring to the rise of networks or the increasing significance of cultural governance strategies, constitute lived experience; but also how that lived experience – and the cultural practices through which people make sense of it – help to constitute those very narratives. In other words, it means telling a *social* story about governance itself.

References

Brah, A. (1996) *Cartographies of diasporas: Contesting identities*, London: Routledge.

Brodie, J. (2002) 'The great undoing: state formation, gender politics and social policy in Canada', in C. Kingfisher (ed) *Western welfare in decline*, Philadelphia, PA: University of Pennsylvania Press, pp 90-110.

Clarke, J. (2004a) 'Dissolving the public realm: the logics and limits of neo-liberalism', *Journal of Social Policy*, vol 33, no 1, pp 27-48.

Clarke, J. (2004b) *Changing welfare, changing states: New directions in social policy*, London: Sage Publications.

Clarke, J. and Newman, J. (1997) *The managerial state: Power, politics and ideology in the remaking of social welfare*, London: Sage Publications.

Clarke, J. and Newman, J. (1998) 'A modern British people? New Labour and the reconstruction of social welfare', paper presented to the Discourse Analysis and Social Research Conference, Copenhagen Business School, Copenhagen, September.

Clarke, J., Smith, N. and Vidler, E. (2005) 'Consumerism and the reform of public services: inequalities and instabilities', in M. Powell, K. Clarke and L. Bauld (eds) *Social Policy Review 17*, Bristol: The Policy Press/Social Policy Association, pp 167-82.

Dryzek, J.S. (2000) *Deliberative democracy and beyond*, Oxford: Oxford University Press.

Everingham, C. (2004) *Social justice and the politics of community*, Aldershot: Ashgate.

Fink, J., Lewis, G. and Clarke, J. (2001) *Rethinking European welfare: Transformations of Europe and social policy*, London: Sage Publications.

Hall, C. (2002) *Civilising subjects: Metropole and colony in the English imagination 1830–1867*, Cambridge: Polity Press.

Hajer, M. and Wagenaar, H. (eds) 'Introduction', in *Deliberative policy analysis: Understanding governance in the network society*, Cambridge: Cambridge University Press, pp 1-30.

Lewis, G. (2000) *'Race', gender and social policy: Encounters in a post-colonial society*, Cambridge: Polity Press.

Marquand, D. (2004) *Decline of the public: The hollowing-out of citizenship*, Cambridge: Polity Press.

Needham, C. (2003) *Citizen-consumers: New Labour's marketplace democracy*, London: The Catalyst Forum.

Newman, J. (2001) *Modernising governance: New Labour, policy and society*, London: Sage Publications.

Newman, J. and Vidler, E. (2005: forthcoming) 'Discriminating customers, responsible patients, expert citizens: consumerism and the modernisation of health care', *Journal of Social Policy*.

Palier, B. (2003) 'Analysing the relationship between globalisation, European integration and welfare states', *Global Social Policy*, vol 3, no 2, pp 146-51.

Phillips, A. (1995) *The politics of presence*, Oxford: Clarendon Press.

Steinberg, D. and Johnson, R. (eds) (2004) *Blairism and the war of persuasion: Labour's passive revolution*, London: Lawrence and Wishart.

Tarrow, S. (1994) *Power in movement: Social movements, collective action and mass politics in the modern state*, Cambridge: Cambridge University Press.

Walters, W. (2002) 'Social capital and political sociology: reimagining politics?', *Sociology*, vol 36, no 2, pp 377-97.

Walters, W. (2004) 'Some critical notes on governance', *Studies in Political Economy*, vol 73 (spring/summer), pp 27-46.

Warner, M. (2005) 'Making public', lecture at Tate Modern, London, 25 February.

Young, I.M. (1990) *Justice and the politics of difference*, Princeton, NJ: Princeton University Press.

Index